PERIOD FIXTU AND FITTINGS
1300-1900

EXCEPT·THE·LORD·BVILD·THE
HOWSE·THE·LABOVRERS·THER·EOF
PREVAIL·NO·TERECTEDBY·RFOR·158o

LINDA HALL

COUNTRYSIDE BOOKS
NEWBURY BERKSHIRE

First published 2005
© Linda Hall 2005
Reprinted 2007, 2011

COUNTRYSIDE BOOKS
3 Catherine Road
Newbury, Berkshire

To view our complete range of books,
please visit us at
www.countrysidebooks.co.uk

ISBN 978 1 85306 742 6

Photographs and illustrations by the author
Editing, additional illustrations, Chapter 1 photos
and photos on pages 72, 76 and 80 by Trevor Yorke

Produced through MRM Associates Ltd, Reading
Printed by Information Press Ltd

CONTENTS

ACKNOWLEDGEMENTS

The following people have generously supplied me with information from their own fieldwork, both published and unpublished, and I am indebted to them for their many and varied contributions, and for allowing me to pick their brains on many occasions.

Thanks go, too, to the house owners who have emailed photographs and other information. I have also gathered information when visiting buildings on conferences organised by the Regional Furniture Society and the Vernacular Architecture Group, and particular thanks are due to the conference organisers. Most of these buildings are private houses and I would like to record special thanks to the many owners and occupants who have welcomed us into their homes over the years, together with our notebooks and cameras. Without them a book such as this would be impossible to produce. Other house owners who have attended my lectures have generously invited me to visit their dated houses, and I have gathered a large amount of material from these visits. Unfortunately, it is not possible to name them all here but their generosity is summed up by the lady in Suffolk who, seeing myself and two American colleagues peering at her dated house, invited us in off the street and let us loose with our cameras and tape measures.

My thanks also go to Dan Miles for ensuring that the paragraph on dendrochronology was accurate; to him and to Mick Worthington for dating a large number of the buildings featured in this book, particularly those in Hampshire, Shropshire and America; and to Carl Lounsbury, Willie Graham and their colleagues in the Vernacular Architecture Forum of America for arranging our recent trip to that country, where I saw many useful parallels. If I have omitted anyone from this list, please accept my apologies; any such omissions are due to oversight, not intention.

Alison Armstrong; Tony Beresford; Malcolm Birdsall; Alan Brodie; Harry Brooksby (and the Royal Commission on the Ancient and Historical Monuments of Wales); Veronica Chesher; Victor Chinnery; John Dallimore (and the Somerset Vernacular Buildings Research Group); Susan Denyer; Ruth Gibson; the late Joan Harding (and the Surrey Domestic Buildings Research Group); Nick Hill; Barbara Hutton; Nina Jennings; Stanley Jones; Laurence Kinney; Michael Kinney; Marion McClintock; David and Barbara Martin; Jeremy Milln; Dr James Moir; Madge Moran; Chris North; John and Jane Penoyre; Dr. Edward Peters; Edward Roberts; Martin Roberts; Pam Slocombe (and the Wiltshire Buildings Record); Peter Thornborrow; John Thorp; Tony Tolhurst: R Tyler; Jane Wade; Brenda Watkins.

Thanks are also due to the following for permission to use photographs taken in their properties: Historic Royal Palaces for allowing access to Kew Palace and Kensington Palace, and to Lee Prosser for arranging this; to the Bishop of Chichester; the Master of St Cross Hospital, Winchester; the Barley Hall Trust, York; Cogges Manor Farm Museum, Oxfordshire; the Norfolk and Norwich Heritage Trust (Dragon Hall); Guildford House Gallery, Guildford; Lord Edward Manners of Haddon Hall, Derbyshire; the Old Merchant's House Trust, Marlborough; Oakwell Hall, Birstall, West Yorkshire; the Ryedale Folk Museum, North Yorkshire; Shibden Hall Museum, Halifax, Totnes

Museum Trust (Devon); the Weald and Downland Open Air Museum, Chichester and the Wycombe Museum, High Wycombe. Thanks to Graeme Cottam, Acting Director of the Centre for the Study of Early English Women's Writing (1600-1830) at Chawton House, Chawton, Hampshire, for permission to reuse many of the drawings I made of their fixtures and fittings; these were originally published in Hampshire Houses 1300-1700 by Edward Roberts (2003). Chawton House is open Mondays to Fridays by appointment only; telephone 01420 541010 or visit www.chawton.org.

Particular thanks must go to Charles Brooking of the Brooking Collection for providing material that I was unable to gain elsewhere. The Brooking Collection is an unparalleled collection of architectural items rescued from salvage yards, skips and demolished and renovated houses, and comprises over 100,000 items from sash pulley wheels to whole doors and sections of staircases. Many are from buildings which have been accurately dated by inscription or documentary evidence. The greater part of the collection is housed at the University of Greenwich in the old Royal Hospital site, but Charles has a smaller display at his home, 44 The Drive, Cranleigh, Surrey, GU6 7LZ. This can be viewed by appointment, and Charles also provides a consultancy service. He can be contacted on 01483 274203. The Brooking Collection website can be found at www.rehmc.gov.uk.

Thanks must also go to Peter Addyman, my then tutor at Southampton University (and then director of the York Archaeological Trust until 2002) who first set me on this path by asking 'Why don't you go and look at houses?' Little did he know where it would lead!

Last, but by no means least, I would like to thank my daughters, Catherine and Elizabeth, for completing some of the drawings, adding dates to photocopies, and cooking meals when I was too busy to do so, and my husband Mike, for his boundless patience and lack of complaint over late meals, a chaotic house and a pre-occupied wife!

NOTE: Where a date shows a hyphen, e.g. 1561-76, this indicates the date range of a single building. Where a date shows an oblique, e.g. 1419/1430 Shropshire, it refers to two different buildings in the same county.

INTRODUCTION

The period house which you may live in or visit is more than just a charming, rustic home. It can reflect the very landscape in its construction, record the fluctuating fortunes of the community in its quality, and illustrate the regional styles and skills of nameless local craftsmen. In its structure are recorded centuries of alterations and additions to meet the demands of growing families, new fashions and the personal whims and aspirations of previous owners. The English period house is a very personal and ever changing piece of living history and much of its character comes from the fixtures and fittings within.

Understanding and dating these parts which make up the whole is crucial to unravelling the history of the house. Whether trawling through reclamation yards and antique shops, or wandering through our glorious country houses, recognising the period of its fixtures and fittings is essential and rewarding. This process, however, is further complicated by regional variations in decoration and materials. Until the Industrial Age, houses were built by local craftsmen using mainly timber and stone from the surrounding countryside, and in styles which may have taken decades to spread out from London. It needs not just knowledge of period fashions but also of the material and detail of fittings in the specific region of the house in order to accurately date the parts. General publications which attempt to guide the owner or visitor to period houses in this quest all too often show photos without labels, giving only vague dates and little information of regional styles. It is partly with these shortcomings in mind that this book has been compiled.

It has come about as the result of many years of visiting and recording historic houses all over the country, from Devon to Yorkshire and from Gloucestershire to Kent. Each chapter covers a different part of the house, detailing its development in a straightforward informative text complemented by hundreds of detailed line drawings and photos of the changing styles and individual parts from the door itself, down to the hinges it was hung upon. Each illustration has the location and date recorded; the latter having been confirmed not just by the obvious inscribed date somewhere on the house but also by documentary evidence and dendrochronology (see page 210).

As the book focuses upon vernacular architecture and the varied work of the local craftsmen the dates span from the medieval period up to the early 19th century when mass production and improved transportation brought standardized designs and imitated decoration across the whole country. There was, however, a short revival of local skills in the last decades of Victoria's reign and a few examples from this era are included.

The fixtures and fittings included in the book come from houses large and small, grand and humble. Remember, though, that the majority of the houses featured are private property with no public access. Please also note that if you are planning to move or replace any part of a listed building, consent is a legal requirement. Period fixtures and fittings have all too often in the past been removed by people who did not realise their true age and value. It is therefore the purpose of this book not only to provide guidance on dating houses from their fittings but also to encourage the occupants of such houses to enjoy and understand the interior features of their homes from the most magnificent fireplace to the smallest latch fastener.

1 A BRIEF HISTORY
OF THE ENGLISH HOUSE

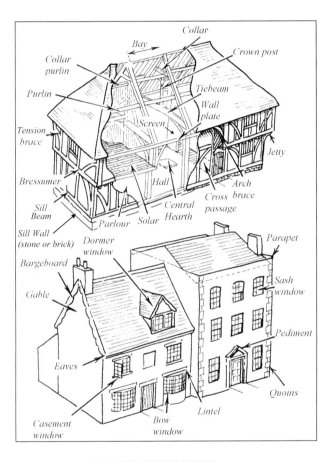

Collar
Bay
Crown post
Collar purlin
Purlin
Tiebeam
Wall plate
Screen
Tension brace
Jetty
Bressumer
Hall
Arch brace
Cross passage
Sill Beam
Central Hearth
Parlour
Solar
Sill Wall (stone or brick)
Dormer window
Parapet
Bargeboard
Sash window
Gable
Pediment
Eaves
Quoins
Casement window
Bow window
Lintel

Fig 1.1 (left): A south eastern timber-framed house (top) and features in a brick and stone town house (below).

Fig 1.2 (below): A reconstructed cottage probably built in the 13th century, which was based upon excavations of the deserted medieval village of Hangleton, Sussex. Like the majority of houses in this period it contained one main living room (although this example had a small partitioned inner room). The life expectancy of peasant cottages is still the subject of debate and it is mostly the better quality medieval houses which survive today.

TYPES AND PLANS OF HOUSES
Medieval

The basic medieval house consisted of an open hall as its main and sometimes only component. It was open to the roof and had an open hearth in the centre of the floor (see

Fig 1.3 (above): A view of a hall with cross wings at either end.

Labels on figure:
Upper end (private chambers)
Louvre (from French l'ouvert) meaning the opening)
Jetty
Oriel window
Lower end (service rooms)
CROSS-WING

Fig 1.4 (below): The 'Jew's House', Lincoln. A rare late 12th century stone building which, despite its name, may not have been built for a Jewish family (two original round-arched windows and the main doorway survive; the other doors and windows are later).

Fig 1.2). Most surviving houses have additional rooms, however, with two-storey units at one or both ends, and a screens or cross passage with opposed doorways at the (socially) lower end of the hall. This separated the hall from the service room or rooms, while at the upper and more private end was the parlour (see Fig 1.1). The two-storey units may be in line with the hall, giving a simple rectangular plan of two or three rooms in a row, or there may be cross-wings at one or both ends.

The partition at the lower end of the hall may have evidence of three original doorways, two in the centre for the buttery and pantry and another at one end of the wall for the stair. In larger houses there may have been a third central doorway leading to a kitchen which in this period was often detached to reduce the risk of fire. At the upper end of the hall there were doorways leading to the parlour and the stair and these were usually positioned at either end of the wall.

Urban houses had to fit into more limited sites with the prime areas divided into long thin plots. The narrow frontage was often used as a shop, with the hall and additional rooms arranged behind. In contrast, wealthy merchants and gentry may have large courtyard houses with wide frontages; the rear ranges may include warehouses and storerooms. The population at this period was primarily rural, however, and the majority lived in single-roomed houses (see Fig 1.2). Many had an integral cow-byre, forming a longhouse, a type that remained popular in the north and west even into the 20th century. A defensive variant in the turbulent border regions of the north was the bastle house, with the living quarters above the byre.

Few medieval houses survive in anything like their original state and the rooms within have often changed their uses several times over the years. The original doorway positions, for instance, can be very important in determining the layout and use of the rooms when first built. They may survive intact, but often at least one has been blocked although the original doorhead may still be in place; even if it has been removed, peg-holes in the studs on either side can reveal its former existence. Another common alteration is that the open hall was given a chimney stack and fireplace, and an upper floor inserted, although not necessarily at the same time. In the areas where houses are of stone it was easy for the new chimney stack to be positioned at right angles to the front wall, preserving the former screens passage with its front and back doorways. In timber-framed areas, however, the new stack is more likely to have been placed in the middle of the passage, creating a lobby entry and providing back-to-back fireplaces in two of the main rooms. In some houses the entire hall was rebuilt at a later date, although the two-storey cross-wings at one or both ends may have been retained.

16th and early 17th century houses

From the end of the 15th century the open hall fell from favour and was replaced by the fully floored house as owners sought more privacy and improved accommo-dation. The change, however, was gradual with variations in date between different parts of the country and different types of house (see chapter 4). An advantage of these new styles of house was that only a single stair was required, which was more likely to be in a central position rather than at one end. This was both easier for access and gave more privacy to the bedrooms, as a stairhead landing or lobby could give separate access to several chambers. Those who could not afford to do this, or were canny with their money, simply converted their old open hall, inserted a new floor and replaced the old open mullioned windows with new, larger, glazed versions. Details such as original doors and doorframes will often reveal whether or not the current first-floor layout is original or a later alteration.

By the second half of the 16th century the country was experiencing strong growth in wealth and population, and a noticeable increase in building took place at first in the prosperous south, spreading to the more remote areas of the north and west by the 18th century. This 'great rebuilding' resulted in new multi-storey houses in the cramped prime locations in towns and cities, with builders limited by narrow medieval plots doing just as they do today, expanding upwards. Three-, four- and five- storey timber-framed structures were erected with jetties looking impressive and increasing the space on the upper floors. Narrow passages down the side gave access to a rear

Fig 1.5 (above): The Guildhall, Lavenham, an early 16th century timber-framed building with close-studded vertical timbers.

Fig 1.6 (below): A 14th century 'Wealden' house with its distinctive recessed central hall, in effect a compact variation of the building in Fig 1.3 under a single roof. (see cut away drawing in Fig 1.1, page 8)

Fig 1.7 (below): A late 16th century farmhouse from Midhurst, Sussex, reconstructed at the Weald and Downland Open Air Museum. Note the central chimney serving two back-to-back inglenook fires.

Fig 1.8 (above): A jettied timber-framed town house dating from 1543 on Castle Hill, Lincoln (the ground floor has been altered at a later date).

Fig 1.9 (below): Wick Court near Gloucester was completed around 1662 on the site of a medieval house. Note it has a symmetrical façade.

Fig 1.10 (below): Cogges Manor Farm, Oxon. The gabled building in the foreground was added in the 17th century to an earlier hall (on the left) which itself had been floored and altered in the 16th century.

courtyard with perhaps a detached kitchen and room for stabling or livestock.

New substantial yeoman and gentry farmhouses commonly had three, four or five ground-floor rooms, with bedrooms on the first floor, and storage and servants' accommodation in attics above. (It was not uncommon for the parlour to be used as the main bedroom until the later 17th century.) These new buildings incorporated large inglenook fireplaces in the hall and kitchen, with smaller fireplaces in the parlour and some bedrooms. New ideas of symmetry first appeared in Elizabethan mansions; by 1700 most new houses had symmetrical façades and rooms arranged around a central entrance hall.

Older houses were modernised or enlarged, and many longhouses were upgraded; either the cattle were moved out and the byre converted to a room, or the direct access between byre and house was blocked. Alternatively, new two or three unit houses were built, with at least a fireplace in the main room and often a second heated room. The majority of houses and cottages of the working population would have been of poorer construction and most have long since gone. The picturesque village house which today we term a cottage was probably built for a successful local farmer.

Later 17th century and 18th century houses

The Great Fire of London in 1666 and others around the country resulted in a series of new building regulations over the following century. Although new timber-framed houses had been banned in London from as early as 1605, this and other regulations had often been ignored in the rush for new housing. Now in the wake of the disaster they were generally adhered to. New houses had to be in stone or brick (which was now more affordable), and took standardized forms, with sizes related to the width of road along which they stood. In the 18th century further steps to reduce the risk of fire spreading along rows of houses resulted in windows being recessed further behind the exterior walls and bans on exterior woodwork such as cornices and door surrounds.

These regulations, new fashions for classical architecture, and the still limited plots for urban building resulted in the dominance of the urban terraced house, usually a two- to four-storey structure with cellar and attic and its principal rooms on the first floor. The regulations and latest fashions tended to originate in the south and spread over the decades to the more distant parts of the country.

The larger town or country house was now typically brick or stone and double pile, with two living rooms at the front and service rooms at the back. This created problems with the roof, as available materials were too heavy for the low pitch required to cover this size of structure in a single span. A variety of solutions was devised, the most common being two parallel roofs. In the late 18th century lighter Welsh slate became widely available, enabling roofs to have a much lower pitch and a wider span. Other Georgian features were new sash windows, classically-styled doors and surrounds, and symmetrical façades with elegant proportions rather than ornate decoration.

Many of these houses were built in the wake of enclosures, when the open field system was replaced by compact blocks of land with a new isolated farmhouse in the middle. The old stone or timber-framed houses back in the village were often divided up to create cottages for the workforce, especially in the 19th century, with additional doors and stairs inserted and sometimes extra fireplaces. Some houses became public houses or shops. Other great changes came if the lord of the manor decided to build a new park around his country house and remove the whole village from his doorstep to a more distant site, where regular pairs of new stone or brick cottages replaced the old and varied housing.

In the north and west there was much rebuilding in the 18th century with updated longhouses, new two-roomed cottages with attics lit by dormer windows, and, in the Yorkshire Pennines, laithe-houses. These double-pile houses combine living quarters, barn, byre and stables all under one continuous roof (laithe is the local name for a barn).

Houses are not and never have been static entities, and there were frequent additions and alterations through this period to update existing houses. New windows are perhaps the most common change, with thousands of sash windows being inserted into older houses in the 18th and

Fig 1.11 (above): An early 18th century brick town house in Lincoln. Note the fashionable features such as the parapet hiding the roof from view, the early sash windows nearly flush with the surrounding brickwork and the corner stones (quoins) contrasting with the brickwork.

Fig 1.12 (below): The Crescent, Buxton, built in a classical style in the 1780s. Note the top row of windows have finer glazing bars and the frame is recessed behind the wall with a plain surround, the style of the later 18th and early 19th century. (The windows below are later.)

Fig 1.13 (above): A timber-framed house with a later fashionable façade added. Notice that the ground-floor window does not line up with the windows above as it would have done if it was a new structure and not one having to fit in with the existing building behind.

Fig 1.14 (below): Edensor village was rebuilt from 1838-42 on a new site by the Duke of Devonshire so that it was out of sight of Chatsworth House. The new houses reflected many of the designs in J.C.Loudon's influential 'Encyclopedia of Cottage, Farm and Villa Architecture'.

19th centuries. Sometimes these were inserted into openings of the same size, in which case the only external clue may be a hoodmould above a sash window (hoodmoulds were only used for earlier mullioned windows). Often, however, the window opening has been altered in size and shape, which may leave traces in the brick or stonework and will certainly leave clues in timber framing. Eighteenth century modernisation often took the form of plastering over any exposed timbers, inside and out; ceiling beams were totally concealed if possible, or plastered and painted white, if not. Many houses in prominent positions or along the new coaching routes had whole new classical façades added to mask an unfashionable timber-framed house. A view down the side or an uneven row of windows will usually reveal the older structure behind.

Windows and doorways were sometimes moved or simply blocked, either to avoid the window tax or because new and more convenient openings had been made elsewhere. In stone- or brick-walled houses the resulting recesses often became cupboards.

19th century houses

The conversion of the country from an agricultural and mercantile economy to an industrial and financial one throughout the late 18th and 19th centuries resulted in a huge shift and growth of population, principally in the towns and cities. Speculative builders, who had appeared in the later 17th century, were responsible for some of the new, if indifferent quality housing rather than the local carpenter or mason. The endless rows of anonymous brick and stone terraces made from mass-produced or widely transported materials to standardized designs, publicised in the growing number of architects' magazines sounded the end of vernacular architecture.

In the towns and cities the terrace had grown in height and depth, with more floors, half basements which raised the front door up a set of steps, and rear extensions with a full suite of service rooms. Stucco (a form of render) covered brickwork and was applied and coloured to imitate fine stone, and was also used to form classical details and decoration as the Victorians relaxed the strict

Palladian rules which had made the Georgian terrace so plain. For the newly rich industrialists and financiers and later the growing middle classes, the semi or detached villa appeared in the new suburbs, at first in the fashionable Classical and Italianate style. Later as the country sought a new identity by looking back to the past, Gothic and Revival styles were favoured. The removal of window taxes in the 1850s resulted in the previously expensive bay window becoming the fashionable accessory of the second half of the 19th century, spreading down from the villa to the middle class terrace, at first as a single-storey feature and later at full height.

Fig 1.15 (above): A Victorian villa with canted (angled) bay windows fitted with large panes of glass and a confused mix of styles between Italianate and Gothic!

For the rural and urban poor, housing had not improved and for some had become worse, with most expecting no more than a single room to accommodate their family. Back-to-back houses, and cottages with a top floor or a side unit for industry, were the best many could expect until health and building regulations in the second half of the century began to improve their plight. These meant that the working class family of 1900 could expect to rent a two up, two down house.

The rapid industrialisation and the mass-production of goods of all types eventually caused a social and artistic backlash, and the later 19th century saw a revival of traditional crafts and buildings based on earlier vernacular styles rather than Classical or Gothic architecture. The revival became known as the Arts and Crafts Movement, and by the late 1890s many fine quality houses had been built, with steeply-pitched tiled roofs, mullioned windows with wrought-iron casements, tall chimneys and the use of local materials. Architects such as Lutyens or Philip Webb were deeply involved in all aspects of the interiors as well, designing all the fixtures and fittings down to the door hinges and latches.

As before, existing houses were still being adapted for the new age. With the growing popularity of coal in the 18th century, fireplaces were reduced in size as coal burns in a smaller area than wood, and iron grates and kitchen ranges were installed. Cupboards were sometimes created in what had originally been part of a large open fireplace, while the new smaller fireplace opening received an up-to-date surround. This process continued unabated until the later years of the 20th century, with

Fig 1.16 (below): Spout Hall, Leek, 1871, designed by Richard Norman Shaw, one of the leading late Victorian architects whose early work was inspired by 16th and 17th century farmhouses and cottages. Note, however, the stone-arched doorway in 14th century style.

Fig 1.17 (below):A series of drawings showing how a cruck-framed house was constructed. The timbers were usually prepared away from the site (1), where the joints were all numbered with carpenters' marks to enable easy re-assembly on site (2). Each pair of crucks was reared in turn and propped in place until it could be joined to the previous truss by the horizontal timbers (3). Finally the wall framing was added, the wattle and daub infill installed and the roof thatched (4).

1
Timber trimmed and split in two.

2
Cruck- frame assembled.

3
House erected one bay at a time.

4
Wattle inserted into frame and covered in daub.

many 17th century open fireplaces being reduced in size several times until they ended up as a tiny opening with a 1950s tiled surround. The fireplace had then become totally out of scale with the room and often looked completely ridiculous. More recently the trend has been to open them up again, which restores the correct proportions to the room but may lose valuable historical evidence along the way. It can also be debated whether it is acceptable to throw out (or hopefully move to a different location) a Victorian fireplace surround that may be a very good example of its type and period in order to return to an earlier phase. It, too, is evidence of the many changes that the house has undergone and is just as valid histori-cally as the first phase, which can pose considerable dilemmas for the would-be restorer and for the researcher or conservation officer alike. (NB. It should be noted that all such work in a listed building requires Listed Building consent.)

In the 19th century rooms were often reduced in size in order to create new entrance lobbies, insert new stairs, or create long passages to avoid having to go through one room to reach another. It is usually fairly easy to spot these insertions: rooms may be oddly proportioned, or a fireplace be set right at one edge instead of nearer the middle of a wall. If there are original ceiling beams, they may have decorative stops at their original ends, usually at the outer walls of the house. If there are additional stops on either side of a partition wall, it indicates that the wall is an original feature and not an insertion.

Doorframes were often modernised to try to make them match any new ones which had been installed, and it is not uncommon to see a 17th century ovolo-moulded doorframe to which has been added a moulded architrave of 19th century design. Doors, too, have frequently been replaced, and there are many 18th, 19th and 20th century doors in older frames. Conversely there may be 17th century doors that have been moved and are now either in older frames or in much more recent surrounds. If the ground floor or the best rooms were being modernised, the old but still serviceable doors may be relegated to the attics or outhouses where they would be less obvious; many a farmer has avoided the cost of a new door in a farm building by installing an old one from the house.

Architecture is not simply about functional buildings; it is also about trying to look fashionable at minimum cost. It is the combination of these two requirements that has led to the wonderful architectural mixtures that make up many of our old houses.

MATERIALS

Timber framing

Medieval houses were built from locally available materials, either timber framing or stone, while the mud or cob walls common in Devon and Buckinghamshire (where it is called wichert) may have been more widespread. Timber framing was either cruck-framed or box-framed. Crucks, common in the north and west and unknown in the south and east, are large curved timbers which run from ground to apex, and are set in pairs to form the main framework of the building. Box-frame construction uses vertical posts joined by tiebeams and wall-plates at the top and by sill beams at the base to form a rigid box. By the 17th century box framing had become the dominant form in all areas where timber framing was still used. The panels were infilled with wattle and daub, a lattice made of either thin hazel twigs or split oak laths and coated with a mixture of mud, straw and other ingredients. When dry the daub was coated in limewash, either white or coloured depending on local tradition, and evidence suggests that the limewash was often carried over the timbers as well to act as a preservative. In the 16th century some houses had brick nogging as infill, or brick may replace the wattle and daub at a later date. In the 18th and 19th centuries timber walls were often concealed behind plaster, weatherboard or tile hanging, or a complete false façade in the latest style (Fig 1.13, page 12).

Stone

Stone was used for medieval peasant houses in areas where it was readily available, such as south Gloucestershire and parts of Devon, but elsewhere timber houses were often rebuilt or clad in stone in the 17th century when its use became more widespread. The band of oolitic

Medieval framing

Close studding

Decorative framing

Fig 1.18 *(above): Types of box framing.*

Fig 1.19 *(below): Examples of bonding (the way a brick wall is laid). English Bond was popular in the 16th and early 17th centuries (also revived in the late 19th), while Flemish was fashionable from the late 17th until the 19th century.*

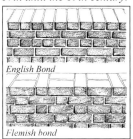

English Bond

Flemish bond

limestone that runs from Somerset across to Lincolnshire produces good quality freestone which can be cut into regular blocks (ashlar) and moulded mullions and doorways. Other types of limestone, sandstones (common in the south Pennines and the Welsh Marches), granite and slate produced poorer quality stone usually used as rubble walling, either coursed or random. In areas with no good building stones, flint was used, sometimes in the form of smooth pebbles from the beach, with brick for the corners and openings.

Brick

Although popular for the grandest mansions in the 15th and 16th centuries, brick was not generally used for mass walling in ordinary houses until the 17th century. The earliest hand-made bricks were thinner than later ones, with varying colours and textures; machine-made bricks from the 19th century onwards are larger and more regular in size, colour and finish, and can appear harsh in comparison.

Cob walls

Mud and clays have been used for walling from prehistoric times, but the use of clay mixed with straw and other ingredients such as dung, chalk and gravel to form cob was still popular in Devon and elsewhere in the 18th century and is currently undergoing a revival. The typically thick walls were built up in layers on a solid stone footing and were protected by overhanging thatch and a coating of lime render.

2 DOORS
Doorways, Hinges and Latches

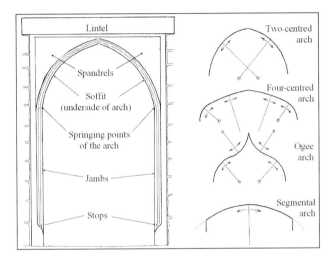

Lintel

Spandrels

Soffit
(underside of arch)

Springing points
of the arch

Jambs

Stops

Two-centred
arch

Four-centred
arch

Ogee
arch

Segmental
arch

Fig 2.1 (left): Parts of a doorway and four types of arches found in doorheads and windows.

Fig 2.2 (below): A medieval stone doorway with a two centred arch typical of the 14th century. The close-up below shows the decorated stop which terminates the chamfer or moulding around the doorway (see page 24).

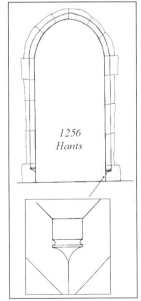

*1256
Hants*

DOORWAYS AND DOORFRAMES

Stone doorways survive in important houses from as early as the 12th century, with well-known examples in towns such as Lincoln, where they are commonly referred to as either 'the Norman House' or sometimes 'the Jew's House'. Most surviving stone doorways date from later in the medieval period and often indicate that the house was of manor house status or above, even if now it is simply a farmhouse. In the 14th and early 15th centuries the two-centred arch was the usual form, but after this the four-centred arch was in general use until at least the middle of the 16th century.

Wooden doorframes were more common, and the majority of them were square-headed. In humbler houses all the doorways would have taken this form, in larger ones only the less important doorways had square heads. Two-centred arched doorframes survive in surprisingly large numbers; they may remain in situ even

Fig 2.3b (below): 1325 Hants has a 'durn' doorframe, in which the jambs are expanded and shaped at the head to form the arch. This type is widespread and is known until at least the middle of the 15th century, and the word 'durn' is even found in a Cornish folk song! (Inside is a close-up of the pyramid stop, see page 25).

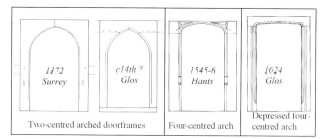

1372 Surrey	c14th ? Glos	1545-6 Hants	1624 Glos
Two-centred arched doorframes		Four-centred arch	Depressed four-centred arch

Fig 2.3a (above): Wooden doorframes: Note the stops on 1545-6 Hants are set very high, a common 16th century feature.

1325
Hants

Fig 2.4 (below right): Ashley Cottage, Hampshire, 1567-8. The partition wall separating the formerly open hall from the parlour contains two blocked doorways; the one on the left has a cambered head and led to the parlour. The one on the right has a straight head and led to the stair to the upper chamber at this end. Straight-headed doorframes are almost universal in medieval buildings for stair doors; as the door would have to open outwards, it would conceal any arch when closed, making a more decorative doorframe a pointless expense.

when the rest of the house has been altered and modernised (they were popular in the 14th century in both Hampshire and Sussex, the latter up to c1450).

The four-centred arch began to replace the two-centred arch in the early 15th century, and in this period both types may be found in the same house. It remained in common use until fashions changed on the accession of Elizabeth I in the mid 16th century. At the same time the shouldered arch is found in some areas (see Fig 2.5b, page 19). The design first appears in stone in medieval castles, when it is commonly called the Caernarvon arch, and occasionally occurs in stone in domestic buildings at the top of the social scale. Most domestic examples are of wood; the type seems especially common in Devon and Somerset, but there are examples in many areas. A likely date range is mid 15th to mid 16th century.

Alongside these was the cambered doorhead, a simpler form in which the doorhead rises to a central point. These 'arches' may be very shallow, with the centre only an inch or two above the springing point. At Ashley Cottage the cambered doorhead is formed in the horizontal rail of the

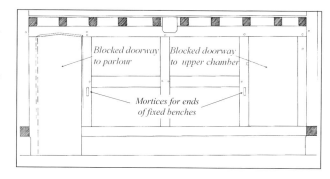

Blocked doorway to parlour

Blocked doorway to upper chamber

Mortices for ends of fixed benches

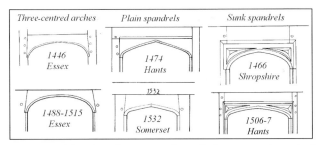

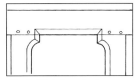

Fig 2.5b *(above): A shouldered arch.*

Fig 2.5 *(above): Three-centred and four-centred arched doorheads. The 1532 example from Somerset is an unusually early example of an inscribed date, which only become common in the later 16th century.*

partition wall, while the jambs are simply structural studs with a slight chamfer.

A simpler alternative to the four-centred arch is the three-centred doorhead and typical simple designs of the 15th century from Essex are shown in Fig 2.5. Some four-centred arched doorheads are plain (1474 Hants and 1532 Somerset), while others have sunk spandrels (1466 Shropshire and 1506-7 Hants). Durn doorframes (see Fig 2.3b) are no longer used, but instead the head of the arch is formed in a single timber tenoned into the jambs.

Ogee doorheads seem more common in the west and the north, and in the far north of Cumbria persist to the end of

Fig 2.7 *(below): Ogee doorheads. On the left, the true ogee with and without chamfers. In the centre, late 16th and early 17th century ogee variants with a tiny central upturn hinting at their origin. On the right, later ogees, some with extra embellishments, and an unusual 'depressed ogee' of 1672 from Somerset.*

Fig 2.6 *(below): Doorframe mouldings. Medieval stone doorways often have a plain chamfer, although some have hollow or double chamfers (1438-42 Hants). Wooden Doorframes, too, are often chamfered, but a more complex moulding was in general use in Hampshire and East Sussex, with chamfers set at much less than 45° with a step and hollow (in Hampshire there are several dated examples between 1474 and 1545). Different stops came into use from the late 15th century; at 1528 Hants the moulding finishes with a flat and step (see page 25).*

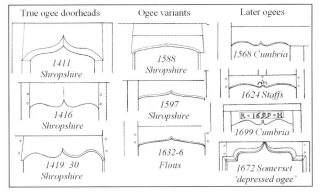

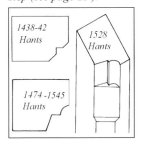

1393
Ludlow,
Shropshire

Fig 2.8 *(above):*
The 1393 Palmers' Guild
in Ludlow has a two-
centred arch with
quatrefoils and
mouchettes in the
spandrels, which has
amazingly survived in a
front elevation otherwise
altered completely to the
Georgian style.

Fig 2.10 *(below):*
Examples of a flat head
with rounded corners and
depressed four-centred
doorheads.

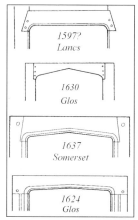

1597?
Lancs

1630
Glos

1637
Somerset

1624
Glos

the 17th century. Many northern examples are of stone and the ogee shape is used for many late 17th century doorheads in Ribblesdale in the Yorkshire Dales. Elsewhere they are mostly of wood and belong to the 15th century, with variants in the later 16th and early 17th centuries. The later examples generally have a less pronounced ogee shape and a late variant from 1672 Somerset, has a 'depressed ogee' arch.

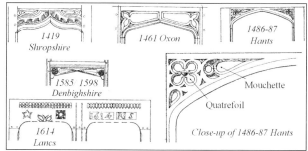

1419
Shropshire

1461 Oxon

1486-87
Hants

1585-1598
Denbighshire

1614
Lancs

Mouchette

Quatrefoil

Close-up of 1486-87 Hants

Fig 2.9 *(above): Examples of decorated doorheads. The remains of an open-hall house behind the Nag's Head, Shrewsbury (1419 Shropshire) has ogee doorheads decorated with mouchettes and foliage. 1614 Lancs is an example from a modest house where the centre of each doorframe has been cut back, leaving the original form uncertain, but the large curves at each side suggest that these too were ogee arches.*

Some doorframes in high status buildings were highly elaborate, with moulded surrounds and decorated spandrels. Even more modest houses may have decorated doorheads, and many East Sussex houses have carved spandrels. These usually take the form of a flower, most often a rose, surrounded by stylised leaves or geometric designs similar to Hants 1486-87 above.

From the mid 16th century the four-centred arch gradually changed and by the 17th century the depressed four-centred arch was a common form for stone doorways (Fig 2.3a); it continued well into the 17th century.

Many wooden doorframes also use either this form or the cambered head, and they may be moulded or chamfered. The depressed four-centred arch has rounded corners and straight sides; the cambered head (Fig 2.11) does not have rounded corners. There are two different methods of jointing the former; in the first, the doorhead or lintel is tenoned between the jambs, often with an angled joint (1597 Lancs, 1637 Som.) The other has the jambs tenoned into the soffit of the doorhead (1624 Glos). Cambered heads show the same variety of jointing as shown in Fig 2.10, but those with moulded frames now have scribed joints. This means that the tops of the jambs are cut away to fit over the moulding of the lintel, giving the appearance of a mitred joint.

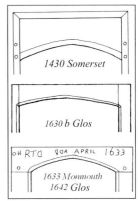

Fig 2.12 (above): A variant type of cambered head has slightly curved sides; 1630 Glos has the lintel tenoned into the jambs, while 1633 Mon/ 1642 Glos has the jambs tenoned into the lintels. 1430 Somerset is almost exactly the same shape as the later variants of the cambered head, showing the potential difficulty of dating by style alone.

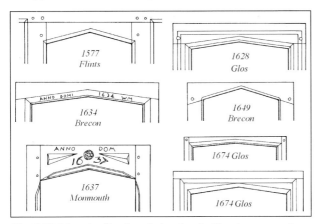

Fig. 2.11 (above): Cambered doorheads. The steeper versions are sometimes called 'peaked heads'.

Square-headed doorways were used alongside arched doorways throughout the medieval period, and from the mid 16th century began to dominate. They may be moulded or chamfered, and wooden doorframes in stone-walled buildings may have a moulded overlintel. It is quite common for a date to be carved on the lintel, such as 1571 Bucks and 1594 Glos, while in Monmouthshire

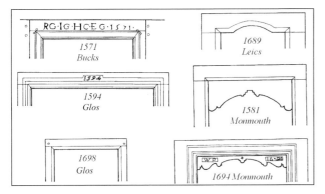

Fig 2.13 (left): A selection of square-headed doorways. 1689 Leics is unusual in having a segmental arch in the centre, while 1581 and 1694 Monmouth illustrate the fashion for decorative boards set within the frame.

1634a Sussex

1677 Yorks

1680a Yorks

(Above) : Medieval forms
survive longer in stone
doorways; at Bateman's
(1634a Sussex) the front
doorway has a fashionable
round arch while elaborate
four-centred arches of
medieval style are used for
the internal doorways.

Fig 2.14 (right): A round-
arched doorway of 1672
from Somerset; it is in a
porch added when an
earlier building was
altered and enlarged.
Granite examples from
Devon are at Middle
Bonehill (1682) and
Corndon (1718), both in
Widecombe-on-the-Moor.

and Breconshire there was a fashion for decorative boards set within a chamfered or moulded frame. Many of these also include dates in the decorative scheme.

Round-arched doorways are common in the early 17th century, influenced by grand Elizabethan houses such as Montacute (1580-1601), or the slightly later Ham House in Surrey of 1610, but are usually only used for the main doorway(s) or the porch. Most examples are in superior houses and are of stone, but some are found further down the social ladder in wealthy farmhouses, and sometimes in brick.

They persist into the late 17th century, and in the Dartmoor area of Devon, where granite is the available building stone, a number of longhouses have simple round-arched doorways, with dated examples of 1682 and even as late as 1718.

1605
Lancs

Fig 2.15 (above):
Gawthorpe in Lancashire
has a pair of doorways in
the screen at the lower end
of the hall which have deep
segmental arches with a
central notch. The
spandrels have inlaid
foliage designs bearing
shields with initials, and
the date 1605 in the centre.

Fig 2.16 (left): An
example of a 'Porch
House' is in Shrewsbury,
dated 1628, and is not an
enclosed porch but rather
a slight forward
projection with a very
deep moulded doorframe
and a moulded cornice
carried on heavily carved
consoles. Above is an oriel
window on carved
brackets (see page 68-69).

Round-arched doorways are also commonly found in hall screens in larger houses of the later Elizabethan period and into the 17th century.

Many houses were given a more important appearance by the use of a two-storey porch, either of timber or stone, a feature which originated in the medieval period and remained popular for much of the 17th century. Timber porches may have lavish carving and some have open

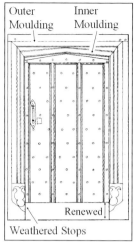

Outer Moulding   Inner Moulding

Renewed

Weathered Stops

Fig 2.17 (above): Many external doorframes have two orders of mouldings, commonly two ovolos or an ogee and ovolo separated by one or two steps. If the doorframe has an arched or cambered head the inner moulding follows the camber while the outer moulding forms a square head (1659 Glos).

Fig 2.18 (right): Sections through different types of wooden doorframe and stone doorway mouldings.

panels in the sides with turned spindles. Often the porch was sufficiently distinctive to give the house its name, and there are many called 'Porch House' all over the country.

Doorway and Doorframe Mouldings

Both wooden doorframes and stone doorways were either chamfered or moulded and the accession of Queen Elizabeth I in 1558 seems to have brought about a change in style. The old hollow and chamfer moulding was now replaced by the ovolo moulding, which is a quarter round with one or more steps on either side. The earliest dated ovolo doorframe is in Winchester and dates from 1560 while a similar doorframe in a Buckinghamshire house has an inscribed date of 1571. Both have double steps on either side of the ovolo (see Fig 2.18) and square heads rather than arches or cambers.

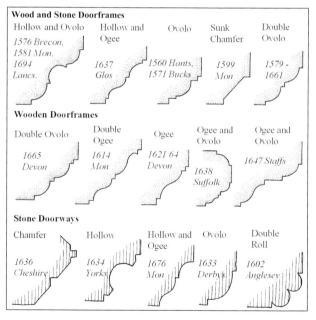

In East Sussex and Hampshire moulded doorframes seem to be largely confined to gentry houses, but in Gloucestershire the ovolo moulding became extremely popular and is found in many of the substantial yeoman farmhouses. Here it is used not just for doorframes, but also for mullions, ceiling beams and fireplace lintels.

Stops

Near the base of the frame, the chamfer or moulding terminates with a stop, which can be plain or decorative. 1560 Hants has a type commonly known as the pumpkin, vase or onion stop, which occurs here in its simplest form. Some late 16th century Hampshire and mid 17th century Gloucestershire doorframes combine the vase with elements such as the truncated or complete pyramid.

Some highly elaborate stops have survived, although often heavily weathered on external doorframes, such as the fluted columns with Ionic capitals in Devon 1635-40.

Most doorframes, however, have much simpler stops, with step stops and scroll (cyma, ogee or lamb's tongue) stops being the most common. Ovolo or ogee mouldings may also have converging stops, where the moulding tapers to a point; alternatively a flat plane separates the scroll or step stop from the moulding. The same range of simple stops is found on ceiling beams and fireplace

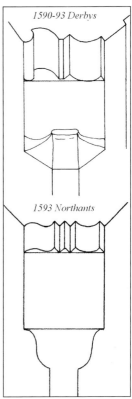

Fig 2.19 (above): Examples of stops on stone doorways.

Fig 2.20b (below): A Gloucestershire stop by the same carpenter in two different houses in the same parish.

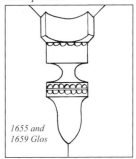

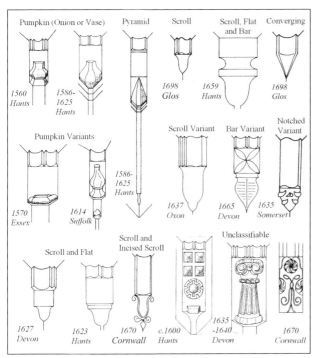

Fig 2.20a (above): Examples of doorframe stops.

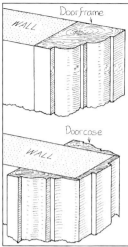

Fig 2.21 (above): A section through a doorframe showing how it is moulded from a solid piece and a doorcase with the moulded members fitted around the wall.

Fig 2.22 (below): Examples of 17th century bolection mouldings. They occur in both wood and stone, and are common in the period 1670-1720. The large S-shaped bolection moulding is usually combined with one or more smaller elements, commonly an ogee and a projecting half-round fillet; small hollow chamfers and bead mouldings are also sometimes used.

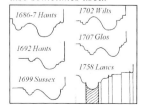

lintels, which rarely have the same elaboration as doorframes. Sometimes unusual stops enable the work of an individual carpenter to be recognised within a restricted area.

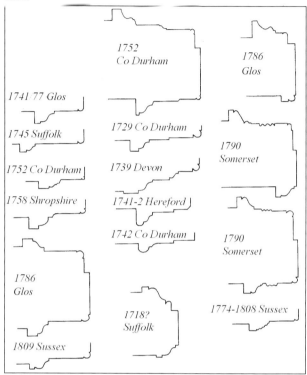

Fig 2.23 : Profiles of 18th century doorcase mouldings.

Doorcases

These differ from earlier moulded doorframes in being applied mouldings set around the door opening rather than a separate doorframe set within the opening (see Fig 2.21). The earliest, in the late 17th century, are bolection mouldings with a prominent profile (see Fig 2.22). At the same time variations on the ogee and/or the bead moulding became popular. Simpler doorcases have a flat plane between the outer ogee moulding and the inner bead, but more elaborate ones have a double plane or step; occasionally the plane is omitted (1718 Suffolk).

Around 1800 the S-shaped ogee moulding underwent a subtle change to a more angular profile that is very characteristic of the 19th century; one of the earliest examples is 1790 Somerset, where it is combined with a shallow reeding.

The wide doorcases of the early 19th century have a completely different type of moulding with a symmetrical design (Fig 2.26b). The earliest, as seen in service rooms at Kensington Palace in 1805, have a recessed central field with a moulding on either side, but much more elaborate designs soon became popular. Often they were added to earlier houses, such as the Wiltshire house described as 'recently rebuilt' in 1789, where the parlour was evidently updated and given a new doorcase in the early 19th century.

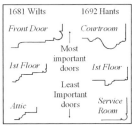

Fig 2.24 (above): Doorcases can reveal the different status of rooms by their variations or complexity. The Wardenry, Farley, Wilts (1681) has a splendid series of original doorcases, with the most elaborate for the main first-floor room and front door but the plainest in the attics. The same sequence occurs at Otterbourne Manor, Hampshire (1692), a former courthouse, with a bolection-moulded doorcase for the courtroom but only old-fashioned doorframes with a bead moulding for the service rooms.

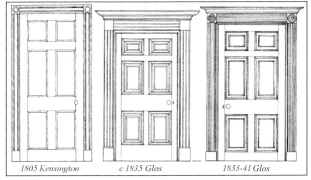

Fig 2.25 (above):Early 19th century doorcases. Many early 19th century doors have a wide doorcase with corner squares, which may be plain but often have concentric circles or floral designs in them. Again these can reveal the hierarchy of the different rooms. The mouldings usually terminate in a plain square block at the base.

In many houses these wide doorcases were only used in the entrance hall and on the first-floor landing; inside the rooms more traditional doorcases were used. These continued the ogee and bead tradition, but often incorporated an extra small bead with the ogee (1812 Hants, 1821 Glos). Others finished the ogee with a small chamfer (Fig 2.26b: 1804 Co. Durham), a feature which became especially popular from the 1830s and continued into the 20th century.

The later 19th century brought larger mouldings and designs that bore little resemblance to anything which had preceded them. Others draw heavily on traditional designs, but include rather more elements than earlier

Fig 2.26a (below): Profiles of 19th century doorcases which incorporate an extra small bead with the ogee.

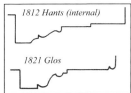

Fig 2.26b (right): A selection of profiles of doorcase mouldings from the 19th century.

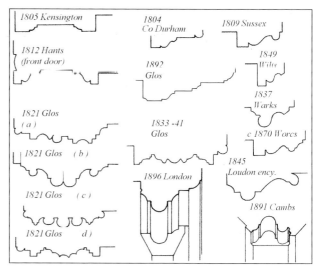

Fig 2.27a (below): Typical late 17th century two-light over-door light from Oxfordshire (1693). It has a central ogee-moulded mullion with an external rebate for the glazing and the doorframe has a small ovolo moulding running down the jambs to the ground with no stops of any kind. The door is an early example of the four-panelled door where all the panels are the same size and retains the original doorhandle (Fig 2.83, page 57).

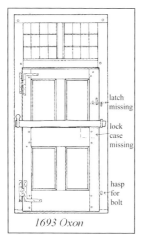

1693 Oxon

examples (1892 Glos). Often these late mouldings stop several inches above the floor, usually at the height of the skirting board, and the doorcase is finished with a wide flat chamfer.

Over-door lights and Fanlights

Over-door lights first appear in the 17th century to light central staircase halls, particularly in double-pile plans where the house is two rooms deep and there may be a long central entrance hall leading to the stair at the back. These 17th century over-door lights usually have wood or stone mullions which match those of the rest of the house, and originally had leaded lights. By the late 17th century it had become quite common for front doorframes to incorporate a two-light window above the door (see Fig 2.27a).

Fanlights became a popular feature throughout the 18th century, although the term 'fanlight' was not invented until around 1770. The name derives from the semicircular shape, although the earliest 'fanlights' were rectangular and if they had a semicircle it was set within a rectangular opening. Before long the opening itself became semicircular in shape and was often incorporated into a doorcase with a broken pediment. Until the middle of the century fanlights were always made of wood, with glazing bars which match those of sash windows. After about 1750

Fig 2.27b: *In the 18th century the over-door light developed into the decorative fanlight of which there is a multitude of variations. These examples are all in Richmond, Surrey, which has a large and varied range of fanlights in houses around The Green; most have rectangular openings with a semicircle as the main element of the design.*

brass and wrought iron were used instead, with cast iron from the late 18th century. These enabled more delicate and intricate designs to be used.

In the 1780s a special alloy of copper, zinc and iron was discovered and was used for cast decoration on fanlights which had wrought-iron ribs. The strange golden colour of the metal led to the name 'Eldorado' being applied to them, and implies that, unlike most fanlights, these were not painted. Some towns had identifiable local styles of fanlights, such as the plain semicircle with just two angled ribs that was popular in Lewes until the early 19th century.

Some early 19th century fanlights incorporate a central lantern, glazed as an integral part of the design. Fanlights were sometimes inserted into earlier houses, and can often be identified by mouldings which do not match the rest of the doorcase. The increased availability of sheet glass from the 1840s led to the gradual demise of the fanlight, although it lingered on in rural areas.

1833 Glos

Fig 2.29 *(above): A simple four-light over-door window can be seen at a Gloucestershire house of 1833.*

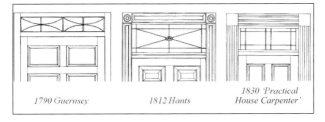

1790 Guernsey   *1812 Hants*   *1830 'Practical House Carpenter'*

Fig 2.28 *(above): At the end of the 18th century and especially in the early 19th many fanlights reverted to the rectangular shape prevalent a century earlier, but with simple glazing patterns instead of mullions and leaded lights. Victorian versions may include coloured or etched glass.*

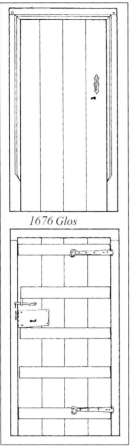

1676 Glos

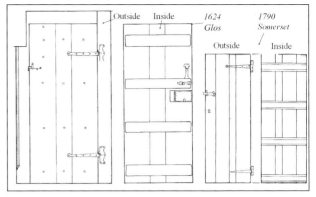

Fig 2.31 *(above): Doors before the 19th century frequently have planks of irregular widths. This is often the result of the availability of timber, in which case the arrangement can be purely random, with a narrow plank on one edge to make up the required width, or two planks of greatly differing widths. Sometimes it was done for deliberate effect, with a narrower central plank (1624 Glos), or with alternate wide and narrow planks (1790 Somerset).*

Fig 2.30 *(above) A typical plank and batten door. This Gloucestershire door of 1676, set in a moulded frame, retains all its original furniture (the lock case and the hasp for the lock bar, latch and latch fastener, handle and hinges).*

DOORS

The earliest and simplest form of door is the plank and batten door, in which vertical planks are nailed onto horizontal battens. There are usually four or five battens, although three is not uncommon, and many are either totally plain or chamfered. Often they have a fairly rough finish and they may not all be the same width.

Numerous plank and batten doors survive from the 16th century onwards, and the simplest are almost impossible to date accurately. The earliest doors generally have the widest planks, with two or three to a door, while by the end of the 17th century four planks are commonly found. Planks gradually get narrower during the course of the 18th century, and in the 19th century doors of six or more planks are common. At this date the boards will be machine-sawn and much more regular in appearance than the earlier hand-sawn variety.

Few recognisably medieval doors survive in domestic buildings, but evidence from churches shows that the earliest doors from the late Saxon and Norman periods were held together by elaborate jointing systems and ironwork, without any battens. In the 13th and 14th

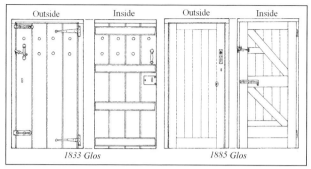

1833 Glos

1885 Glos

Fig 2.32 *(above): 19th century plank and batten doors. The 1833 Glos example is a cellar door pierced for ventilation. In the 19th century the planks are now much narrower; in the early 19th century they still have a small bead moulding down one edge of each plank, as they did in the 18th century, but by the later 19th century that has gone. The 1885 Glos example has plank and batten internal doors, but the external doors are ledged and braced.*

Fig 2.34 *(below): Examples of medieval doors. The ironwork on the front door of Elsie Briggs House in Westbury-on-Trym, Bristol, suggests that it is contemporary with the 15th century doorway – the iron cross is the symbol of Bishop Carpenter of Worcester, who was connected with Westbury in the mid 15th century. The date of the door at Manor Farm, Breadstone, Glos is less certain; the doorway is 15th century, and the door handle is a type not usually found after the 16th century, but the double scroll hinges and the applied battens are more usual in the later 16th and 17th century. The original door at Porch House, Thornbury, Glos is no longer in situ, but is preserved inside the open hall. Its date is uncertain, but late 14th or early 15th century seems likely.*

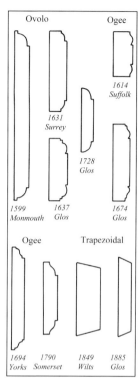

Fig 2.33 *(above): Profiles of door battens. Battens are often moulded in the 17th and 18th centuries, but many have a simple chamfer or are completely plain. In the 19th century they are trapezoidal.*

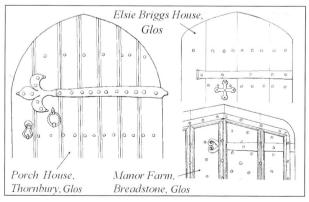

Elsie Briggs House, Glos

Porch House, Thornbury, Glos

Manor Farm, Breadstone, Glos

Fig 2.35 (right): *Examples of 16th and 17th century double thickness doors. Note vertical planks on the outside faces and horizontal or diagonal on the inside. Note the carpenter's marks /, // and /// on the planks of 1641-42 Hants.*

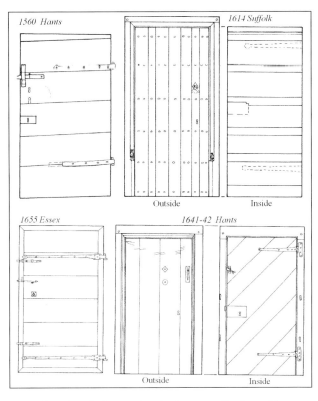

centuries church doors often had narrow D-shaped battens or a complete framework to which the planks were fixed.

Most external doors and some internal doors (1560 Hants above) were double thickness, with vertical planks on the outer face and horizontal 'counter boards' on the inside. Most doors are three or four planks wide, but occasionally narrower planks were used, as at 1614 Suffolk above; here the inner horizontal planks are alternately wide and narrow, an unusual arrangement. The same effect can be seen at 1623 Hants, where the narrow 'planks' are in fact moulded battens, with the gaps between them filled in with thick planks. Diagonal internal planks were sometimes used from the mid 17th century, such as 1641-42 Hants, and several examples occur in 1680s Quaker meeting houses in both England and America. In better quality work there may be a narrow frame around the counter boards, as at 1655 Essex (Fig 2.35), which also has exceptionally long strap hinges.

Applied fillets are often used to cover the joints between the planks, which helps to make the door draught-proof and keep the rain out of the joints. For this reason they are most commonly used on external doors, but by no means exclusively so. Hinges are usually set on the outer face of the door and pass beneath the fillets. Simple vertical fillets are common, and this seems to be the normal type in the 16th century with frequent examples up to the mid 17th century and continuing into the later 17th century. Some have a central horizontal fillet forming panels, usually six in number. 1638 Suffolk has unusually narrow planks for this period, and has twelve panels; the outer ones are narrower, and on one side are so narrow as to be scarcely discernible.

Fig 2.36: Strangers' Hall, Norwich has a good series of dated doorheads, (1493, 1570 and 1592) with almost identical arches so not helpful for dating purposes but a useful warning!). The 1493 doorhead could be read as 1393, but because there is a very clear 3 at the end, the squiggly number is actually a 4, written like half an 8.

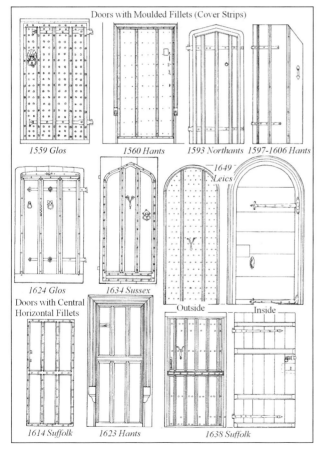

Fig 2.36 a (left): Doors with applied fillets ('cover fillets' or 'cover strips') 1593 Northants, 1597-1606 Hants and 1614 Suffolk are internal doors. 1638 Suffolk, like 1614 Suffolk (Fig 2.35), has unusually narrow planks for the period; either local fashion or a shortage of large trees in the area may be responsible.

Doors are larger than the doorframe as they close flush against the back of the frame; rebates in wooden doorframes are rare until the late 17th century. If a door has applied fillets, the outer fillet forms a frame which fits tightly within the doorframe. If the doorframe or doorway is arched the frame made by the fillets will form a matching shape, as on the 1593 Northants and 1634 Sussex examples (Fig 2.36). Sometimes a door with this feature will be set in a square-headed doorframe and so has clearly been moved from its original location.

Fig 2.37 (right): Doors with applied fillets forming six or more panels. Nails were usually prominent, forming a decorative pattern, but they are not visible on the second-floor door at Kew Palace (1631 Surrey). This door has two planks of unequal width, so the central fillet does not cover the join, but as it is an internal door this is less important. Unusually for this period, the planks are pine. Another internal door (1614 Suffolk) has a very narrow central plank which is entirely covered by the central fillet. 1586-1625 Hants is also an internal door, while 1637 Glos has internal and external doors of this design.

1614 Suffolk   1631 Surrey   1669 Sussex

1637 Glos   1586-1625 Hants   1623 Hants   1655 Essex

A more elaborate version of the door with cover strips has two or three horizontal fillets forming six or more panels, depending on the width of the door. They are particularly common in the later 16th and the first half of the 17th century, but persist into the second half of the 17th century and the nails are usually prominent giving a decorative effect.

The profile of the earliest applied fillets or cover strips have hollow mouldings and are quite narrow. Both ovolo and ogee mouldings were used from the late 16th century and are common in the first half of the 17th century. Some are extra wide and include a central recessed section, giving a very rich appearance to the

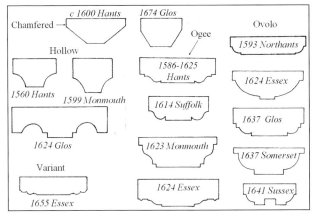

Fig 2.38 (above): Profiles of a selection of fillet mouldings from the 16th and 17th century.

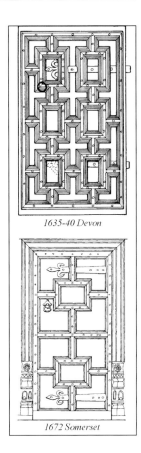

1635-40 Devon

1672 Somerset

Fig 2.39 (top right): Applied fillets can be arranged in a highly decorative manner to create elaborate geometric patterns, such as the wonderful door of the Sloping Deck restaurant in the Butterwalk, Dartmouth, a row of four houses built between 1635 and 1640 by merchant Mark Hawkings. This was the door to Hawkings' own house in the centre of the row, which was more elaborate than those on either side. In Somerset, Weston Farm, Wambrook was remodelled in 1672 and given a porch with a datestone and several decorative doors and doorframes. The front doorframe has highly decorative stops, while the door has a double 'square-within-a-square' design.

door. Doors with applied fillets gradually went out of fashion in the second half of the 17th century.

There are many ways of decorating a door, and it should be remembered that when new the oak would have been a much lighter colour than it is now, and it would certainly not have been covered in layers of gloss paint. Much of the decoration that now seems hardly visible would have been far more prominent when first produced. A common type of decoration is shadow or scratch moulding running down the edges of the planks (see Fig 2.40). Often the nails holding the planks to the battens are arranged in a pattern, such as the simple zigzag at 1616 Surrey or the double zigzag at 1648 Lancs (see Fig 2.42).

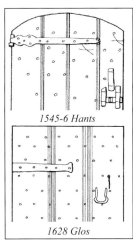

1545-6 Hants

1628 Glos

Fig 2.40 (bottom right): Shadow or scratch mouldings running vertically alongside the joints in the planks at 1545-6 Hants and 1628 Glos.

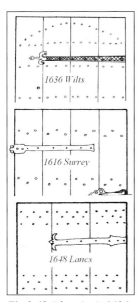

Fig 2.42 (above): At 1636
Wilts the nails at the top of
the door are arranged in
an arch shape, suggesting
that the doorframe is, or
was, also arched.

Fig 2.43 (below): 1674
Glos is a variant of the
door with applied moulded
fillets, with the addition of
carved decoration on the
top rail, which is shaped
to fit the cambered head of
the doorframe.

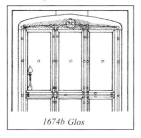

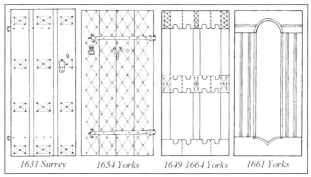

Fig 2.41 (above): Decorated 17th century doors with shadow or
scratch mouldings, nails arranged in patterns or incised
decoration.

Sometimes the nails are joined by incised lines which
may form an all-over lozenge design as at 1654 Yorks (see
Fig 2.41). This may have been very common, but the
incised lines are often hard to see and many have undoubt-
edly been overlooked. The attic door at Kew Palace (1631
Surrey) has groups of five nails joined to form a saltire
cross within a rectangle, and is a good example of another
decorative technique whereby two of the three planks are
reduced in thickness at one edge to give a panelled effect
(see Fig 2.44). Sometimes the top rail of the door is carved
into a decorative shape, with a round arch at 1661 Yorks
above.

A more elaborate design occurs at two West Yorkshire
houses (1649 and 1664), in which top, bottom and middle
rails are all given exaggerated ogee designs; in addition the
nails are joined by incised lines. This is likely to be the
work of an individual carpenter working in a limited area,
as nothing like it is known elsewhere.

Door planks can be joined in a variety of ways. The
simplest is for the planks to butt against each other, but as
the wood shrinks as it dries out this method leaves
draughty gaps between the planks. Good quality doors may
have tongued and grooved planks, which have been found
in Hampshire from the 14th to the mid 17th century.
Rebated planks are common at least from the 17th century
and they continue right through into the 20th century. The
date of introduction of this type is not known. From the late
17th to the mid 19th century door planks frequently have a
small bead moulding down one edge. In the 17th century

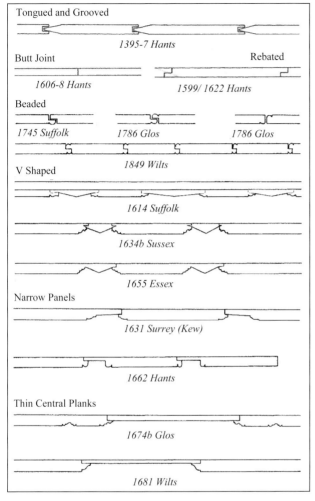

Tongued and Grooved

1395-7 Hants

Butt Joint

Rebated

1606-8 Hants

1599/ 1622 Hants

Beaded

1745 Suffolk   1786 Glos   1786 Glos

V Shaped

1849 Wilts

1614 Suffolk

1634b Sussex

1655 Essex

Narrow Panels

1631 Surrey (Kew)

1662 Hants

Thin Central Planks

1674b Glos

1681 Wilts

Fig 2.44 (left): Profiles of door planks showing the various types of joints and moulding. Other dated examples with triangular sections are 1618-21 Surrey and 1624 Bucks; thin central planks also occur at 1674a Glos, 1678b Glos, 1686b Glos, 1693 Oxon and 1743 Westmorland . N.B 1655 Essex is a remodelling of an earlier house, so the door may be earlier.

Fig 2.45 (below): Profiles of shadow mouldings.

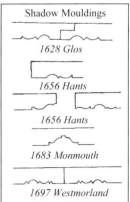

Shadow Mouldings
1628 Glos
1656 Hants
1656 Hants
1683 Monmouth
1697 Westmorland

there are a number of decorative techniques which involve reducing the thickness of the planks to create recessed vertical panels. In the first half of the 17th century one type has a triangular projection in the narrow panels, with small mouldings on either side. The triangular section may be part of the main plank (Essex 1655) or a separate section inserted between the planks (Fig 2.44: 1634 Sussex). Others in the middle of the century have a similar design but with a flat section instead of the projecting triangle (Fig 2.41: 1631 Surrey and Fig 2.44: 1662 Hants). In the last quarter of the 17th century another type of door became popular, in which the central plank is thinner than the two outside planks; the latter are moulded, with moulded fillets applied across the centre plank to give the appearance of sometimes two but usually three panels in the centre (Fig 2.46 bottom row: 1674 Glos).

Fig 2.46 (right): Doors with false or applied panelling.

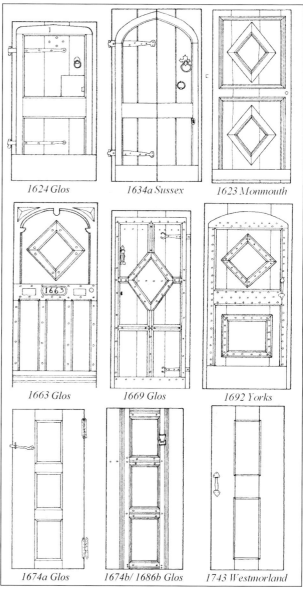

1624 Glos   1634a Sussex   1623 Monmouth

1663 Glos   1669 Glos   1692 Yorks

1674a Glos   1674b/ 1686b Glos   1743 Westmorland

A type of door which became very popular in the late 17th century is the two-panelled door. Its antecedents can be found in the early 17th century, when a number of doors have applied mouldings forming an outer frame which is divided in two by a horizontal timber. These, like the doors with applied fillets, are plank and batten doors embellished to resemble panelling. Some have applied mouldings forming lozenges, a popular motif in the 17th century (1623 Mon, 1663 Glos and 1692 Yorks), while 1669 Glos incorporates a lozenge into a door with applied mouldings forming six panels.

Panelled Doors

In the later 16th and 17th centuries doors of true panelled

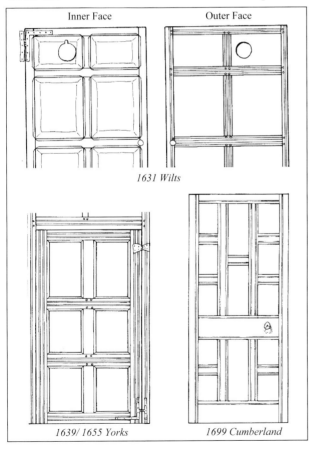

Inner Face   Outer Face

1631 Wilts

1639/ 1655 Yorks   *1699 Cumberland*

Fig 2.47 (left): True panelling (small panels). The door at Woolmore Farm, Melksham, (1631 Wilts) has a circular hole near the top, with a moveable cover on the inner face of the door. It is too high to be a peep hole and was almost certainly to help control the draught to the fireplace to enable the fire to burn well. An unusual panelled front door can be seen at The Registry in Carlisle (1699 Cumberland). It has shadow mouldings on the rails and stiles, but the design is a variant of the two-panelled door and, as an external door, the construction is more robust.

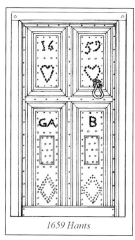

1659 Hants

Fig 2.48 *(above): A mid 17th century four-panelled door with an unusual arrangement of two shorter panels on top and two longer ones below. This heavily decorated and dated door is formed by applied mouldings rather than true panelling. Very unfortunately it was stolen from the empty house some years ago and its current whereabouts are unknown. A true panelled door with the same four-panelled arrangement is in a Wiltshire house of 1648.*

construction are found, in which thin panels are set into a framework of rails and stiles. Many are cupboard doors set into panelled rooms, and so match the rest of the panelling, but some internal doors also have this construction whether or not the room is now panelled. They are generally lighter in construction than plank and batten doors, and may have carved motifs within the panels or as a frieze at the top.

The shallow mouldings of the rails and stiles may be repeated on both sides of the door, but the inferior face may have a simple chamfer around the panels, while the panels themselves are roughly finished and bevelled at the edges (Fig 2.47:1631 Wilts). This is especially true of cupboard doors.

The two-panelled door became the normal type, at least for superior rooms, from about 1670 to 1730, with examples in smaller houses until the middle of the 18th century. Common variants have one, two or three small

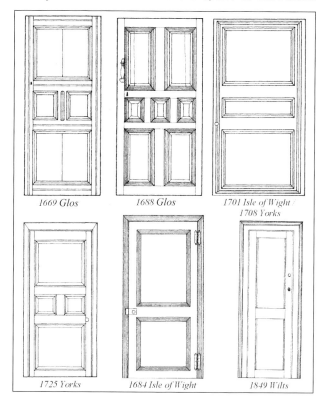

1669 Glos *1688 Glos* *1701 Isle of Wight / 1708 Yorks*

1725 Yorks *1684 Isle of Wight* *1849 Wilts*

Fig 2.49 *(right): Two-panelled doors and variants.*

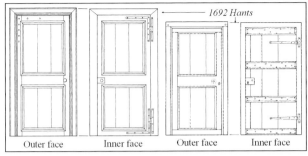

Outer face   Inner face   Outer face   Inner face

Fig 2.51 (above): Otterbourne Manor, Hampshire, 1692. Many two-panelled doors have true panelling, but others are of plank and batten construction with applied mouldings; Otterbourne Manor has both types, true panelling for the high status rooms (left) and applied panelling for the less important ones (right).

Outer face   Inner face

Fig 2.50 (above): An early two panelled door.

panels between the two main ones while others are embellished with geometric shapes, as at 5 The Close, Winchester (Fig 2.52). It even persists for cupboard doors until the mid 19th century (Fig 2.49: 1849 Wilts), but now has flush rather than recessed panels.

The panels, unlike those of the earlier small-frame panelling, are now wider than the available planks and so are made up of two or more pieces of timber. Often the wood has shrunk and there are now gaps between the planks, but originally the joints would have fitted tightly and been almost invisible. For this reason no attempt is made to have planks of even widths. Usually the panel is fielded on the main face of the door, with a small ovolo or ogee moulding around the frame, although late 17th century doors may have a heavy bolection moulding; often the same moulding occurs on the rear face with plain recessed panels. For important doors both sides will have fielded panels; lesser doors have plain recessed panels on the main face and no mouldings at all on the back.

Fig 2.52 (right): 5 – 8 The Close, Winchester is a street of four large houses built for cathedral canons in 1660-2 . Two retain their original front doors, which follow the two-panel pattern with applied mouldings forming geometric shapes; each door has a different pattern. The doors show the first move away from the double thickness door which has a complete layer of horizontal planks on the inside; here there are narrow gaps between the wide battens.

Outer face

1662 Hants

Inner face

1722 Glos

Fig 2.53 *(above): Oxwick Farm, Yate, Glos 1722. This eccentric house has round-arched doors throughout, with true panelling for the more important rooms and plank and batten doors for the attics. One of these has the words 'Cheese Roomes' painted on it, to claim exemption from the window tax. This has been found on other doors in Gloucestershire attics, and there are some elsewhere in the country. Often the paintwork has faded over the years or become covered with dirt, and one new owner inadvertently scrubbed off most of the words before noticing the OO and realising what she had done!*

Early in the 18th century the six-panelled framed door became the standard design that was to last until well into the 19th century. The proportions are always broadly the same, with two small panels at the top, larger ones at the bottom and the longest in the middle. The top panels may be square or rectangular, and sometimes there is little difference in size between the bottom and middle panels. Panels are usually fielded with an ovolo- or ogee-moulded frame, and follow the same pattern as two-panelled doors. Front doors may be embellished with elaborate architraves (Fig 2.54) of stone or wood, while interior doors have moulded wooden architraves.

From the late 18th century the four-panelled door begins to grow in popularity (Fig 2.56: 1786 Glos) and by the Victorian period has superseded the six-panelled door

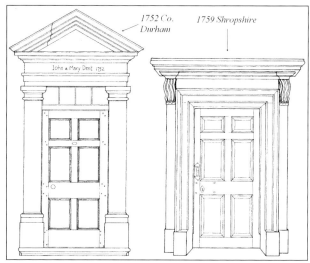

1752 Co. Durham   *1759 Shropshire*

John & Mary Dent 1752

Fig 2.54 *(above): Once porches had fallen out of fashion in the early 18th century, it became common for doors to be protected by a hood of either wood or stone, carried on carved brackets. At the beginning of the 18th century the shell hood was popular, later superseded by the flat hood. In the middle of the century pedimented doorways were popular. These two mid-18th century doors have grand doorcases; 1752 Co. Durham has columns with a pediment, while 1759 Shropshire has a flat hood carried on carved consoles. It also has a vertical door handle of a type more usually found on internal doors at this period; external doors normally have either drop handles or round brass knobs.*

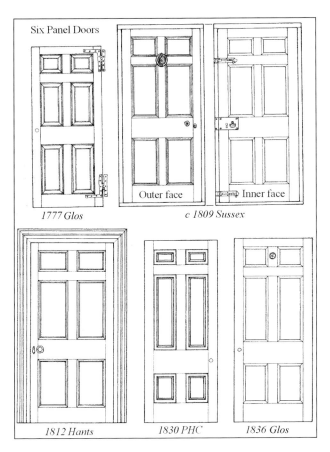

Six Panel Doors

1777 Glos

Outer face   Inner face

c 1809 Sussex

1812 Hants   *1830 PHC*   *1836 Glos*

Fig 2.55a (left): Standard six-panelled doors occur throughout the 18th and the early 19th century, with panel mouldings of varying degrees of complexity, depending on the status of the house or the status of the individual room within the house. The panels on the inner face are nearly always simpler than those on the outer face, so that the entrance hall will have the plain panels of the front door (c1809 Sussex) but the best face of the doors to the main rooms.

Fig 2.55b (below): The parts of a panelled door.

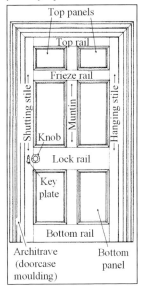

Top panels

Top rail

Frieze rail

Shutting stile

Muntin

Hanging stile

Knob

Lock rail

Key plate

Bottom rail

Bottom panel

Architrave (doorcase moulding)

almost entirely. The proportions are characteristic of the period, with tall upper panels and much shorter lower panels. In the earlier part of the period the front door will usually still have six or even eight panels, but the interior doors have four (Fig 2.56: 1812 Hants and 1833 Glos).

From the 1870s the panel edges are often chamfered and stopped rather than moulded, and some doors are three panels wide instead of two (Fig 2.56: c1870 Worcs). At the end of the 19th century, the 18th century-style six-panelled door was again popular for front doors, and there are many variants which include glazing in the upper panels.

In the late 19th century door design was often influenced by earlier periods, but it was rare for one style to be copied exactly. Instead a 'mix and match' approach was adopted, which could lead to one side of a door being classical in

Fig 2.57a (above): 2 Church Square, Whitby, dated 1881. While still using the traditional six-panel form, this door is typical of the later 19th century with its Gothic details and the chamfers and stops around the panels, nicely picked out by the current paint scheme.

Fig 2.57b (below): Late 19th century 'mix and match' style.

1891 Cambs

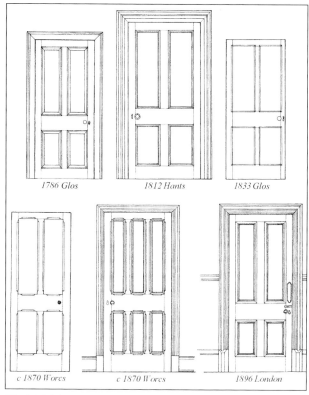

1786 Glos   1812 Hants   1833 Glos

c 1870 Worcs   c 1870 Worcs   1896 London

Fig 2.56 (above): Examples of 19th century four-panelled doors. Note how at 1870 Worcs one door is three panels wide and has chamfers and stops around the panel edges, a fashion in the later 19th century.

appearance while the other owed more to the Jacobean period.

In Cloister Court at Sidney Sussex College, Cambridge, designed by J.L.Pearson in 1891 (Fig 2.57b), the doors have the same arrangements of panels on each side, but on one side the panels are raised and fielded while on the other they have an ovolo-moulded fillet with a recessed central panel. The overall style is also a mixture, with the top half of the door resembling the 17th century doors with applied fillets, while the lower half has a narrow central panel reminiscent of the late 17th century two-panel variants. The bottom section is three panels wide in a style typical of the late 19th century.

1892 Glos

Fig 2.58 (above): At Tower House in Almondsbury, Glos (1892) the doors have the same moulding on both sides; however, one side has the classical six-panel design while the other has a mock-Jacobean geometric pattern. Both sides have an eared doorcase with pediment.

Door Panel Mouldings

From about 1670 doors with both true and applied panelling have prominent bolection mouldings around the panels (Fig 2.60), and as with earlier versions, they mirror the wall panelling of the period and indeed are often an integral part of the design. Many have plain recessed panels, but in more important houses the bolection moulding is combined with fielded or raised and fielded panels. Both have an angled plane or field between the moulded edge and the raised panel in the centre, and in the earliest examples this field is set at a very shallow angle (Fig 2.61:1648 Wilts and Fig 2.60: 1671 Lancs).

Raised and fielded panels have the face of the panels set forwards from the plane of the door (Fig 2.60: 1694 Yorks), while the fielded panel is set behind or level with the plane of the door (Fig 2.61: 1718 Suffolk). In the 1690s a small

Fig 2.59 (above): The Arts and Crafts movement produced some wonderfully elaborate doors, such as those in a Middlesex vicarage designed by J.D.Sedding in 1886. Mock Gothic arched doors combine the heavy medieval-style criss-cross framework on the back with the narrow planks typical of the 19th century, and the framework is all tenoned and pegged in traditional fashion. The accompanying ironwork is suitably elaborate, and while heavily influenced by earlier periods, could not be mistaken for 17th century work. Apart from the heavier nature of the ironwork, the designs tend to be bolder and brasher, and the hand-made nails of earlier times have been replaced by machine-made screws.

Fig 2.60 (right): Profiles of late 17th century bolection door panel mouldings.

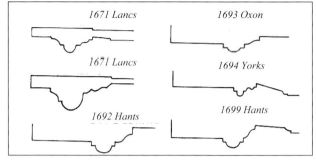

1671 Lancs

1693 Oxon

1671 Lancs

1694 Yorks

1692 Hants

1699 Hants

quarter-round moulding may surround the raised part of the panel. At the same period doors in lesser houses or to less important rooms have simpler ogee and/or bead mouldings around plain recessed or sunk panels (Fig 2.60: 1692 Hants). Others mimic panelled doors with applied bolection mouldings, or with a simple ogee moulding.

Fig 2.61 (right): Profiles of fielded door panel mouldings.

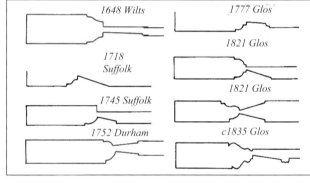

1648 Wilts

1777 Glos

1821 Glos

1718 Suffolk

1821 Glos

1745 Suffolk

1752 Durham

c1835 Glos

Fig 2.62 (below): Late 17th century applied mouldings.

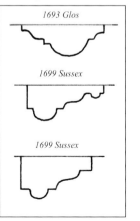

1693 Glos

1699 Sussex

1699 Sussex

The ogee moulding with the fielded panel first appears in a four-panelled door at 1648 Wilts, where both the moulding and the field around the panel are very shallow. The style does not become really popular until around 1700, and occurs first in two-panelled doors and is then almost universally used for standard six-panel doors. There are numerous slight variations, depending on the status of the house and the status of the room within the house. The most elaborate versions are always used for the most important rooms, with the simplest reserved for the attics and service rooms. Usually the raised face of the panel is surrounded by a step, but occasionally this is omitted (1718 Suffolk) or replaced by a tiny quarter round moulding (1777 Glos).

In the early 18th century the frame around the panels often has an ogee moulding, but the quarter round is widely used throughout the century and into the 19th century. The door may have moulded and fielded panels on both sides, but often the inferior face will have simple recessed panels. These may have the same moulding as the outer face or a different moulding (Fig 2.61:1821 Glos); simpler doors have no moulding at all on the rear face (Fig 2.61:1745 Suffolk). In the early 19th century more elaborate mouldings became popular, and the fielded panels may have an extra moulding providing a raised frame to the panel (Fig 2.61: c1835 Glos).

Recessed or sunk panels are common in the late 17th and early 18th century, and on the rear face of the door the panel may have slightly bevelled edges to reduce the thickness where it enters the frame (1710 Westmorland). The type continues through the 18th century for less important doors and then becomes extremely common in the 19th century with a variety of mouldings. These often include a small bead around the edge of the panel. In the late 18th and the early 19th centuries the moulding is often

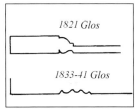

1821 Glos

1833-41 Glos

Fig 2.63 *(above): In the early 19th century the flush panel is also popular, where shallow mouldings separate the frame from the panel. Sometimes the entire door is treated in this way, but front doors often have the lower panels flush and the upper ones recessed.*

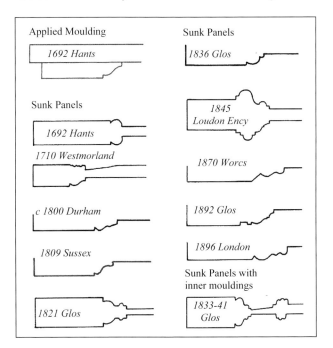

Applied Moulding

1692 Hants

Sunk Panels

1692 Hants

1710 Westmorland

c 1800 Durham

1809 Sussex

1821 Glos

Sunk Panels

1836 Glos

1845 Loudon Ency

1870 Worcs

1892 Glos

1896 London

Sunk Panels with inner mouldings

1833-41 Glos

Fig 2.64 *(left) : Profiles of recessed or sunk panels. 1845 Loudon Ency. is an example of one of the exceptionally elaborate door mouldings which were illustrated in Loudon's Encyclopaedia of Cottage, Farm and Villa Architecture, showing how separate moulding strips are applied to a plain panelled door. Many of the 19th century mouldings are applied in this way, although the application of many layers of paint over the years can make it hard to tell if the moulding is an integral part of the frame or a separate timber.*

very small, but it becomes larger again later in the 19th century. More elaborate doors also have an applied projecting moulding forming an inner frame to the panels (Fig 2.64: 1833-41 Glos). Sometimes the front door still has fielded panels while the interior doors all have recessed panels. In the late 19th century the moulding is often combined with either a chamfer (Fig 2.64: c1870 Worcs and 1896 London) or a sunk channel (Fig 2.64: 1892 Glos).

DOOR FURNITURE

Hinges

Doors are generally hung on long strap hinges which have a loop at the end which hangs on a stout iron hook called a pintle set into the wall or doorframe (Fig 2.66:1545-6 Hants and 1598 Surrey). The loop is usually formed by bending the end of the hinge around on itself, but sometimes the end of the hinge is carried around to the other side of the door, leaving a loop in the process. Hinges on smaller doors may have a base-plate instead of a pintle, with a smaller loop attached to a vertical plate nailed to the doorframe. This plate may be a plain rectangle, but often has a curved or wavy outline, and the type is commonly called a T-hinge (1743 Surrey). At the other end of the strap the hinge usually terminates in a decorative end, although there are a few absolutely plain hinges of various dates (Fig 2.65).

One of the earliest datable types, found in the second half of the 16th century, has an expanded end decorated with curves or ogees, and often the other end is also

***Fig 2.65** (right): Examples of strap hinges with plain ends.*

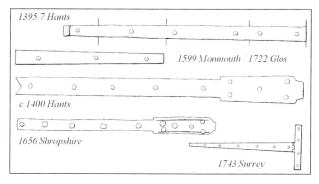

1395 7 Hants

1599 Monmouth / 1722 Glos

c 1400 Hants

1656 Shropshire

1743 Surrey

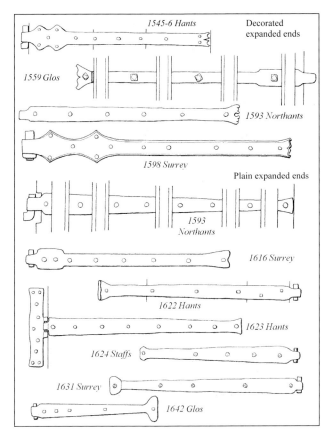

Fig 2.66 (left): Examples of strap hinges with expanded ends.

Within the figure:
1545-6 Hants — Decorated expanded ends
1559 Glos
1593 Northants
1598 Surrey
Plain expanded ends
1593 Northants
1616 Surrey
1622 Hants
1623 Hants
1624 Staffs
1631 Surrey
1642 Glos

expanded both to look decorative and to provide a larger hanging loop. Plainer expanded ends continue until the mid 17th century, and now the hinge usually tapers slightly, the taper becoming more pronounced as the century progresses. Sometimes the extreme tip of the hinge is folded back on itself, a type that seems common in Hampshire (1622 Hants).

Occasional hinges occur with lozenge-shaped ends, but the type that is found throughout the country from the 16th century or earlier to the mid 18th century is the spearhead end. Shapes vary from short and squat to long and thin and many have a small step between the end and the shaft. One of the latest dated examples found so far is 1740 in Henley, Oxfordshire.

Highly decorative hinges are especially popular from about 1620 to 1675 (Fig 2.68), with most being variations

Fig 2.67 *(right):*
Examples of strap hinges
with lozenge and
spearhead shaped ends.

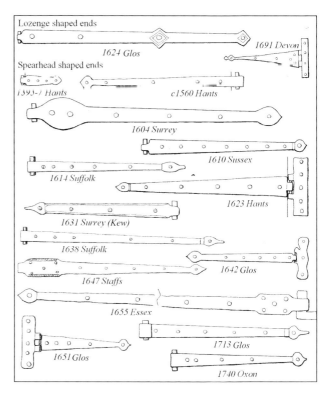

Lozenge shaped ends
1624 Glos
1691 Devon
Spearhead shaped ends
1595-7 Hants
c1560 Hants
1604 Surrey
1610 Sussex
1614 Suffolk
1623 Hants
1631 Surrey (Kew)
1638 Suffolk
1642 Glos
1647 Staffs
1655 Essex
1713 Glos
1651 Glos
1740 Oxon

on a fleur-de-lis design. 1656 Shropshire (Fig 2.68) has a most unusual design, with large scrolls at the butt end and dramatic slender S-shapes at the other. Some hinges are covered with incised zigzags or cross-hatching and some are chamfered. Chamfers and decoration may have been more common than we think; many hinges are either weathered or covered in paint or varnish, thus disguising much of the finer detail.

The heart or double scroll design seems to be especially common in Gloucestershire (Fig 2.69), where it is also used for window catches. Strangely the dated hinges are all between 1630 and 1680, while the window catches are 1678 to 1710, but the sample is too small to draw any meaningful conclusions. Blacksmiths, unlike carpenters and masons, did not travel far and so local styles are more likely to have restricted areas.

The strap hinge with a round end is found alongside the other types throughout the 17th century (Fig 2.70). As

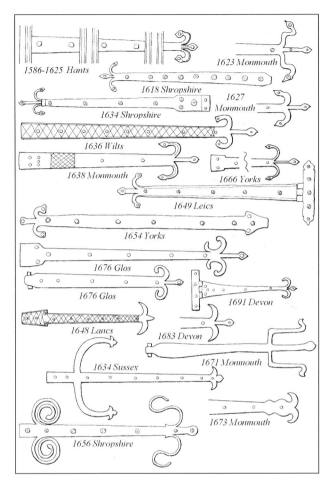

Fig 2.68 (left):
Examples of highly
decorative strap hinges.
These seem to be more
popular in the west.

Labels within figure:
1586-1625 Hants
1623 Monmouth
1618 Shropshire
1627 Monmouth
1634 Shropshire
1636 Wilts
1638 Monmouth
1666 Yorks
1649 Leics
1654 Yorks
1676 Glos
1676 Glos
1691 Devon
1648 Lancs
1683 Devon
1671 Monmouth
1634 Sussex
1673 Monmouth
1656 Shropshire

Fig 2.69 (below):
Examples of heart-shaped
or divided scroll strap
hinge ends.

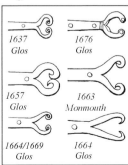

1637 Glos	1676 Glos
1657 Glos	1663 Monmouth
1664/1669 Glos	1664 Glos

with the others, the taper becomes more pronounced as the century goes on, but in this case it reaches almost absurd proportions by the early 18th century. T-hinges with round ends seem to be more common than other types and become very popular in the 18th century, and the strongly tapered versions continue into the early 19th century.

By the later 19th century standardised machine-made hinges with a uniform taper largely replace the hand-made wrought iron hinge, fixed with screws. At the same time, however, the Arts and Crafts movement promotes a return

Fig 2.70 (right):
Examples of round end
strap hinges. Some 18th
century examples have
such a strong taper that
the round end is barely
still connected to the shaft.

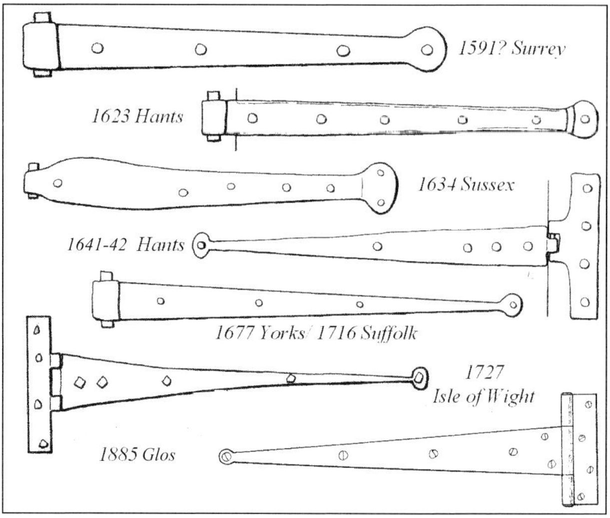

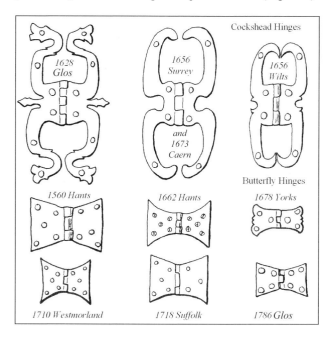

Fig 2.71 (below):
Examples of strap hinges
with baseplates. Some 'T-
hinges' are not actually a
T shape but have much
smaller rhomboid
baseplates, like half of a
butterfly hinge.
Occasionally the baseplate
is more decorative and
resembles half a
cockshead hinge.

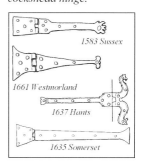

to the old-fashioned hand-made product, often with
definite chamfers and elaborate decoration.

Cockshead and butterfly hinges are generally used for
lighter cupboard doors, and butterfly hinges are
particularly common on spice cupboard doors (Fig 2.72).

Fig 2.72 (right): Examples
of cockshead and
butterfly hinges.

Cockshead hinges seem to be most common in the later 16th and the early 17th centuries, but have proved surprisingly elusive in dated contexts. They derive their name from the resemblance of the terminals to a cock's head, with the nail forming the eye and the two points the beak and the comb. Simpler derivatives, with inward-turning ends, occur in Surrey and Wiltshire houses, both of 1656. Butterfly hinges were popular throughout the 17th and 18th centuries, and in the later period were also used on shutters. By the end of the 18th century simple small rectangular hinges replace the more attractive butterfly hinge on shutters.

H-hinges are very common, especially in the second half of the 17th century and the early 18th century. Like the butterfly hinges, they were used for lighter internal doors and cupboard doors as they are not robust enough for heavy external doors. Many are beautifully finished with tiny chamfers, but often they have been painted over and such detail is concealed. During the course of the 18th century the decorative ends are lost and the plain H-hinge becomes the ubiquitous form, continuing into the machine-made era.

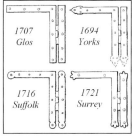

Fig 2.74a (above): *Examples of L-hinges. These come into use in the late 17th century, and some of the earlier examples have decorative ends. These are relatively rare, however, and plain L-hinges are the norm throughout the 18th century and into the early 19th century. Like the H-hinges, they can vary in size from 4 inches to 10 inches long, depending on their location.*

Fig 2.74b (below): *A cast-iron door knocker c1800 (Brooking Collection).*

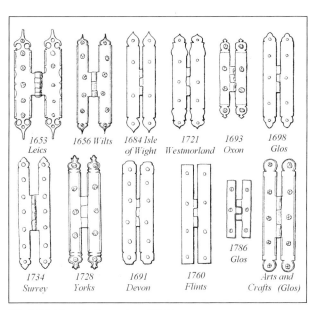

Fig 2.73 (above): *Examples of H-hinges.*

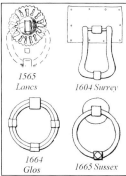

1565 Lancs *1604 Surrey*

1664 Glos *1665 Sussex*

Fig 2.75 *(above): Examples of ring knockers. Sometimes only the back plate survives, while the ring itself is missing, as at Hoghton Tower (1565 Lancs).*

Fig 2.76 *(below): 19th century door knockers.*

c1780-1810 Brooking Collection *1812 Hants* *1841 Glos*

c1809 Sussex *1841 Glos* *1841 Glos*

Victorian brass door knockers

Victorian iron door knockers

Door Knockers

Original door knockers survive surprisingly often, and fall into two main categories, the spur knocker (Fig 2.77) and the round or ring knocker (Fig 2.75). Spur knockers can be quite plain (1649 Leics and 1654 Yorks) but may have decorative fixing plates, and the shaft may have incised or moulded rings. One even has the date 1634 and the initials 'WM' incorporated in the design.

Ring knockers bear a superficial resemblance to drop handles, but are not attached to a latch, and usually have a heavy knob at the base with which to knock. In the early 19th century the ring knocker returned to popularity, but now with an integral circular back plate decorated with concentric rings or floral designs. Victorian knockers tend to be heavier and are often brass or painted cast iron.

Drop Handles

Medieval wrought iron drop handles are common on church doors, but relatively rare in domestic contexts. The earliest, such as Bramley Manor, Hants (1545-6) shows the pierced decoration typical of medieval designs, albeit in a heavily weathered and simplified form. It is unusual in having a round handle; more often the circular form is used

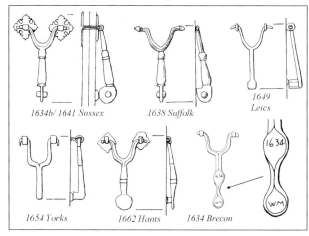

1634b/1641 Sussex *1638 Suffolk* *1649 Leics*

1654 Yorks *1662 Hants* *1634 Brecon*

Fig 2.77 *(above): Examples of spur knockers with the front elevation to the left and side to the right, and a close-up of 1634 Brecon.*

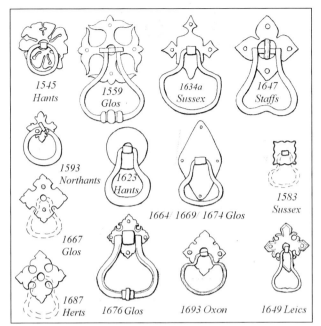

Fig 2.79 (below): A Gloucestershire gentry house of 1678 has a highly decorative triangular backplate on an attic door, which may be unique.

Fig 2.78: Examples of drop handles.

for the knocker while the handle has variations on a stirrup shape. The backplates take a variety of forms, many based on the lozenge or, less often, the square. A few Hampshire examples have a plain circular backplate; their distribution elsewhere is not known. Many drop handles are on external doors, when the handle is quite sturdy, but more delicate examples are used for internal doors (e.g. 1693 Oxon and for dog-gates as at 1649 Leics). Drop handles are frequently replaced and often a later upright handle will be set alongside an earlier drop handle. In many cases all that survives of the drop handle is the backplate, and

Fig 2.80 (below): At Berden Hall, Essex (1655), the drop handle does double duty and also serves as the knocker; an extra large nail with its own decorative backplate has been provided on the door rail.

Fig 2.81: Examples of 18th and early 19th century brass drop handles.

sometimes not even the plate but simply its impression in the wood, with a central hole and often a semi-circular mark below it where the handle used to swing.

In the 18th century the drop handle is almost exclusively used for internal doors, cupboards and shutters, and it is now much smaller and made of brass. The basic design hardly changes and continues into the Regency period in the early 19th century. Drop handles are usually fixed directly to the end of the latch, but sometimes operate a small rocker bar below the latch.

Fig 2.82 (below): Upright door handles with expanded ends which are either decorated, rounded or leaf shaped. They are sometimes called Suffolk latches. Other examples of large leaf-shaped ends are 1702 Wilts, 1713 Glos, and 1743 Westmorland.

Upright Door Handles

The earliest type of upright handle has large decorative ends which are nailed to the door; the handle is usually flat

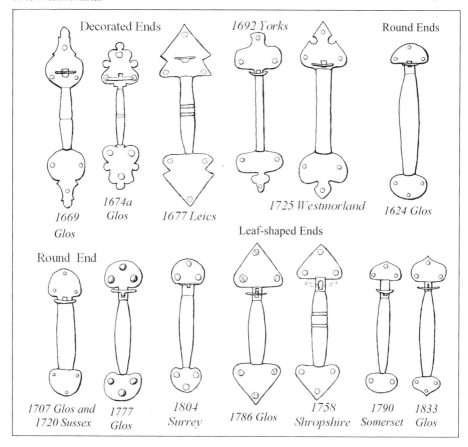

Decorated Ends   *1692 Yorks*   Round Ends

1669 Glos   *1674a Glos*   *1677 Leics*   *1725 Westmorland*   *1624 Glos*

Leaf-shaped Ends

Round End

1707 Glos and 1720 Sussex   *1777 Glos*   *1804 Surrey*   *1786 Glos*   *1758 Shropshire*   *1790 Somerset*   *1833 Glos*

in section, but may be round. A flat or curved thumb-plate operates a lifting bar which passes through the door to raise the latch, and none have so far been found in dated contexts before the mid 17th century. These examples often have highly decorative ends and may have one or more incised lines across the centre of the handle. Simpler forms have smaller rounded ends, with most belonging to the 18th century. At the same time, handles with large leaf-shaped ends were popular, especially in the 18th century when the ends can be very large. Earlier versions dating from the 17th century are slightly smaller and have a more curved shape. This style returns at the end of the 18th century and continues into the 19th before the advent of machine-made handles. Arts and Crafts handles of the

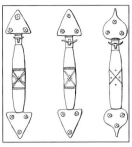

Fig 2.83b (above): Arts and Crafts door handles from Gloucestershire.

Fig 2.84 (below): Examples of iron pull handles. To avoid unnecessary wear and tear on the door handle or latch, doors were often fitted with a pull handle. A few were of wrought iron, with decorative back plates, and the 17th century examples illustrated are both on large heavy doors; the west door of Shere church in Surrey is dated 1626, while Cold Overton Hall, Leics., is dated 1649. In each case the handle is mounted in sockets top and bottom so that it swivels.

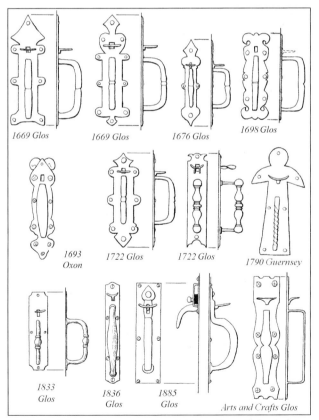

1669 Glos
1669 Glos
1676 Glos
1698 Glos
1693 Oxon
1722 Glos
1722 Glos
1790 Guernsey
1833 Glos
1836 Glos
1885 Glos
Arts and Crafts Glos

Fig 2.83a (above): Examples of upright handles with backplates, sometimes called Norfolk latches.

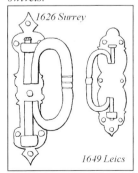

1626 Surrey

1649 Leics.

Fig 2.85 (below): Examples of wooden pull handles. Far more common than iron pull handles (Fig 2.84) are simple wooden pull handles which are nailed onto the door and project at an angle. Most are plain, but occasionally the edges are given carved decoration, and the tops usually have a rounded projection to give a better grip.

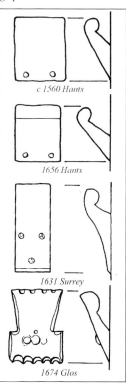

c 1560 Hants

1656 Hants

1631 Surrey

1674 Glos

late 19th and 20th centuries are usually even more decorative than 17th century handles, with incised lines and saltire crosses on the centre of the handle. The difference is partly due to the fact that, being newer, they have suffered less wear and so the decoration still stands out clearly. It is a useful reminder of what many of the older features would have looked like when new.

The alternative type of upright handle has a decorative backplate to which the handle is fixed (Fig 2.83) and in almost every case the handle is not flat but round in cross-section. Again the earliest in dated contexts belong to the second half of the 17th century, but this probably just reflects a lack of recording rather than a lack of earlier handles. In the 19th century backplates become much simpler, and Fig 2.83: 1885 Glos is a standard machine-made type found on numerous doors throughout the country. As with other features, the Arts and Crafts movement brought a return to hand-made items; the illustrated example is very distinctive, with its flat handle and an outline that bears little resemblance to earlier examples.

Knob handles come into fashion in the 18th century, when small brass knobs are a common alternative to the drop handle, with larger ones used for external doors. In the early 19th century, handles in larger houses may have tooled decoration such as concentric circles on the base of the handle. The knob handle took many different forms in the Victorian period, with new materials such as ceramic and glass being used, as well as metal.

Door Latches

Numerous iron latches survive in 17th and 18th century houses, and the most decorative are the spring latches with elaborate backplates (Fig 2.86). These are operated by a rocker bar attached directly to a drop handle, while above the latch an L-shaped spring holds the latch in place. The spring latch was also popular in the 18th century, when the standard type in many houses was the brass knob or drop handle attached directly to a short, wide, heavily-tapered latch. The whole assembly is mounted on a square or rectangular backplate, which often includes a bolt as well. The spring is usually above the latch, but can be below

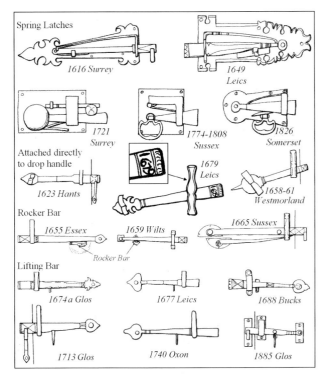

Fig 2.86 (above): Examples of iron latches.

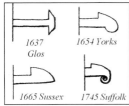

Fig 2.87 (above): Examples of simple latch fasteners. This type is basically an iron bar with a notch in it, driven directly into the doorframe. Most are undecorated, but occasionally there is a small curl below the end, as 1745 Suffolk.

Fig 2.88 (below): The more common type of latch fastener has a thinner bar which curves down from the end of the main bar and is nailed to the doorframe; the main bar is driven directly into the frame. As doors closed flush against the back of the frame, all latch fasteners have to allow for the thickness of the door as well as the latch. 1745 Suffolk (Fig 2.87) has a rebated doorframe and therefore a small notch for the latch.

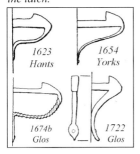

(1721 Surrey). These latches continued in use in the Regency period, but sometimes the backplate has a tapered shape with a round end (1826 Somerset).

In the 17th century the spring latch is not common and most are simple bar latches. Some are lifted by rocker bars, but most drop handles are attached directly to the end of the latch by what is in effect a large split pin, whose ends are bent outwards to hold the assembly together. Others are operated by a lifting bar set usually about a third of the way along and attached to the thumb-plate of an upright handle. A latch holder set close to the edge of the door holds the latch in place. These holders are simple flat hasps whose ends go directly into the door, and sometimes they are beautifully decorated with tiny chamfers and nicks. It is not uncommon for the latch fastener to have been renewed (1659 Wilts, 1688 Bucks), or for the holder to survive but with no latch. The latches themselves are usually decorated with incised lines and saltire crosses, a feature said by a

20th century blacksmith to represent the cross of St Andrew between the door jambs, barring the way to any evil spirits that may wish to enter. As such it is a type of apotropaic 'evil-averting' mark. The mark gradually goes out of favour during the 18th century, but was revived by some of the Arts and Crafts blacksmiths.

By the beginning of the Victorian period, latches, like other ironwork, were machine made and standardised. The latch is attached to a small rectangular base plate and usually has a small round knob attached with which to lift the latch. The latch holders now have returned ends which, like the base plate, are screwed to the door.

Fig 2.89 (right):
Examples of wooden latches with front view and a side profile.

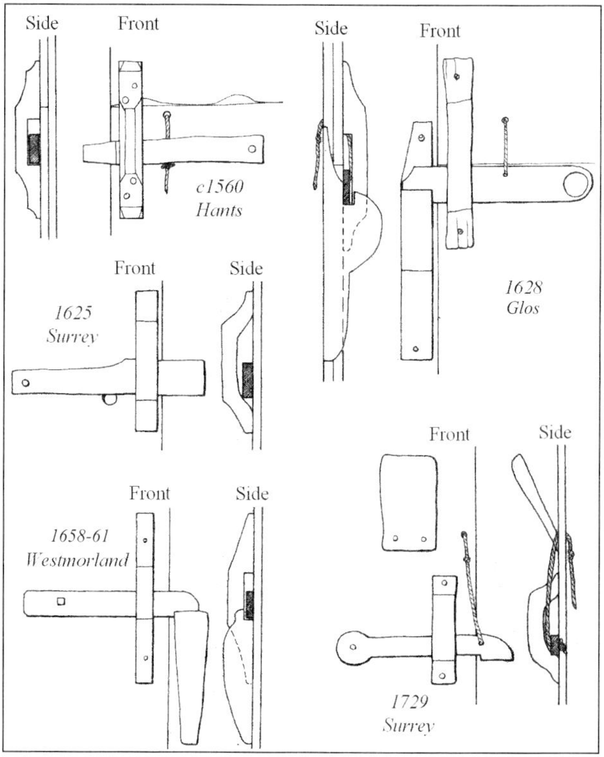

Fig 2.90 (below):
Examples of wooden latch fasteners.

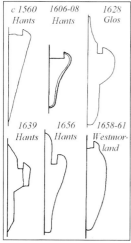

Wooden latches are hard to date, but many survive in 17th and early 18th century contexts (Fig 2.89). Most are on internal doors, but 1628 Glos has a massive one on the original back door. There are two methods of raising a wooden latch, either a string (or perhaps a leather thong) which passes through a small hole above the latch (c1560 Hants), or a large finger hole below the latch (1625 Surrey). The finger hole is also used with iron latches in farm buildings.

Most wooden latches also have a wooden latch fastener, a solid block nailed onto the doorframe (Fig 2.90). Some have a wide notch to account for the door thickness (1606-08 Hants), but some have a more sophisticated design with a thinner notch cut into the block a door's thickness away from the frame (1628 Glos). It is not uncommon for wooden latch holders and fasteners to survive when the latch itself has gone. Sometimes wood and iron are mixed, and this may indicate that an original wooden feature has broken and been replaced by iron. (Fig 2.98).

Lock Cases

Although often an old door will have lost its original lock case, a number still survive in situ, often on internal doors, and occasionally they still have the original key. Replacement lock cases can be recognised by the fact that they are smaller than the markings on the door planks, with much smaller keys; often they are fixed on with over-elaborate iron straps, whereas the originals are simply nailed on. Decoration includes simple incised lines

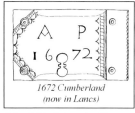

1672 Cumberland
(now in Lancs)

Fig 2.92 (above): This dated lock case, now separated from its original location at Rydal Hall in the Lake District, is one of a number said to have been given to her tenants in the North West by Lady Anne Clifford, Countess of Pembroke. The suggestion is that she kept a master key and so could always let herself into a tenant's house if she needed somewhere to stay!

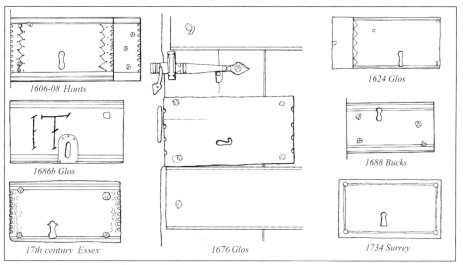

1606-08 Hants

1624 Glos

1686b Glos

1688 Bucks

17th century Essex

1676 Glos

1734 Surrey

Fig 2.91 (above): Examples of lock cases.

1631-6 Oxford

(Above): This keyplate shows a marked resemblance to a pair of seahorses, joining dragon scrolls and cockshead hinges as zoomorphic forms.

Fig 2.94 *(below): 19th century keyplates with covers.*

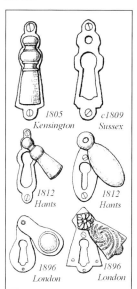

1805 Kensington

c1809 Sussex

1812 Hants

1812 Hants

1896 London

1896 London

(1606-08 Hants), shallow mouldings along top and bottom edges (1686 Glos), and tiny chip marks along the edge (17th century Essex). 1686b Glos has the initials IT incised on it and unusually it has a metal keyplate, a feature not normally seen on lock cases. In the 18th century brass lock cases came into fashion, incorporating lock, latch and handle in one unit.

Keyplates

Keyplates come in a variety of shapes and sizes, with some very decorative examples in the late 16th and early 17th centuries. The sizes reflect the changes in the size of the

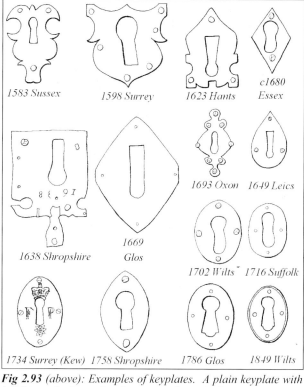

1583 Sussex

1598 Surrey

1623 Hants

c1680 Essex

1638 Shropshire

1669 Glos

1693 Oxon

1649 Leics

1702 Wilts

1716 Suffolk

1734 Surrey (Kew)

1758 Shropshire

1786 Glos

1849 Wilts

Fig 2.93 *(above): Examples of keyplates. A plain keyplate with 1638 inscribed on it has been reused upside down on a door in Much Wenlock in Shropshire, and appears to have lost some decoration at the top (now the bottom) edge. Kew Palace (1734 Surrey) has some beautifully inscribed brass keyplates which bear the initials of Prince Frederick, with a crown and a star.*

keys, with the earliest ones being much larger than 18th and 19th century examples. Plainer keyplates are common in the second half of the 17th century, when varieties of lozenge were popular. By 1700 the oval keyplate had largely taken over from earlier designs; one of the earliest is 1655 Essex (Fig 2.80), where it is made of iron, but brass gradually became the usual material and continued into the 19th century. From about 1800 the elongated keyplate with integral cover came into fashion and remained popular right through the 19th century. Some Victorian ones are decorated, but many are plain. These are all fastened with screws, whereas the earlier ones have hand-made iron nails or small brass pins. Earlier ones, of course, may have been refastened with screws if the original fixings failed at some point; the same applies to all the other types of ironwork.

Bolts and Drawbeams

A few 17th century bolts are mounted on backplates, and at Great Fosters at Egham, Surrey (1598) the bolt is

Fig 2.95 *(above): A few 19th century keyplates are highly elaborate, such as the delicate brass ones used on cupboard doors at c1809 Sussex.*

Fig 2.97 *(below): Moorend Farm, Hambrook, Glos (1676). This beautifully decorative bolt and handle are on the inner face of the door to the back stair, and the fact that the end of the handle is partly covered by the bolt shows them to be contemporary.*

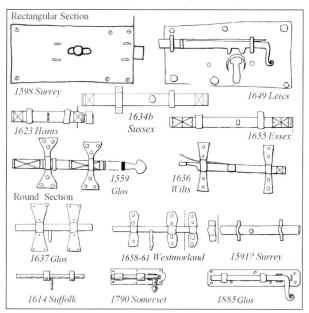

Fig 2.96 *(above): Examples of bolts. Note security springs on 1636 Wilts and 1649 Leics.*

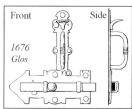

Fig 2.98 (right): Wooden bolt, Bramley Manor (1545-6 Hants) is an unusual example of a wooden bolt with decorative carving; the fact that half of the bolt has been broken off indicates why they are rare items. On the left is Sevington Manor (1597-1606 Hants) which has a bolt and latch that mix iron and wood; this may indicate that original wooden elements were broken and replaced with iron at a later date.

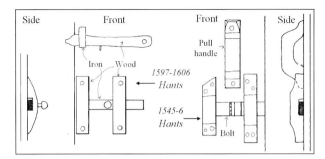

Fig 2.99 (below): A drawbeam which slides out of the wall in a stone-walled house from South Gloucestershire, dated 1659.

actually set into the door and covered with an iron plate. A small knob protrudes through the plate to enable the bolt to be moved. This degree of sophistication is rare and is not found in the average house.

Most bolts are attached to the face of the door by two iron hasps (e.g. 1559 Glos), and the type used seems to depend partly on the cross-section of the bolt. Bolts of rectangular cross-section have hasps which have pointed ends driven directly into the door (1623 Hants). Bolts of circular cross-section, however, are more likely to have hasps with expanded ends which are nailed to the door (1637 Glos). Both types have some sort of knob or bar attached to the bolt with which to move it, and rectangular bolts are often decorated with incised lines and saltire crosses in the same way as latches (1655 Essex). Bolt design changed totally in the 19th century, with round-sectioned bolts set on a backplate and held in place by two closed hasps and an open 'guide rail' at the knob end. The knob is now attached to a short shaft (1790 Somerset), or the end of the bolt is extended to form a sort of handle (1885 Glos).

Many houses have, or had, heavy drawbeams to provide extra security in addition to that provided by locks and bolts. The fact that many 17th century yeoman farmers kept large amounts of cash in the house and in effect acted as lending banks for their poorer neighbours may be one reason for this. In stone-walled houses the drawbeams are set into the thickness of the wall, and often only the slot survives. Houses with thinner walls may have removable drawbeams, which are slotted into a closed hasp at one end and then dropped into an open hasp at the other (Fig 2.27).

Drawbeams seem to go out of favour in the middle of the 18th century. Sometimes internal doors also have drawbeams when extra security or privacy is required. Llanmihangel Place and Llancaiach Fawr, both in South Wales, are large houses with first-floor parlours. In each case there is a stair set within the thickness of the wall leading between the parlour and the underground cellar; the stair bypasses the ground floor and both the cellar doors and the parlour doors have drawbeams. This presumably enabled the owners and their friends to indulge in private drinking parties without fear of being interrupted!

Fig 2.101: Llancaiach *Fawr Glamorgan – this door may date from the 1628 alterations but could be earlier. It has nails arranged in interesting patterns.*

Fig 2.100 Cambridgeshire - This 1603 door and doorhead, copied in 1995. Rather a nice touch!

Fig 2.102: Algar's Manor, Iron Acton, Glos has its original front door and frame, though moved from its original position (tree-ring dated to 1559/60).

3 WINDOWS
IRONWORK AND SHUTTERS

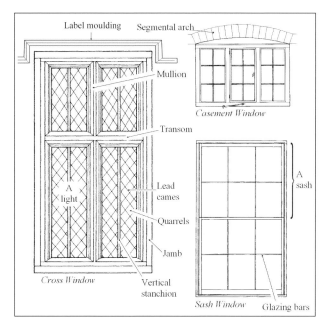

Fig 3.1 *(left): Drawings of a cross, casement and sash window with labels of their parts.*

Label moulding
Segmental arch
Mullion

Casement Window

Transom

Lead cames

A light

Quarrels

Jamb

Cross Window

Vertical stanchion

A sash

Sash Window
Glazing bars

TYPES OF WINDOWS
Medieval

The word 'window' derives from 'wind eye', the place where the wind comes in. This reflects the fact that in the medieval period the vast majority of houses had unglazed windows with glass found only in select buildings like royal palaces. In 1250 Henry III wanted the glazed windows of the chapel at Sherborne Castle to be altered 'so as to open and shut', and he also required opening windows at Guildford and in the hall at Northampton. These must be the earliest references to opening casements, but none are known to survive from this early period.

Medieval windows survive in many stone houses of

Fig 3.2 *(below): Ashleworth Court, Glos, (circa 1460), featuring large transomed windows with traceried heads.*

Fig 3.3 (above): At Upbury Farm in Yetminster, Dorset, the tall window which originally lit the open hall can clearly be seen between the later windows inserted when an upper floor was put into the hall.

Fig 3.5 (below): Unglazed windows can be found at a surprisingly late date in service rooms such as dairies, as shown in this example from the rear dairy of Tankerdale Farm, Steep, Hampshire, built in 1622. Another is in a Sussex cottage of 1694.

manorial status or above, and all have evidence of a strong iron grille which prevented anyone from breaking in. Occasionally the grilles survive, (Fig 3.4) but more often holes in the window surround show where they have been removed.

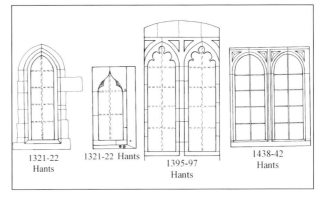

1321-22 Hants   1321-22 Hants   1395-97 Hants   1438-42 Hants

Fig 3.4 (above): Examples of stone windows from Hampshire.

The window shape developed from the simple lancet and the more elaborate ogee of the 13th and early 14th centuries to the 15th century cusped head and finally to the four-centred arch with sunk spandrels found in the later 15th and early 16th centuries.

Larger transomed windows with traceried heads can be seen in buildings of superior status (Fig 3.2) although such windows have either been glazed at a later date or else blocked and replaced with more up-to-date windows. There are, however, sufficient medieval references to glazed windows to suggest that at least in London and other major towns they were not that uncommon. In larger medieval buildings where halls have more than one window, the one lighting the high table may be a projecting bay window usually with canted (angled) sides, which increases the amount of available light.

Many more houses had wooden windows and a surprising number have survived, at least in part. The simplest and originally the most common type had simple square mullions set diamond-wise in the frame. The open hall had tall transomed windows, often divided by a central stud or square mullion (Fig 3.7: 1446 Essex); the other rooms had horizontal windows of anything from two to eight or ten lights.

Diamond mullioned windows were of necessity unglazed and, as it has proved almost impossible to add satisfactory glazing at a later date, few have survived intact. The evidence for their former existence survives in abundance, however, in the form of diamond-shaped mortises in the headbeam and sill of the frame, often revealed during restoration work. Sometimes the mortises are not diamond shaped but triangular, with the mortise sited nearer to the inner face of the sill so as to minimise the risk of damage by rainwater entering the mortise.

Fig 3.6 (above): Re-used timbers at Berg Cottage, Barkway, Herts, showing a mortise (top right) for a diamond mullion. Re-used timbers often contain mortises for diamond mullions, although it is often not clear if the timbers in question have been re-used from the same house or brought in from elsewhere. Sometimes a house is clearly a new build on a particular site: recent restoration work at the above cottages dated 1687 has revealed a large number of re-used timbers, all numbered with carpenter's marks which refer to their current location. Such re-use of medieval and later timbers is common and carpenters must have kept a supply from houses that were demolished.

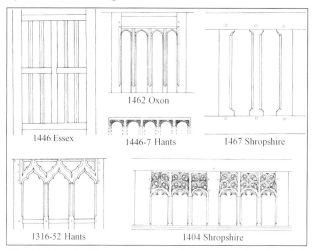

1462 Oxon

1446 Essex

1446-7 Hants

1467 Shropshire

1316-52 Hants

1404 Shropshire

Fig 3.7 (above): Wooden windows from the medieval period. The example of 1462 from Oxfordshire is the upper half of a tall hall window, but the part below the mid rail has been replaced by a later window. The five-light window head of 1446-7 from Hampshire was found in the attic of a building in Odiham; the small triangles in the spandrels are pierced right through. There is no proof that it belongs in the building in which it was found, but the fact that it is exactly the right size to fit in one of the existing window openings strongly suggests that it does. Moat House, Longnor (Shropshire), dated 1467, has a very unusual two-light window to one of the upper chambers. The mullion and the jambs are chamfered and stopped, with the stops curving outwards to make each light narrower top and bottom.

More elaborate wooden windows can be found, often surviving in the less conspicuous side walls, and examples are known in both timber-framed and stone-walled houses. Ogee shapes occur in the 14th century (Fig 3.7: 1316-52

Fig 3.8 (above): The hall window at Oakwell Hall, Birstall, Yorks. The house was built in 1583, but the hall was altered in the mid 17th century.

Hants) while cusped window heads seem to belong to the 15th century (Fig 3.7: Shropshire 1404). Simpler still are the four-centred arched heads found in other 15th century windows (Fig 3.7: 1462 Oxon).

Mullioned and Transomed Windows

The advent of affordable glazing in the 16th century greatly altered the appearance of houses and the size and number of windows. Mullioned windows of two to five lights became common, and the lights were now much wider than they had been previously. Wide transomed windows of six to twelve lights were especially popular in the Elizabethan period and continued into the 17th century.

In the Lancashire and Yorkshire Pennines even wider transomed windows occur in the larger houses, with anything up to twenty lights; such windows are common in the first half of the 17th century and are still occasionally found in this area in the second half. In this wealthy area the open hall regained popularity in the early 17th century and houses were built with enormous hall windows to illuminate the galleries and plaster ceilings with which many of the houses were furnished. A number of these have double transoms for the large hall window, such as Oakwell Hall (Fig 3.8).

Oriel Windows

Fig 3.9 (below): Carved bracket below oriel window dating from the 16th century. Newport in Essex has a religious scene which includes a Virgin and child and an angel playing a harp.

Oriel windows project forward from the wall face and are carried on decorative carved brackets. They come in a variety of sizes, from modest three or four light mullioned windows to larger transomed affairs. Oriels usually occur on timber-framed buildings, although the occasional stone oriel may be seen in buildings at the top of the social scale. When such a window has been removed from a timber-framed building the evidence may still be seen in the form of mortises for the brackets below the sill. Not all oriels had decorative brackets; plaster coving may conceal plain brackets (Fig 3.11), while some early 16th century oriels have a solid wooden sill which may be carved with figures or other decoration (Fig 3.9).

Another form of projecting window is the planted-on

window, carried on a heavily moulded sill and pegged onto the outer face of the wall; it does not project as far as a true oriel (Fig 3.10).

Oriels continued to be a popular form of display well into the 17th century. Occasional later 17th century oriels are found, but they are rare and went out of fashion until they returned with the vernacular revival of the 1870s.

Flanking Windows

It is quite common for both oriels and flush windows to have smaller mullioned windows on either side called flanking windows and they occur from the mid 16th to the mid 17th century. In Sussex they are found in superior houses from circa 1560 and by the end of the century were used in all houses regardless of status.

Fig 3.10 (above): A planted-on window on an early 17th century house in Cheshire.

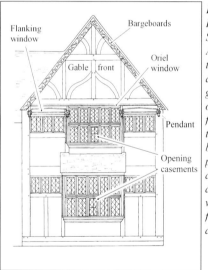

Fig 3.11 (left): Priory Cottages, Steventon, Oxon, A reconstruction of the former appearance of the gable end; the two oriels and their flanking windows, the gable front, the barge boards and pendants were all added in 1570-1 to an earlier cross-wing. The upper flanking windows are now blocked.

Fig 3.12 (below): The Butterwalk, Dartmouth, was built between 1635 and 1640 by Mark Hawkings. Three of the four properties were leased to other tenants, but his own house in the centre of the row is distinguished by the fine oriels on the first and second floors. The former have brackets in the form of heraldic beasts, the latter have strange human figures.

Many flanking windows have subsequently been blocked and are only visible on the inside or not at all; evidence often comes to light during repair and restoration work. Flanking windows created a complete run of glass across the face of the wall and the effect was particularly dramatic in towns where there could be whole rows of houses with large amounts of glazing. In this case the flanking windows were often as tall as the main window.

Bay and Bow Windows

Bay windows, unlike oriels, extend the full height of each storey and may be continuous through two or more storeys. Most of the late 17th century examples in Bristol have Ipswich windows in which the centre light has a semicircular arch within the square frame (Fig 3.13). Similar bays and full-height flanking windows can be seen in Tewkesbury, but without the Ipswich windows.

Circular bay windows occur in some of the most important 16th and early 17th century houses, but being very expensive to produce, did not travel down the social scale and do not reappear until the bow windows of the late 18th and the early 19th century. At that period they were popular in towns, with many having a shallow curve and only projecting forwards a short way so as not to obstruct the pavement. They are especially common as late 18th and early 19th century shop windows and can indicate that what is now a purely domestic property was once a shop. The bow window also proved popular in the new seaside resorts and spa towns where they permitted the occupant a better view.

In the second half of the 19th century after the repeal of duties on glass and tax upon windows the previously expensive bay window returned with a vengeance, and

Fig 3.13 (above): St Bartholomew's Hospital, Christmas Steps, Bristol, has a simple Ipswich window with a semicircular arch in the central light. This type of window is found in its most elaborate form at the Ancient House, Ipswich, hence the name; here the bays have rounded sides and the wall below the window, plain in the Bristol example, is covered with decorative plasterwork. Between the windows is a coat-of-arms of Charles II, dating the oriels and the plasterwork to circa 1670. There is even an Ipswich window made entirely of brick in Watlington Town Hall, Oxon of c1665.

Fig 3.14 (above): Examples of Victorian bay windows from a single storey canted bay from the 1860s (left) to full height bays from the 1880s (middle) and 1900s (right).

thousands upon thousands of them can be seen lining the streets of our Victorian suburbs. Single storey canted examples were used at first with full height bays for the grander houses but by the end of the century they had worked their way down the social ladder with single storey examples on modest terraces and full height on better middle class houses.

Straight-sided bays were also popular and both continued into the 20th century. Many are decorated with exuberant plasterwork or terracotta in the form of foliage capitals and moulded lintels, while others have plain or polychrome brick arches, varying from a shallow segmental arch to full-blown pointed Gothic with hood moulds and decorative label stops.

Fig 3.15 (above): A single storey bow window.

Mullioned Windows

In the 16th and 17th centuries houses outside the towns were far more likely to have simpler mullioned windows of either stone or wood. Wooden mullions were used in all timber-framed buildings and in stone buildings in areas such as Devon and south Gloucestershire where good quality stone for mullions was not available locally. The construction of the windows varied slightly; those in timber-framed walls were built as part of the wall while in stone walls the window had a complete frame set into the stonework below a wooden over-lintel. In better quality houses the over-lintels may be chamfered or moulded with decorative stops at either end.

Fig 3.16 (below): Wooden mullioned windows from a timber-framed house in Hampshire and a stone-walled house in Gloucestershire. Each has a single opening casement.

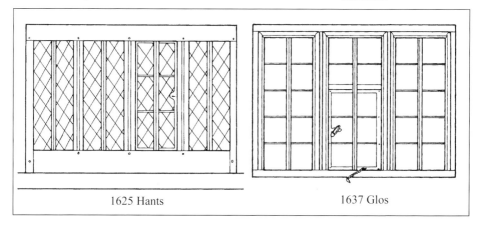

| 1625 Hants | 1637 Glos |

Fig 3.17 (above): Almshouses, Moretonhampstead, Devon, built of granite in 1637. The arcade doorway and mullioned windows are all of the same material.

Fig 3.18 (below): Pendick's Farm, Tytherington, Gloucestershire, largely built in 1664, showing windows of diminishing size.

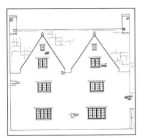

Stone mullions were used in areas of better quality stone such as the Pennines and the oolitic limestone belt which passes through the Cotswolds and up to Lincolnshire. Here the stone could easily be carved into moulded mullions and hoodmoulds. Hoodmoulds are a projecting moulding above a window or doorway designed to divert the rainwater away from the opening. They usually have down-turned ends and may have interesting carvings in the label stops at the ends, particularly in the Yorkshire and Lancashire Pennines. By the end of the 17th century individual hoodmoulds had gone out of fashion and instead a single moulded string course runs across the entire face of the wall above the windows. Sometimes it takes a turn upwards over the front door, depending on the relative heights of the door and window openings.

In the Lancashire and Yorkshire Pennines round-arched heads to the window lights are a distinctive regional feature, found in the 16th century in Lancashire but apparently persisting later in Yorkshire. In this area some very wide mullioned windows are found, with five to eight lights being common and more not infrequent. Some Pennine and Cotswold houses have a larger central mullion called a king mullion, generally a feature of the first half of the 17th century. Stone mullions were also used for high status houses in other areas. In south Gloucestershire, for example, stone mullions are common within about five miles of the oolitic limestone scarp of the Cotswolds, but over that distance their use is restricted to houses of the gentry or wealthy yeomen who could afford the additional transport costs. Less tractable stone such as granite could also be used for mullions and doorways (Fig 3.17).

Stone mullions were also used in some larger brick houses, either to provide a pleasing contrast of colour and material, or because the house was originally rendered to resemble stonework. This is most common in the later 17th century. At earlier periods the mullions were sometimes made of brick and plastered over to look like stone, although if the brickwork was of good quality with fine joints it may have been left exposed.

In the 16th and early 17th century the size of the window is likely to reflect the importance of the room but by the mid 17th century in much of England the influence of classical architecture made symmetry more important and windows were arranged to produce the most pleasing external appearance. This sometimes resulted in a window being split between two rooms, most commonly service rooms such as dairy and buttery, or first-floor chambers. In Gloucestershire, where the gabled farmhouse was the standard type throughout the 17th century, windows were sometimes arranged in diminishing sizes, from four lights on the ground floor to single light windows high in the gables (Fig 3.18). Similar arrangements can be seen in the gable ends of houses set end on to the street.

In the Pennine areas of Lancashire and Yorkshire a symmetrical façade seems to have commanded far less importance in the 17th century, and as late as circa 1700 there are houses with unbalanced façades. This area also boasts some very distinctive local types of window. In the mid 17th century three or four-light stone-mullioned windows with an ogee arch spanning all the lights occur in the Burnley area while some gentry houses of the same period in the Halifax region have distinctive rose windows in the porch.

Simple chamfered mullioned windows continued to be used in stone regions throughout the 18th and into the 19th century for smaller houses and cottages. Windows of this date can be distinguished by their uniformity, lack of hoodmoulds and square shape; it is rare to find anything other than two-light windows at this period, although there are occasional examples with three-lights. Both wood and stone mullions returned in the late 19th century, when the Arts and Crafts movement began to take its inspiration from vernacular buildings.

Cross Windows

From the mid 17th century the four-light transomed window called a cross-window began to make an appearance, although it had sometimes occurred in earlier houses (Fig 3.19b). By the end of the century the cross-window was the standard type in all the larger townhouses and farmhouses.

Most of the earlier cross-windows have the transom just above the centre, while by the end of the century it was often much nearer the top of the window, although this is

Fig 3.19a (above):
Woodlane Hall, Sowerby, West Yorks, dated 1649, has a splendid porch, with a rose window. Dated examples occur between 1638 and 1650.

Fig 3.19b (below):
Gawthorpe, Padiham, Lancs, built in 1605. The main façade has large transomed windows; smaller four-light transomed windows were used in the sides of the bays and the porch where space was limited. This seems to be the case with all cross-windows before 1650 – they were used as an alternative to the larger mullioned and transomed windows where space would not permit anything wider.

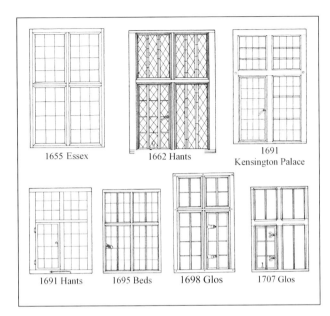

1655 Essex   1662 Hants   1691 Kensington Palace

1691 Hants   1695 Beds   1698 Glos   1707 Glos

Fig 3.20 (above): Stanford House in Chipping Campden, Glos, dated 1705, has a rather unusual arrangement of individual cross-windows to the right of the door and paired cross-windows to the left. It is possible that this is an alteration, with the paired windows having been moved closer together to reduce the amount of window tax to be paid.

Fig 3.21 (above): Cross-windows. The two Gloucestershire examples are of stone, the others are wood.

Fig 3.22 (below): Oval window with date at Northwick House Farmhouse, Pilning, Glos.

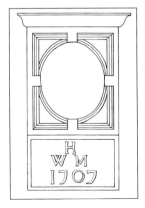

not an invariable rule. Cross-windows are equally common in both wood and stone, and reached a peak of use in the 1690s, remaining popular until about 1740 in most areas and in the north for even longer.

Already, however, the new sash windows were beginning to come into fashion, and Kensington Palace, built in 1691, has sash windows at the front and cross-windows at the back facing the courtyard (Fig 3.21). Although cross-windows are common, many more have been replaced by sash windows in the 18th or 19th centuries; as the proportions of the window openings were the same this was an easy way of making a house look up-to-date.

Commonly found with cross-windows in the stone areas of Gloucestershire, Somerset, Northamptonshire, Yorkshire and Lancashire is the small oval window, usually set high in a gable and sometimes combined with a datestone. They are usually carved from a single piece of stone although very occasionally they were made of wood, and occur from the 1660s to the 1720s, with a dramatic peak in the 1690s.

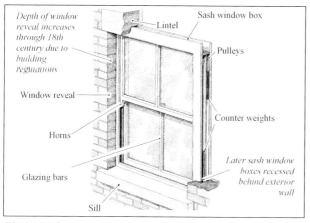

Fig 3.23 *(above): A Victorian sash window with labels of parts.*

Labels in figure: Depth of window reveal increases through 18th century due to building regulations; Lintel; Sash window box; Pulleys; Window reveal; Counter weights; Horns; Later sash window boxes recessed behind exterior wall; Glazing bars; Sill

Sash Windows

Sash windows are variously claimed to have been invented in England or Holland in the 1670s, and are only found in these two countries and in America. They were installed at Whitehall Palace circa 1670 and in Dyrham Park near Bath in 1692, and soon became extremely popular although the rate of adoption of the new style varied across the country. In most of the earliest examples, only the lower sash can be moved, and this was common until the mid 18th century. Various devices such as wooden pegs or small hooks

Fig 3.24 *(above): The earlier style sash window at the top has its timber sash box exposed while the later example at the bottom has it recessed and hidden behind the masonry.*

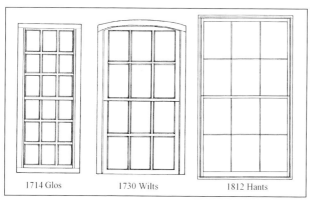

1714 Glos   1730 Wilts   1812 Hants

Fig 3.25 *(above): Examples of sash windows. Note that the glazing bars become thinner and the individual panes larger from the early example on the left to the later on the right.*

were used to prop them open while others were hung on sash cords and counterbalanced with lead weights concealed in the boxing on either side. From the late 18th century the weights are more often cast iron. The cords ran over pulleys, which until the 1760s were generally wooden; after that the more durable brass or cast iron were used. At first the weights ran in a groove hollowed out of a solid wood jamb, but later boxes were constructed to contain them.

In early sash windows this boxing is set flush with the outer face of the wall and forms a wide frame to the window. After the London Building Act of 1709 the frame was supposed to be set back at least four inches from the wall face to reduce the risk of fire spreading along rows of terraced houses. The 1774 Act further stipulated that the boxing should be concealed behind the masonry, leaving only the side members of the actual sashes visible. This creates a very different appearance between early and late sash windows.

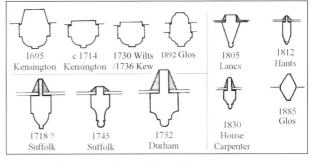

| 1695 Kensington | c 1714 Kensington | 1730 Wilts /1736 Kew | 1892 Glos | 1805 Lancs | 1812 Hants |

| 1718 ? Suffolk | 1745 Suffolk | 1752 Durham | 1830 House Carpenter | 1885 Glos |

Fig 3.27 (below): A house in Marlborough featuring windows with segmental arches in the brickwork and a square head to the frame.

Fig 3.26 (above): Profiles of glazing bars.

These Acts initially only applied to London and although the larger cities soon followed suit, smaller towns and rural areas took longer to absorb the new ideas; its use as an aid to dating is therefore limited. Even in London it was impossible to enforce where sash windows had been inserted into older timber-framed structures, whose walls were not thick enough to allow for any recessing of the windows. Conversely, in Bath, it was usual to set the boxing behind a moulded stone architrave from an early date and exposed boxing is rare in the city.

In some single-hung sash windows the top sash could

move down a short way, where it was held open by a small stop on the frame. By the middle of the 18th century the double-hung sash was becoming usual, in which both the top and the bottom sashes are moveable.

The earliest glazing bars which subdivide the sashes are wide and may be anything up to 2 inches by 2 inches (5 x 5 cm), with ovolo mouldings on the inside and are common up to the 1730s (Fig 3.26: 1730 Wilts). The outer face is rebated for the glazing, with the putty giving a chamfered appearance. The panes of glass are small and each sash commonly has nine panes; however, twelve or sixteen are not unknown.

Fig 3.28a (above): Houses in Upgang Lane, Whitby, with late 18th century stair windows, each with 41 panes of glass.

Later windows have larger panes of glass, usually six in each sash although eight over eight is common, with much thinner glazing bars. By the early 19th century glazing bars may be as little as half an inch (1.25cm) across and as well as the ovolo a variety of mouldings were used, sometimes different ones on each floor of the house, with the most elaborate in the most important rooms.

Sash fasteners fixed to the centre of the meeting rail were introduced some time in the 18th century, when they were made of wrought iron, but became very common in the 19th century, when they were made of brass and many designs feature in late Victorian catalogues.

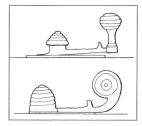

Fig 3.28b (above): Sash fasteners c1870 Worcs.

Although most sash windows have square heads, variations are also common. First appearing in the 1690s, the segmental arch (Fig 3.27) was especially popular in the 1720s and 1730s, with occasional examples turning up as late as the 1790s. From about 1730 the round-headed window was used in specific locations, usually at the back to light the staircase or over the front door. In the 1790s and early 1800s some urban terraces have round-arched windows on the ground floor, with square-headed windows in the upper storeys. Stair windows may be larger than those elsewhere in the house, and Whitby had a fashion for extremely long thin windows running almost the full height of the wall above the front door, with the staircase balustrades carried across the windows at each half landing (Fig 3.28).

Fig 3.29 (below): A Venetian window from the George Hotel, Tideswell, Derbyshire.

At the end of the 18th century it became fashionable to have windows reaching down to the floor; these first appeared in London in the 1770s, in developments such as Bedford Square, and reached Bath by the 1790s. Often

Fig 3.30 *(above): A house in Broad Street, Ludlow, Shropshire, with massed Venetian windows. Note the varied patterns of the glazing bars, ogee in the two windows above the front door and radial elsewhere.*

Fig 3.31 *(below): The Ivy House Hotel, Marlborough, has two Venetian windows on the first floor, with a single round-headed sash between them, all featuring intersecting glazing bars. The ground floor has two triple sash windows under a single segmental arch, while the small dormers in the roof have wooden casements.*

earlier windows were altered to take account of the new fashion, and small wrought-iron balconies protected first-floor windows. By the Regency period these became the height of fashion, with many wonderful designs surviving in towns such as Cheltenham and Sidmouth. At the same time the full-height casement or French window was sometimes used instead of the sash, being rather more convenient for use as a door.

Sash windows are sometimes arranged in pairs or even in threes, a fashion which may have begun in the second half of the 18th century in order to reduce liability for window tax; windows less than a foot (30cm) apart were taxed as a single unit. Marks in the stonework or brickwork show that sometimes windows were moved closer together to fall within this ruling. Tripartite windows occur in the later 18th century, while stepped tripartite windows, in which the central light is taller than the others, can be found earlier in the century and had been common in the 17th century in the Lancashire and Yorkshire Pennines.

A particular form of triple window is the Venetian window in which the taller central light has a round arched head. It is usually used for the most important first-floor room or for the grand staircase, but occasionally builders or architects have gone over the top and used it for every window on the main façade (Fig 3.30). Most Venetian windows date from the 18th century, becoming especially popular in the second half of the century and are usually found in larger houses.

Gothic motifs and styles came into use from the 1750s and were popularised by Horace Walpole in his house at Strawberry Hill, completed in 1776. From then on Strawberry Hill Gothick (the 'k' being added to differentiate it from later Victorian Gothic styles) was much copied and windows with arched or ogee heads are found. Sometimes the actual glazing bars intersect at the apex to give a row of pointed arches, a feature often used for the central light of a Venetian window (Fig 3.31), which may even occur as late as the 1840s.

Margin lights, narrower panes of glass around the edge of a window, became popular from about 1800 and were often glazed with coloured glass, red or blue being especially popular, with etched stars in the corners. They were also popular above canted bay windows which came into fashion in the 1850s as they lined up neatly when the façade was viewed straight on.

A major change occurred at the beginning of Queen Victoria's reign in 1837 when much larger sheets of cylinder glass and then plate glass became cheaper and more readily available. At first it was still too expensive for general use and sashes with small panes continued to be used for many houses. After the abolition of window tax in 1851 and the duty on glass in 1857 plate glass came into more general use. Each sash could now have only two panes of glass, usually divided vertically but sometimes

Fig 3.32 (above):
Victorian sash windows
were often set in pairs; this
Italiante-style window is a
good example.

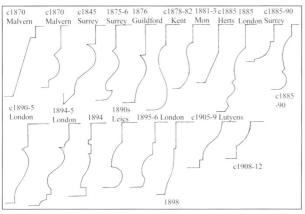

Fig 3.33 (above) : Profiles of sash window horns.

horizontally and later just a single pane of plate glass. These sheets of glass were heavier than the small panes and the absence of glazing bars put a strain on the sash frame. To counteract this the sash horn was invented, a

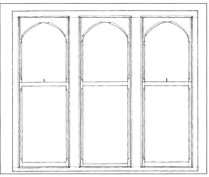

Fig 3.34 (left):
circa 1870 Worcs.
A triple sash
window with
arched tops on the
upper sash.

Fig 3.35 (below): In the
1894 Building Act there
was a relaxation in the
rules on recessing wooden
window frames behind the
external wall and,
although some had already
appeared, there was a
fashion for using
projecting windows and in
the early 1900s for the
return of flush sash
windows. The example
below dates from 1901.

Fig 3.36 (above): A house in Wingham, Kent, dated 1717, has a casement window with slender wooden mullions and large lights with 15 panes of glass in each.

small projection below the joint on each side of the sash. Sash windows have frequently been repaired or renewed and unfortunately the replacements often have both horns and small panes of glass, two things which should never occur together.

Victorian sash windows took a variety of forms, depending on the prevailing style of the time. In the early Victorian period, the Italianate style was popular, with large round-headed windows set within stuccoed walls. In the 1850s the High Victorian period began, with its fashion for all things Gothic and emphasis on polychrome brickwork and moulded terracotta decoration. Windows often had pointed arches, either in the brickwork above the window or for the actual opening, and sometimes the sashes themselves were given arched heads. Straight lintels were often chamfered or moulded.

From circa 1875 the Queen Anne Revival became popular, with a return to plainer brickwork and sash windows, with thick glazing bars and small panes of glass. Sometimes only the upper sash was treated in this way, with the lower one filled with a single sheet of plate glass, a style which became widespread by the end of the century. At the same time mullioned and casement

Fig 3.38 (below): A house of 1758 in Litton, Derbyshire, with large mullioned windows with plain architraves and wooden casements within; but these may not be original as they have large panes of sheet glass.

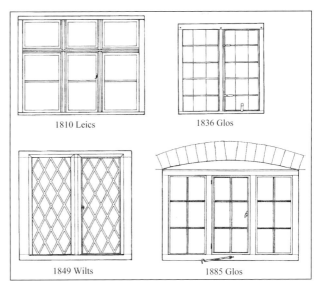

1810 Leics

1836 Glos

1849 Wilts

1885 Glos

Fig 3.37 (above): A selection of 19th century casement windows.

windows returned to popularity with the vernacular revival of the Arts and Crafts movement, led by architects such as Norman Shaw and influenced by William Morris.

18th and 19th Century Casement Windows

Smaller houses and cottages with ceilings too low to accommodate the new style for tall cross-windows and then sashes continued to use the wooden mullioned window, which remained popular throughout the 18th and 19th centuries at this social level. At this period the mullions tend to be slimmer and the window lights larger, with two- and three-light windows being the most common. In areas where stone mullions had been the norm they continued through the 18th and into the 19th century; by the end of the period they were no longer moulded or even chamfered, but had plain square cross-sections and no architraves or hood moulds.

Fig 3.39 (above): Churchill House, Alcester, Warwickshire, dated 1688. Despite its modest size, this house has a highly decorative façade. Although the present sashes are modern replacements (the glazing bars are too thin for 1688), the attic dormers retain their original casements with leaded lights and reveal the pleasing reflections and variations in colour found with early glass. The ground floor was altered in the early 19th century.

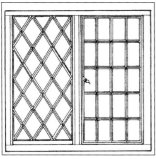

Fig 3.40 (left): A house of 1885 in Gloucestershire has iron casements with iron glazing bars resembling diamond leaded lights , a feature which occurs from the late 18th century. Examples are illustrated in pattern books of the period such as Batty Langley's 'The Builder's Jewel', published in 1754.

Casements (the hinged, opening section of the window) had been made of wrought iron but wooden versions may have first come in around 1680 although many iron casements may have been replaced with wooden ones at a later date. Most wooden casements appear to date from the 19th and 20th centuries, with slender wooden mullions separating the lights and large panes of sheet glass with one or two horizontal wooden bars (Fig 3.37: 1810 Leics). Segmental arches are common over 19th century casement windows in both brick and stone buildings.

Iron casements were still commonly used for the less important windows; in Norwich from the 1830s to the 1880s it was quite common to have sash windows at the

Fig 3.41 (below): The Vicar's Cottages, Chipping Campden, Gloucestershire. These 1833 cottages have cast-iron casements with decorative glazing, set under traditional hood (label) moulds.

Fig 3.42 *(above) :This timber-framed house in Lincoln has had sliding sashes inserted into the upper floor, probably in the later 18th century when the ground floor was given bow-windowed shop fronts. The dormer above this has a vertical sash.*

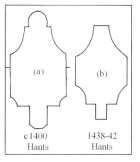

Fig 3.43 *(below): The profiles of two stone mullions from medieval buildings in Hampshire: (a) the hall of St Cross Hospital, Winchester, circa 1400 and, (b) the Bishop's Palace, Bishop's Waltham, 1438-42.*

(a)	(b)
c 1400	1438-42
Hants	Hants

front and casements at the back. It was equally common for servants' rooms in the attics to have casement windows in small dormers even if the rest of the façade had sash windows.

Dormers set within the roof slope are common from the early 18th century, and although occasional examples are fitted with squat sash windows, casements are the norm. They may have either gabled or hipped roofs, and in the larger houses are sometimes given decorative pediments.

Many late 19th century cottages and almshouses have wooden mullions, iron casements, turnbuckle catches and hook stays just like those of earlier periods, with either leaded lights or cast-iron glazing bars. In larger houses, wooden casements and the multi-paned sash with thick glazing bars reappeared, while in the 1880s and 1890s, elongated stone-mullioned windows were common. The Vernacular Revival, which began in the 1870s, made such features extremely popular, and the Arts and Crafts Movement continued their use into the 20th century with the work of architects such as Philip Webb, Norman Shaw and Edwin Lutyens, who used and adapted vernacular styles.

Horizontal Sliding Sash Windows

Although by 1900 the sash window seems to have become universal, an alternative for rooms with low ceilings was the sliding sash, which usually has one fixed and one moveable sash which slides horizontally. They are commonly called Yorkshire sashes as they are particularly common in that county, but examples can be found throughout the country. They were simple to make and relatively cheap as they did not require either sash cords and weights or hinges, handles, stays or catches. When closed they look little different from casement windows and can easily be overlooked. Few are in dated contexts but most appear to date from the 18th or early 19th century.

THE WINDOW IN DETAIL
Mullions

Windows are divided into a number of lights by vertical

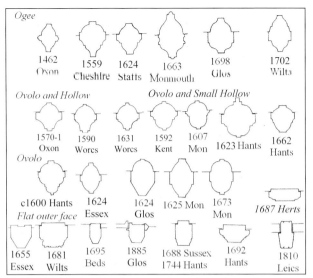

Fig 3.44 (above): A selection of profiles through wooden mullions (outside face at the top).

Fig 3.45 (above): Little Moreton Hall, Cheshire. Three different glazing patterns can be seen in the amazing double bay window with the date 1559 carved in Roman numerals along the top. It was at the forefront of the latest fashions, with the windows installed having the new ovolo moulding on the outer face of the mullions and the more conservative hollow and ogee on the inside (Fig 3.44). Variations of this design can still be found as late as the early 18th century.

mullions and may be further subdivided horizontally by a transom. Medieval mullions either had the simple diamond profile (always made of wood), or a more complex moulding with chamfers, hollow chamfers, rolls and ogees. Few wooden ones survive (Fig 3.44: 1462 Oxon), but several 16th century wooden mullioned windows exist in eastern Sussex. No two are exactly alike,

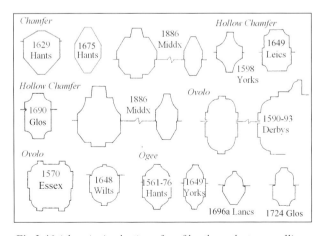

Fig 3.46 (above): A selection of profiles through stone mullions.

suggesting that they were individually commissioned, with the house owner choosing whichever design he liked best. Stone mullions have survived in many manor houses, courthouses and the like and commonly include a large internal rebate to accommodate hinged shutters (Fig 3.43).

The succession of Queen Elizabeth to the throne in 1558 seems to mark a sudden change in architectural details such as mouldings, and the new ovolo moulding became hugely popular for mullions, doorways, beams and fireplaces and ovolo mullions remained the standard type in the later 16th and throughout the 17th century. Date ranges for their use, gleaned from published information, are 1576-1682 (East Sussex), 1594-1686 (Gloucestershire), 1597-1741 (Northants), 1605-1673 (Monmouthshire), 1614-1691 (Wiltshire) and 1615-1694 (Banbury region of Oxfordshire) and there are early stone examples at New Hall, Essex, and Hardwick Hall, Derbyshire. Some mullions have the ovolo moulding only on one face, with a chamfer or hollow chamfer on the other; in almost all cases the ovolo is on the outside. Chamfers and hollow chamfers occur throughout the period and can be hard to date; simple versions continued to be used in stone regions throughout the 18th and into the 19th century for smaller houses and cottages.

Fig 3.48 (below): At Haddon Hall, Derbyshire, the long gallery has windows with simple diamond leaded lights, but the panels are deliberately set at strange angles so as to catch the light and make the glass sparkle.

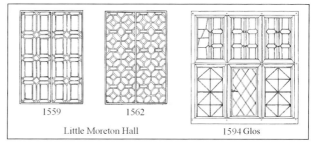

1559   1562

Little Moreton Hall   1594 Glos

Fig 3.47 (above): Glazing patterns used in the late 16th century, with two designs from Little Moreton Hall, Cheshire, 1559 and 1562, and a second-floor window at Morton Grange, Thornbury, Glos, of 1594.

A new type of mullion first appeared in the mid 17th century, with the outer face flat with a small rebate for the glazing (Fig 3.44). Such windows are particularly common from about 1680 and they continue into the 18th century, often being used for the cross-windows that were fashionable at this time. The earliest have a large chamfer or ovolo on the inner face, but in later examples the moulding is much smaller, with a small ogee or a round bead moulding (Fig 3.44: 1688) being the most common

Glazing

Medieval windows were sometimes filled in with wooden lattices, oiled linen or thin sheets of horn, but these are only known from documentary references. William Harrison in his *Description of England*, published in 1577, says that such things were now rarely used 'bicause glasse is come to be so plentifull'. The earliest window glass takes the form of diamond leaded lights, which was the most economical method as it enabled even tiny pieces of glass to be used around the edges of the window. The Elizabethans love of pattern led to the development of elaborate glazing designs, such as those at Little Moreton Hall in Cheshire (Fig 3.47).

Diamond leaded lights sometimes include one or more panes that are pierced lead, used to provide ventilation (several can be seen at Hampton Court Palace). Diamond panes, called quarrels, continued in use throughout the 17th century, but square or rectangular panes gradually

Fig 3.49 (above): Ventilator quarrels at Haddon Hall, Derbyshire, (top) and Stoke Charity church, Hampshire, (bottom); the latter has a rather pleasing spider's web design and is used in several windows in the church.

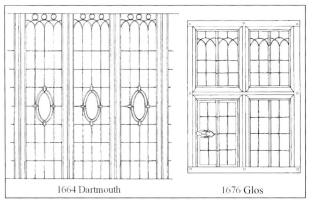

1664 Dartmouth   1676 Glos

Fig 3.50 (above): Decorative glazing of the later 17th century. The Dartmouth example of 1664 may be partly restoration, but the design is similar to that at Moorend Farm, Hambrook, Glos, dated 1676. This second-floor window had been blocked to avoid the window tax and unusually they did not bother to remove the glass before blocking it.

took over from about 1660. Nevertheless diamond panes are sometimes found even in the 18th century. The 1734 *Builder's Directory* refers to long quarrels and square quarrels, implying that they were still in common use. Many windows have had their glazing renewed at a later date, so early diamond lights are relatively scarce; many of those that do exist are the result of late 19th or 20th century restoration work, but may reuse old glass.

Early glass can be recognised by its distinctive greenish or yellow colour, the pleasing irregularity of the surface and the presence of small bubbles and imperfections in the glass. Sometimes people have scratched graffiti on glass panes, leaving their name and perhaps a date. This, of course, is not necessarily the date at which the glass was installed; it merely shows that it was in place by the inscribed date. Some 17th century houses have decorative glazing, which seems to have been revived in the days after the Restoration of Charles II to the throne in 1660; there was much looking back to the good old days of Good Queen Bess and a consequent revival of Elizabethan style.

The panes of glass were held by lead cames and the whole structure was thus somewhat flexible. For this reason, and for security, windows usually had a vertical stanchion of either wood or iron in the centre of each light and the leaded lights were tied to these by fine wire. Many stanchions have been removed, but the diamond-shaped holes can still be seen in the window frame. Double stanchions are occasionally found, but horizontal saddle bars took over instead and are common in the larger lights found in later windows. Saddle bars are usually square in section and often have flattened ends turned at right angles to enable the bars to be nailed to the window frame. They are smaller than stanchions; the latter are an inch or more square (25-30 mm), whereas saddle bars are only a quarter to half an inch in section (6-12 mm). Sometimes round-sectioned saddle bars occur and these appear to be later, often dating from the 19th century. It is hard to give specific dates, however, as windows may have been repaired and altered many times.

There was a dramatic change in glazing in the 1840s as new, much larger, sheets of cylinder glass and then plate glass (first invented in the late 17th century but very expensive) became cheaper and more readily available. At first it was still too expensive for general use and small

Fig 3.51 (below): Iron hinges from casement windows, hung on unusually decorative pintles.

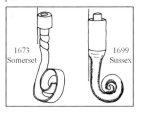

1673
Somerset

1699
Sussex

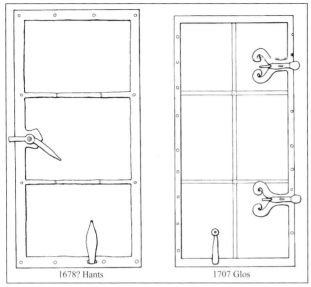

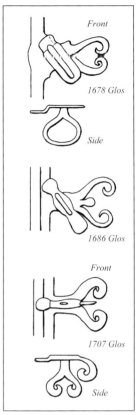

Fig 3.52a *(above): Wrought iron casements. The pattern of holes in the Hampshire example shows that it always had rectangular leaded lights, and marks on the horizontal saddle bars show where these were tied on by wire. The Gloucestershire example, although probably later, has far more holes in the frame, implying that it originally had diamond leaded lights.*

panes continued to be used for many houses but after the abolition of the window tax in 1851 and the duty on glass in 1857, plate glass came into more general use.

In the later 19th century the influence of people like William Morris led to an interest in stained glass, and coloured windows were used in many larger houses. The use of stained glass was often restricted to the front door, entrance hall and staircase, or the upper sections of the main windows.

Fig 3.52b *(above): The heart-shaped window catch seems especially common in Gloucestershire in the late 17th and early 18th centuries.*

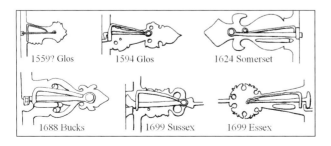

Fig 3.53 *(left): Examples of horizontal spring catches.*

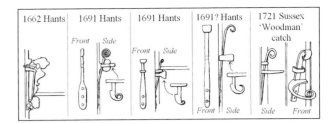

Fig 3.54 (right): Vertical window spring catches. Some examples from the Alton area of Hampshire date from the 1690s, and the type became particularly popular in the south-east in the 18th century. In Sussex it is commonly known as the Woodman catch.

Ironwork

The vast majority of 16th and 17th century windows had only a single opening casement, whatever the size of the window, and they may be less than the full height of the window. These casements were made of wrought iron and were hung on iron pintles similar to the much larger ones used for doors. In a wooden mullioned window the pintles were driven straight into the mullion whereas stone-mullioned windows usually had a complete iron frame which included the hooks for hanging the casement. These windows could be lifted off if needs be and the evidence of probate inventories shows that until some time in the first half of the 17th century they were regarded as movable items, not fixtures. The lead cames were attached to the frame by a series of holes, and the arrangement of these sometimes shows that rectangular panes have replaced diamond lights.

The iron casement needed three attachments, a catch to hold it shut, a stay to hold it open and a handle to move it

Fig 3.55 (right): Turnbuckle catches. The designs may vary according to region. The heart-shaped double spiral common in Gloucestershire (see Fig 3.56) is less common elsewhere. However, insufficient examples have been recorded for accurate assessments to be made. The swivel catches of the Surrey examples in the bottom row may be later replacements. Several have lost their catches, leaving only the decorative base-plates.

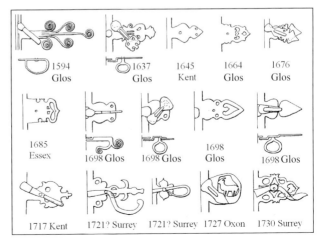

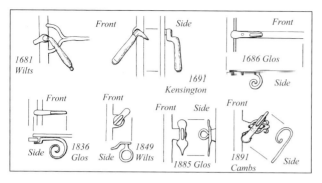

Fig 3.56 (left): A selection of later window catches with simpler designs. The simple spiral catches are hard to date accurately (1686 Glos) as there is no way of being certain if the casements are original or were renewed sometime in the 18th century or later.

Fig 3.58 (below): A simple yet sophisticated window arrangement of 1699 in Kent (detached from its original location) which has a pair of opening casements with horizontal saddle bars and the date 1699 pierced in the centre but these are not the backplates of catches. The windows are held shut by a long iron bar attached to the left-hand casement with two small projections on the bar holding it against the central iron strip. The base of the bar extends at right angles with a circular plate at the end; a knob on the front of this plate turns a smaller one behind, which engages a projection on the right-hand casement.

from one position to another. Catches are fixed onto the frame at the mid point, although larger casements in the later 17th and 18th century may have two catches. The earliest type seems to be the spring catch, which continues to the end of the 17th century. It is usually fixed horizontally but is occasionally used in a vertical position. A V-shaped iron bar, wrapped around a pivot, acts as a latch and a spring, and similar designs sometimes occur in door latches. The latch engages a small iron fastener set into the mullion or window frame. A later type of vertical spring catch has a springy bar fixed to the mullion or frame and a spiral-ended catch on the casement; the bar is pushed in towards the frame to release the window.

The turnbuckle catch consists of a baseplate, usually decorative, attached to the casement, with a swivel catch attached to it. In wooden windows the catch either engages

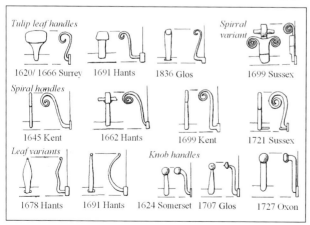

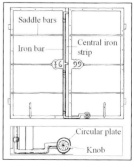

Fig 3.57 (above): Examples of 17th and early 18th century casement window handles.

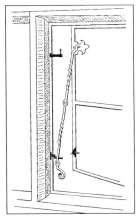

Fig 3.59 (above): Many 19th century houses and cottages in the Stroud area of Gloucestershire have this unique type of window furniture which combines the functions of catch, stay and handle. Two iron pins are fixed to the window frame, one horizontal and one vertical, with a third near the bottom of the casement. Attached near the top of the casement is a long iron bar with three or more holes at intervals along its length; the shank between the holes is twisted. The lower hole can be used on the bottom pin to hold the window slightly open, while any of the holes can be used with the top pin to give further adjustments up to fully open. To hold the window shut, the bar is passed over the two pins on the frame and the lower hole is engaged with the pin on the casement.

a small iron plate set into the mullion, or enters a slit in the mullion. In stone-mullioned windows the catch engages the outer metal frame of the window. These catches take a variety of highly decorative forms and may even include dates or initials. The swivel catch may match the backing plate or may have a contrasting design; often the catches have been lost and replaced with later ones or not replaced at all.

In the late 17th century a simple L-shaped bar catch came into use, with one of the earliest examples being at Kensington Palace in 1691. Simpler versions of the turnbuckle occur in 18th century casements and continue into the late 19th century in country cottages. The Arts and Crafts movement led to a revival of this type and elaborate versions were produced, such as the ones of 1891 from Cloister Court at Sidney Sussex College, Cambridge.

Attached to the bottom of the casement is a handle, used to open and shut the window without adding to the wear and tear suffered by the catch. They come in a variety of forms, notably the tulip leaf, the spiral and the knob.

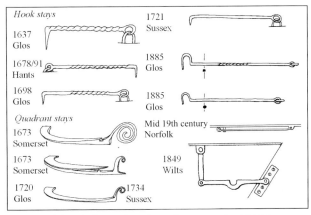

Fig 3.60 (above): Examples of window stays. A mid 19th century casement from Norfolk is an early example of a stay attached to the casement rather than the sill (Brooking Collection).

Some incorporate a hole in the base for a casement stay, while others have a small separate plate containing the hole. These are used with hook stays (Fig 3.60), long iron bars fastened to either the inside or the outside of the window sill. Hook stays may have a shank of square

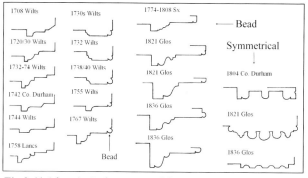

Fig 3.61 (above): Architrave mouldings.

Fig 3.62 (above): Blue Boy House, Hawkesbury Upton, Glos, 1755, has two-light stone mullioned windows with external architraves. Note also the round-headed stair window in the centre.

section twisted into a spiral, or a simpler shank that is round in section; the latter seem to be the later type. These stays usually hold the window fully open, but sometimes two or three stays of different lengths are provided to give more variation.

The other type is the quadrant stay, a quarter circle of flat iron bar attached to the outside of the window sill. These may have a notch in the end or a thicker section to hold the casement fully open; if more scope was required for holding a window partly open, a spring stay could be provided. This had an upper flexible bar, only attached at the sill end, which could be depressed to allow the casement to open but would spring back into place to hold it at whatever position was required. Dating stays is rather problematical, but quadrants are generally found in later 17th and 18th century contexts while hook stays are found in the early 17th century and continue into the 19th century.

Architrave Mouldings

In the later 17th and the 18th century, windows may have external moulded architraves, and towns on the limestone belt such as Stamford have many examples. Designs for external architraves can be found in 18th century pattern books, such as James Gibb's *Rules For Drawing* published in 1732. Eared architraves, which have a small projection at each upper corner, give more elaboration to a façade. Moulded architraves are most commonly found with cross-windows and sash windows, but sometimes smaller houses have mullioned windows with architraves.

Fig 3.63 (below): Medieval shop front in Lavenham, Suffolk. The upper half of each window is covered by a shutter which, when raised, provides a canopy over goods displayed below while the counter for the goods is formed by the downward-hinged shutters which covered the lower half of each window.

In the late 18th and early 19th century plain unmoulded architraves are common, especially in the northern half of England and in Scotland; they are often painted white in contrast to the body of the wall, which may be natural stone or, more usually, rendered and painted a darker colour. Alternatively, the wall may be a light colour and the architraves unpainted. Many houses in the early 19th century abandoned the architrave altogether and, with none of the sash boxing visible, the effect is totally different from earlier styles.

Shutters

Fig 3.64 (above): A vertical sliding shutter held by a rope and wooden block, which has been reconstructed at Bayleaf at the Weald and Downland Open Air Museum, Sussex.

Medieval unglazed windows had a variety of shutters which fall into two main types, hinged or sliding. Few have survived intact, but the evidence of their former existence can often be found. Hinged shutters may open sideways, upwards or downwards and the pintles on which they were hung often survive in medieval stone windows. There may also be a substantial iron hasp set into the central mullion which would hold a small bar to keep the shutters closed. Sometimes, instead of an iron hasp, the stonework is expanded at this point to provide a hole for the bar. Occasionally an iron hasp or hook can be found on one of the ceiling joists above a window, in a position suggesting that it was a fastener for an upward-hinged shutter. The actual shutters are simple constructions with planks nailed to horizontal battens and with iron strap hinges, and are basically the same as many doors.

Fig 3.65 (below): Reproduction of a medieval shutter which hinges upwards at the Bromsgrove Merchant's House, re-erected at the Avoncroft Museum, Worcs.

The alternative type is the sliding shutter, which was extremely common in timber-framed buildings up to circa 1600. Often the tall windows in the open hall had hinged shutters for the upper portions and sliding shutters for the lower half. This was for practical reasons; sliding shutters take up less space and are less likely to get in the way, but would be impossible to open and close at the upper level of the hall window. The main horizontal structural timbers (the mid rail and the wallplate) are thicker than the body of the wall and therefore allow for the construction of a long groove about an inch (25mm) wide to take the upper edge of the sliding shutter. The base of the shutter is held in a groove in a separate timber pegged or nailed to the face of the wall.

When these shutters went out of fashion, the applied rails were taken down to allow for removal of the shutters, so very rarely survive unless there was enough space for the shutter to be slid out at the end. However, careful examination of the timbers below a window will often

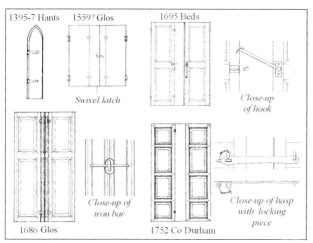

Fig 3.67 (above): Examples of 17th and 18th century shutters.

Fig 3.66 (above): Medieval sliding shutters still surviving in situ in Essex (top) and Sussex (bottom). The former has survived because both top and bottom grooves are in structural timbers and it would have been too difficult to remove them. The latter has survived intact from the 16th century because the building was never modernised.

reveal the marks of nails or peg holes showing where the rails have been. The upper grooves have sometimes been filled in with plaster and painted over, or hacked off altogether leaving a rough surface or an unexplained rebate.

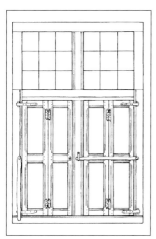

Fig 3.68 (left): Early shutters at The Wardenry, Farley, Wilts, built in 1681 with large wooden-mullioned cross windows. Unlike most, these shutters fit within the mullions rather than passing over them, and the upper lights are unshuttered. Each shutter is composed of two leaves of equal size, hinged together with decorative H-hinges. The simple shutter bars overlap in an iron hook on the centre mullion.

Fig 3.69 (below): An iron shutter stay on the outside wall of a Surrey house.

Fig 3.70a (above): White Friars, Sandwich, Kent, with external shutters with stays in the middle of the long sides.

Fig 3.70b (above): Pintles and hasp for shutters, Glos 1664 (although these may be later additions).

Fig 3.70c (below): American shutter stays are set at the bottom of the shutter and are often highly decorative. This example in New Castle, Delaware, is one of the plainer designs.

Less common are vertically sliding shutters, used where space was restricted or where there was a continuous run of windows (Fig 3.64).

It has been suggested that from the mid 16th century windows were either shuttered or glazed, but not both. While this is hard to prove, there is certainly little evidence for shutters from the late 16th to the late 17th century. Many stone-walled houses of this period have deep window splays which could accommodate shutters, but whitewashed splays helped to maximise the available light and were popular with or without shutters (occasional evidence for shutters survives, see Fig 3.70b).

External shutters still common in Europe and America may have been far more popular than surviving examples suggest. Most survivors are in towns (eg Cambridge, Oxford, Abingdon, and Sandwich). Surviving examples appear to date from the 18th or early 19th centuries, and evidence for others can be found in the form of iron shutter stays on the outside wall; they are usually found halfway up the long sides in England and at the bottom in America.

In the early 19th century some houses had external blinds which folded up into a decorative pelmet-like box at the top of the window. Although the blinds have long since gone, many of the boxes remain.

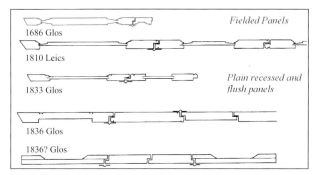

Fielded Panels

1686 Glos

1810 Leics

Plain recessed and flush panels

1833 Glos

1836 Glos

1836? Glos

Fig 3.71 (above): Profiles of shutter mouldings

In the 1680s there was a return to the use of shutters with glazed windows. 1686 Glos in Fig 3.67 has two features which mark it out as an early example. One is the method of fastening: a small iron bar, a quarter of an inch square in cross-section, is inserted into the space between the closed shutters and an iron hasp set in the central mullion. The other is the fact that the shutters are composed of two leaves each, but the leaf which covers the centre of the window is only about three inches wide. In spite of this it is fully panelled to match the main leaves, an amazing piece of craftsmanship, whereas in all later shutters the central leaves are plain (Fig 3.67: 1695 Beds and 1752 Co. Durham). There is no internal architrave or boxing for the shutters to fold back into; they simply hinge back into the window reveals. This explains the very narrow central leaves as the window reveals are slightly smaller than half the window width. Once shutters had an internal framework there was more scope for adjusting the size of the individual leaves.

Internal shutters became a standard feature of 18th century houses and continued until the 1840s, with hinged shutters which fold back into architraves to form the window reveals. These often incorporate window seats. The main leaves are panelled on the outer face, so that they

Fig 3.72 (above): Simple plank shutters without architraves continued to be used in service rooms as in this 1752 example from County Durham.

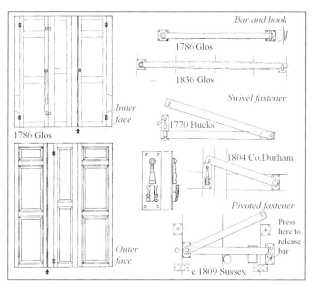

Fig 3.73 (above): Examples of shutter bars. 1786 and 1836 Glos have shutter bars with no security devices. Circa 1770 Bucks and 1804 Co. Durham have swivel catches which have to be moved to one side to allow the bar to be lifted. Circa 1809 Sussex has a security device which has to be depressed at the base to release the bar.

Fig 3.74 (below): In the early 19th century some houses have vertically sliding shutters or 'sash shutters', which work on the same principle as the sash window and are housed in the wall below the window. This example is in an early 19th century house in Buckinghamshire.

form a panelled surround to the window when folded away. The mouldings vary, but the fielded panel is common in the 18th century, with plain recessed panels or flush panels in the early 19th century.

The number of leaves depends on the width of the window. A common arrangement is to have two panelled leaves, with one extra leaf to produce the required width to cover the window. This third leaf is usually a plain unadorned plank. Others have two leaves each side, while some have one leaf on one side and three on the other. In this case the third leaf is a simple narrow plank, while the second one is panelled, but to a simpler design than the main leaves. All the leaves are rebated so that they fit neatly together. It has been suggested that so many shutters were required in the 18th century that the main panelled leaves were mass-produced to standard sizes by

Fig 3.75 (below): Press button security devices. An alternative version in an 1833 house in Gloucestershire has a projecting knob and a slot in the end of the bar which rests over the knob. A retractable pin above the knob holds the bar in place, but is withdrawn when the button is depressed.

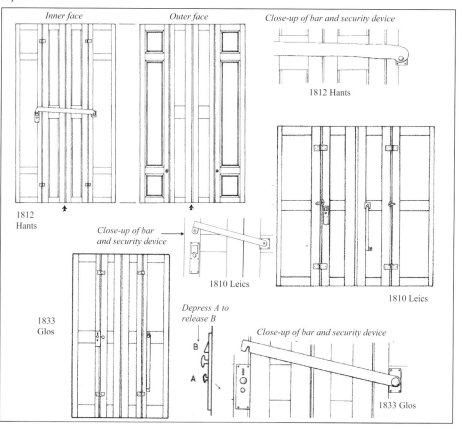

Inner face

Outer face

Close-up of bar and security device

1812 Hants

1812 Hants

Close-up of bar and security device

1810 Leics

Depress A to release B

1833 Glos

1810 Leics

Close-up of bar and security device

1833 Glos

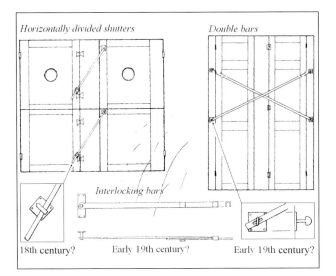

Horizontally divided shutters   Double bars

Interlocking bars

18th century?   Early 19th century?   Early 19th century?

Fig 3.76 (left): Bradley Manor, Wotton-under-Edge, Glos, has a great variety of shutters and shutter bars, none precisely dated but interesting in their methods of fastening. One room has two very long bars which engage with each other. Another has two bars attached to the frame rather than the shutters; they cross diagonally and slots in the ends pass over small pins which turn to hold them fast. Yet another room has split shutters with one diagonal bar on each; these have no security devices but sit in open hasps.

specialist joiners, leaving adjustment to the size of the window to be made on site by cutting the plain central leaves. This assumes that window heights were more standardised than their widths.

Hinges are usually plain H-hinges or rectangular hinges, but in the late 17th and early 18th century the more decorative H-hinges and butterfly hinges are used. Plainer plank shutters with strap hinges were used in service rooms such as dairies in farmhouses, and these simply fold back into the window reveal, with no moulded architrave to house them. Various instruction books give details of shutter construction, such as Peter Nicholson's *New Practical Builder* of 1825. Some shutters were divided horizontally so that the lower half could be kept closed for privacy, with the upper half open for light and ventilation. Sometimes the panels are pierced with ovals, circles or heart shapes to allow a small amount of light in, even when the shutters are closed.

When closed, the shutters are held in place by an iron bar across the centre. In most cases the bar is fixed to one shutter while the other has some form of housing for it. Crudely carved recesses in the opposite shutter leaf accommodate the projecting parts of the ironwork when the shutters are folded back. Occasionally the bar is removable and is held in hasps on either side of the

Fig 3.77 (below): 19th century shutters with removable bars.

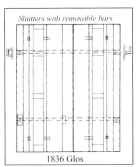

Shutters with removable bars

1836 Glos

Fig 3.78 (below): A house in Bury St Edmunds has a solution to the problem of securing split shutters; the bar is itself split to form an elliptical shape which will hold both shutters closed.

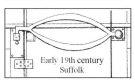

Early 19th century
Suffolk

window although this is rare in England. The simplest form of attached bar is a long hook which engages in a loop (Fig 3.67: 1695 Beds) while rather longer bars with the end resting in an open hasp are shown in 1786 and 1836 Glos, Fig 3.73.

More often there is some form of security device to prevent the bar from being opened from the outside by anyone passing a knife or other implement through the gap. The most common types are the press button and swivel fasteners. The swivel fasteners have a small bar suspended from the fixing plate of the housing; it has to be swivelled to one side to allow the bar to be opened or closed. Most are plain (Fig 3.73: 1770 Bucks), but some can be decorative (Fig 3.73: 1804 Co. Durham). Press-button fasteners have a concealed pin within the housing which engages a hole in the end of the bar; a press button below the housing will release the pin. More unusual examples are shown in Figs 3.76 and 3.78 . The fact that so much ingenuity was expended on making shutters secure from outside penetration suggests that burglary is not just a modern phenomenon. Interestingly, such security devices seem to be unknown in America.

4 STAIRCASES
BALUSTRADES, POSTS AND RAILS

Fig 4.1: *The principal parts of a staircase: (A) risers, (B) treads, (C) newel post, (D) balusters, (E) closed string, (F) dog gate and (G) handrail, (H) open string and (I) curtail step.*

TYPES OF STAIRCASE
Medieval straight and spiral staircases

The earliest wooden stairs were straight flights simply constructed with steps of solid baulks of wood, triangular in section, nailed onto sloping bearers and a few survive in medieval houses such as Crook Hall, Durham. Stone spiral stairs are common in medieval castles, but the few very early stone houses which survive appear to have had external straight flights of stairs. Brick was increasingly used for the larger houses from the 15th century, and brick spiral stairs may have an integral handrail of moulded bricks (see Fig 4.3), as at Chenies Manor House in Buckinghamshire.

The medieval open-hall house needed a separate stair at one or both ends to reach the upper chambers; these were usually a straight flight, set within the ground-floor room and reached either by a door from the screens passage of the open hall or from within the room. Although most of these stairs have since been rebuilt or

Fig 4.2 (below): Colville Hall, White Roding, Essex: a medieval straight stair in a former courthouse.

Tread

Bearer

Fig 4.3 (above): Lavenham, Suffolk: A brick stair with integral handrail.

Fig 4.4 (below): Plans showing types of staircase.

replaced with stairs sited elsewhere, the evidence for their former existence may survive in the form of blocked doorways. In areas where the medieval houses were built of stone, the stair may be a stone spiral built into an end wall or in a projecting turret set on one of the long walls. Two alternative forms of access to the upper chambers were either a gallery across the open hall leading from one chamber to the other, or a ladder or stair from the hall. The gallery meant that only one stair was needed, and there is evidence for a number of these in Hampshire; one still survives at the Red Lion in Southampton. A number of houses have original doorways leading from the upper chambers into the upper part of the open hall with no evidence for a gallery. Sometimes empty mortises imply a wooden platform and a fixed stair rising within the open hall, as at Stokesay Castle in Shropshire. However, the frequent absence of any such mortises and the lack of space in smaller houses are evidence for the use of ladders, although no actual ladders have survived.

Once the open hall had been given a chimney stack and an upper floor, only a single stair was required. This change from the open-hall house to the fully floored house took place gradually from the end of the 15th century, with variations in date between different parts of the country and different types of house. In Hampshire the change

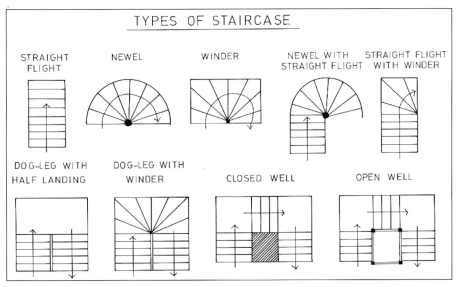

TYPES OF STAIRCASE

STRAIGHT FLIGHT   NEWEL   WINDER   NEWEL WITH STRAIGHT FLIGHT   STRAIGHT FLIGHT WITH WINDER

DOG-LEG WITH HALF LANDING   DOG-LEG WITH WINDER   CLOSED WELL   OPEN WELL took place first in the towns, when the first fully-floored houses were built around 1480 and the last open hall in 1533. In the countryside the manor houses led the way, with the first floored hall dating from 1491-96, and the latest open hall from 1505. Further down the social scale the gentry and some yeomen were building floored halls from the mid 16th century. Many open halls remained open for a considerably longer period, however, and documentary evidence implies that most rural dwellers were still living in open halls in 1600. Elsewhere open halls were in use for even longer, and there is even a house in rural Devon which has never had an upper floor put into the hall.

Fig 4.5 (above): View of a medieval open hall showing the open hearth, a fixed bench, and ladder access to the upper chamber.

Winder stairs

In the new style of house with a complete upper floor, the stair was more likely to be in a central position rather than at the ends. This was both easier of access and gave more privacy to the bedrooms, as a stairhead landing or lobby could give separate access to several chambers. Many houses now had an attic floor as well, and often the main stair simply continued on up. Sometimes the attic stair was in a different location, in an end wall or in the upper part of a tall porch. Larger houses often had two stairs, a main one for the family and guests and a back one for the farm workers or servants.

The stairs incorporated in these modernisations were usually simple winder stairs built next to the new chimney stack. The stack was generally brick in areas of timber-framed houses and the accompanying stair was constructed of timber, often with an under-stair cupboard. In areas of stone building, the stairs next to the fireplace are sometimes of stone, but may have wooden treads and risers on top of a rubble core. The space below the stair sometimes houses a bread oven in the side of the fireplace. Equally often, however, a stone house has a wooden stair with a cupboard below. A winder stair has triangular-shaped steps which wind around a small square post which usually serves as a doorframe (see Fig 4.6); to avoid draughts these stairs were often shut off by doors top and bottom (see Fig 4.6). It is a very versatile and compact type of stair and can be tucked into the corner of a room as well as beside a stack.

Fig 4.6 (below): A winder stair.

Fig 4.7 (above): Glos: A late 16th or early 17th century newel stair with solid oak treads.

Fig 4.8 (below): Hill House, Olveston, Glos. Newel stair with the mast newel carved to match the turned balusters (c1635).

Occasionally it is found in a turret or a central entrance hall, positions where a more elaborate stair might be expected. It remained in common use in smaller houses and cottages well into the 19th century. Where space permitted many were replaced by straight stairs in the 19th and 20th centuries and the empty recesses where the original ones stood may survive as cupboards.

Newel stairs

The true newel stair is similar in form to a winder but has a large central newel post, circular or octagonal in section and about six inches in diameter, into which the treads are tenoned. This post is commonly called a mast newel from its resemblance to a ship's mast; this does not mean that it is a reused timber from a ship and, although in ports such as Dartmouth or along the east Yorkshire coast, such reuse of timbers is relatively common, it does not generally occur inland. The newel stair is usually found in the more prosperous houses and often rises through more than one storey to serve attics as well. Many are located in relatively spacious turrets or within a rear wing, and they occur roughly from the mid 16th to the mid 17th century. The treads may be solid baulks of oak but later versions have separate treads and risers. In the 17th century there may be a short balustrade of turned balusters at the stair-head, and occasionally the newel post itself is carved to match (see Fig 4.8). Simple plain balustrades are also found, often consisting of a simple handrail and one or two horizontal rails, but these can be hard to date; anything from the 17th to the early 19th century is possible. Others have simple balusters which either take the form of vertical planks, as in a Hampshire example of 1625, or are square in section and set diamond-wise. At all periods stairs in more modest houses may have simple rectangular handrails. The handrails mostly have flat tops, and in the early 17th century may be embellished with shallow scratch mouldings along the sides. Others are chamfered, a feature found at any period (see Fig 4.64).

Well stairs

Although a newel stair could be surprisingly spacious, the well stair became the favoured type in larger houses. The earliest version seems to be the closed well (see Fig 4.4), which may have a solid masonry core around which rise short straight flights separated by quarter landings. More often the core is timber-framed with the panels infilled with wattle and daub, and may incorporate cupboards to make good use of the space. Hampshire examples date from circa 1560 and 1597-1606; another of 1561-76 was lost in a fire in 1969.

The closed well soon developed into the square open-well stair, which became a feature of display with square newel posts at each corner with elaborately carved pendants and finials. One of the earliest and largest is at Knole in Kent, dating from 1605-08, and it includes a rare painted balustrade which is an exact copy of the real one (see Fig 4.11).

Fig 4.9 (above): An Essex closed-well stair; the wattle and daub infill is missing, revealing the short straight flights climbing around the central framework. The stair has solid oak treads. Dated examples exist at Lawford Hall, Essex (1583) and Wigborough Manor, Somerset (1585). One of the earliest closed-well stairs dates from 1558 at Broughton Castle, Oxon, and there is another in the Guildhall at Sandwich in Kent built in 1579. Chastleton House, Oxon (1607-12) has two stair turrets, one with an open-well stair and the other with a closed-well secondary stair.

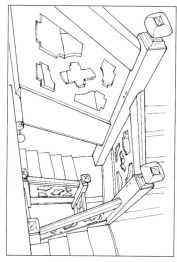

Fig 4.10 (left): An open well stair from a Shropshire house which has been tree-ring dated to the period 1625-59. It has a simple pierced balustrade with geometric patterns.

Occasionally an open-well stair has a real balustrade on both sides, a very expensive feature indicative of considerable wealth on the part of the owner. Examples are Hatfield House, Hertfordshire (1611), a Bucks manor house of 1624 and the Prince Rupert Hotel, Shrewsbury (c1631). In the 18th century there may be wall panelling rather than a balustrade, again a feature of the better quality houses.

Dog-leg stairs

Where space is restricted or the ceilings unusually high,

the quarter landings may be replaced by continuous winders to provide the extra height, but it is more usual to find a dog-leg stair instead. This has two parallel flights separated either by a half-landing or by winders, and takes up a rectangular space rather than the square space of an open-well stair (see Fig 4.12). Simple versions have a timber-framed partition between the two flights, and the corner posts are usually chamfered or moulded and stopped to match the doorframes. Many have open balustrades instead, and there are some ingenious designs to cope with the junctions at the newels. Some simply have two separate newel posts standing side by side, while others have a double-width newel to accommodate both handrails. If space is more limited, the lower handrail and the upper string are designed to cross over each other into a single newel post.

Both open-well and dog-leg stairs are used as features of display, with elaborately carved handrails and strings, turned or carved balusters and decorative pendants and finials. They are commonly positioned directly opposite the front door either in a large entrance hall or in a turret on the rear wall, and were clearly designed to make an impression on visitors.

Fig 4.11: Above is a stair-case from the Merchant's House, Marlborough, Wilts. The house was rebuilt after the great fire of 1653, and the date 1656 is scratched in the attic of the main range. The stair and rear wing were added soon afterwards. The painted balustrade includes large ball finials on the newel posts; the real ones were chopped off and removed at some unknown date. Below is a Buckinghamshire open-well stair of 1624. It has a balustrade against the wall and huge finials, all features designed to impress.

Open-string stairs

The Queen's Stair at Kensington Palace was revolutionary in being one of the first open-string stairs in the country. In open-string stairs the balusters stand on each tread instead of on a sloping closed string, giving a much more open appearance to the stair. The balusters, two or three to a tread, vary in height, and the variation can be made in several ways. In the High Wycombe example (Fig 4.13), the number of turned elements below the main column varies, while in many stairs the turned or twisted column varies in length. Alternatively the length of the unturned blocks at the base of the baluster may vary as in the Victorian example (Fig 4.17). In the Queen's Stair the entire tread end projects and is given a gently curving underside (Fig 4.15), but this design soon gave way to applied brackets for decoration (see page 131).

A characteristic feature of many open-string stairs was the curtail step, a bottom step which was wider than the rest with a curved end (Fig 4.16). The hand rail, too,

1723
Bristol

1731
Sussex

Fig 4.12 (above): This Gloucestershire dog-leg stair of 1698 has a double newel post with ball finials, a wide handrail and turned balusters.

Fig 4.13 (below): An open-string stair of 1740-43 from High Wycombe, Bucks, with decorative brackets. Note how the number of turned elements on the lower half of the baluster increases over the set of three on each tread so that the upper half remains the same all the way up.

Fig 4.14 (above): Two 18th century open-string stairs. Note how the twisted or turned sections vary in height so the lower half remains level and the top stays in line with the handrail.

curved around, often with a cluster of balusters supporting it. Often the central baluster of the cluster was of iron to provide sufficient strength. Sometimes a curtail step was added to an earlier stair, as in the main stair of 1734 at Kew Palace.

The open-string stair remained popular in Victorian times, but a characteristic of the period was to mix and match elements from varying eras. A good example is the stair in St Saviour's Vicarage, Sunbury-on-Thames, Middx, designed by the architect J.D. Sedding and dated 1886 (Fig 4.17 left). The turned section of the balusters is Jacobean in style, but has been combined with the long

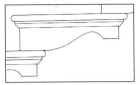

Fig 4.15 (above): The curved tread ends of the Queen's Stair at Kensington Palace, 1691.

Fig 4.16 (below): A curtail step in a Cumbrian house of 1840.

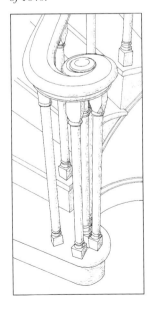

unturned end blocks of a century later. The panelled newel post is reminiscent of late 17th century designs, the finial is faintly Jacobean in flavour, while the toad's-back handrail and the carved brackets are identical to early 18th century designs. Despite the odd mixture the design is actually very successful. Less so is the stair of 1896 from Hampstead, north London (Fig 4.17 right), where the balusters, instead of standing on the treads, are carried past the ends of the steps to terminate in little turned pendants. The slender balusters with multiple decorative elements remained popular well into the 20th century, and many Edwardian houses show similar designs.

Pendant

Fig 4.17 (above): Late 19th century stairs from (left) St Saviour's Vicarage, Sunbury-on-Thames, Middx (1886) and (right) a house in West Hampstead, London (1896). Note how in the left-hand example the unturned blocks at the base of the balusters vary in height so the central turned section rises parallel to the handrail.

THE STAIR IN DETAIL:
BALUSTERS
Turned Balusters

Turned balusters are those which have been made from a block of wood turned on a lathe to create a spindle pattern and the earliest dated examples known so far are those at Grove Place, Nursling, Hampshire, of 1561-76 (Fig 4.18).

These are mirror balusters, in which the top half exactly mirrors the bottom half. The shafts are slightly tapered and decorated with fine incised lines, and the entire length is turned. In slightly later balusters, the top and bottom blocks are left square and are quite short in relation to the length of the baluster. Turned mirror balusters are common until circa 1655, with occasional examples thereafter; the same is true of the fine incised lines which decorate the shafts. The shafts are usually tapered, with slender rings at each end (see Figs 4.19 a and b). Not all balusters of this period are symmetrical, however, and some have single shafts, often tapered and wider at the top, or double shafts unequally divided. In the latter case one may be straight-sided, the other tapered (see Fig 4.22, page 110).

Baluster design changed dramatically around 1655 with the introduction of the vase and bottle shapes for the main shaft. This effectively reversed the direction of the taper, with balusters now being wider at the bottom than the top. The vase is elegantly curved, the bottle shape more angular, but both are popular until circa 1700 (see Fig 4.24, page 111). Like the earlier balusters, they are generally turned from a three-inch square block, although in the 1670s and 1680s larger ones are occasionally found. These vase and bottle shapes are sometimes used for mirror

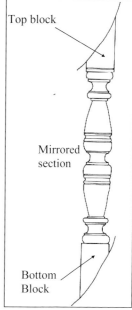

Fig 4.18 (above): Grove Place, Nursling, Hants. A turned mirror baluster dating from 1561-76. The top and bottom blocks are turned, although later examples are invariably square.

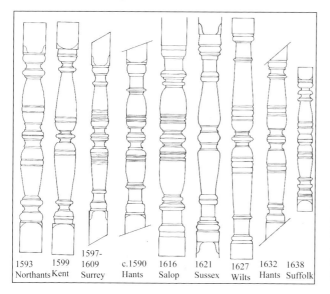

1593 Northants	1599 Kent	1597-1609 Surrey	c.1590 Hants	1616 Salop	1621 Sussex	1627 Wilts	1632 Hants	1638 Suffolk

Fig 4.19 a (left): Examples of turned mirror balusters. 1616 Salop and 1638 Suffolk are turned spindles in the side walls of porches.

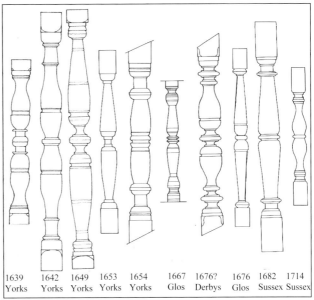

1639 Yorks	1642 Yorks	1649 Yorks	1653 Yorks	1654 Yorks	1667 Glos	1676? Derbys	1676 Glos	1682 Sussex	1714 Sussex

Fig 4.19b (above): Examples of turned mirror balusters.

Fig 4.20 (below): In late 16th and 17th century balusters, the top and bottom blocks are left square and are quite short in relation to the length of the baluster. The shafts are usually tapered, with slender rings at each end.

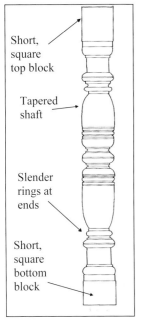

Short, square top block

Tapered shaft

Slender rings at ends

Short, square bottom block

Fig 4.21 (above):The balusters at a Buckinghamshire manor house are joined by round arches, a feature only found in the highest quality stairs. Despite that, much of the carving is rather crudely done. The baluster design puts the stair firmly in the period 1620 to 1640, confirmed by a recent dendro-date for the roof of 1624.

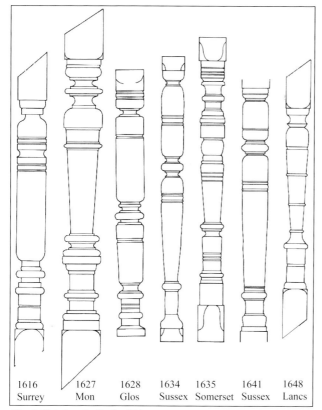

1616	1627	1628	1634	1635	1641	1648
Surrey	Mon	Glos	Sussex	Somerset	Sussex	Lancs

Fig 4.22 (above): Early 17th century turned balusters.

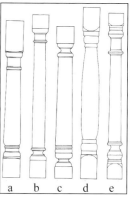

Fig 4.23(above):A simpler variant of the turned baluster that appears in the 1630s is the gun-barrel baluster, with a tapered column with minimal decoration. Dated examples are (a) the west gallery balustrade and stairs at All Saints' Church, Odiham, Hampshire, (1632), (b) a 1634 balustrade in Kent (c) the altar rails at St Andrew's Church, Lyddington, Rutland, (1635), and (d) the gallery in the open hall at Bryndraenog, Radnorshire, (1636). A similar design occurs in the hall gallery at New Hall, Elland, Yorkshire, (e) a multi-period house with a 1670 plaster overmantel in the hall. The similarity of the balusters to those above and the use of fine incised lines suggest that the gallery pre-dates the plasterwork. Pevsner refers to a date of 1640, which seems stylistically more likely.

balusters, which are commonly referred to as dumb-bell balusters and are found until circa 1700.

After 1700 the bottle shape disappeared, but the vase continued to be popular in a more slender form. Alongside it is the tapered column, which often incorporates a small vase or urn shape below the column. Both designs continued throughout the 18th century, getting gradually more slender towards 1800. The unturned blocks top and bottom became gradually longer in relation to the length of the shaft, and some balusters include a narrow unturned block between the main column and the decorative elements below it. This feature is more often found with tapered columns or twisted balusters than in the vase-shaped balusters (see Fig 4.27a, page 112). In the later 18th century simple columns with minimal decoration top

Fig 4.24 *(right): Later 17th century turned balusters. Some of the earliest dated vase balusters are at St John's College Oxford (1631-36), with a very similar painted version at Kew Palace (1631). The balusters of the Oxford stairs are all tenoned and pegged, a mark of high quality.*

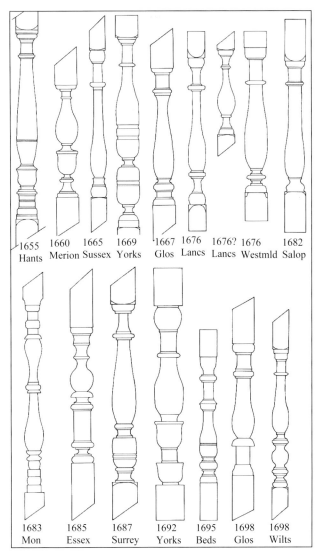

| 1655 | 1660 | 1665 | 1669 | 1667 | 1676 | 1676? | 1676 | 1682 |
| Hants | Merion | Sussex | Yorks | Glos | Lancs | Lancs | Westmld | Salop |

| 1683 | 1685 | 1687 | 1692 | 1695 | 1698 | 1698 |
| Mon | Essex | Surrey | Yorks | Beds | Glos | Wilts |

Fig 4.25 *(below): A dumb-bell baluster of circa 1656 at The Merchant's House, Marlborough, Wilts (a), a vase baluster of 1691 (b) and a bottle-shaped baluster of 1699 (c), both from Hampshire.*

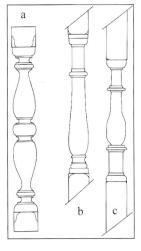

and bottom become common. Sometimes these simpler balusters are found in the upper flights of stairs, leading to the servants' quarters in the attic, while the main flight has a more elaborate design (see Fig 4.27b).

All types of baluster were generally nailed to the handrail and string on the sloping flights, and could therefore be removed leaving little trace; they were usually tenoned into the straight handrail on the landings, however.

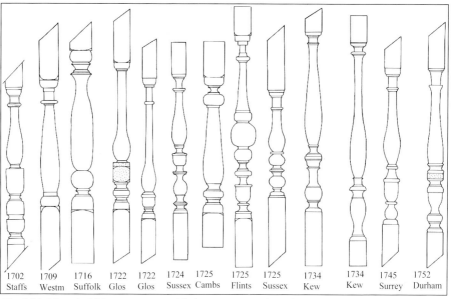

1702	1709	1716	1722	1722	1724	1725	1725	1725	1734	1734	1745	1752
Staffs	Westm	Suffolk	Glos	Glos	Sussex	Cambs	Flints	Sussex	Kew	Kew	Surrey	Durham

Fig 4.26 *(above): 18th century turned balusters – vase shaped (stippling represents square unturned sections).*

Fig 4.27a *(below): 18th century turned balusters – tapered column (stippling represents square unturned sections)..*

Fig 4.27 b: 18th century turned balusters - plainer designs. (a): 1743 Westmorland, (b): 1759 Glos, and (c): 1786 Glos.

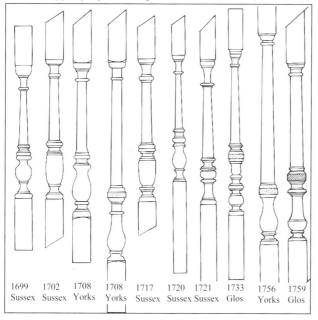

1699	1702	1708	1708	1717	1720	1721	1733	1756	1759
Sussex	Sussex	Yorks	Yorks	Sussex	Sussex	Sussex	Glos	Yorks	Glos

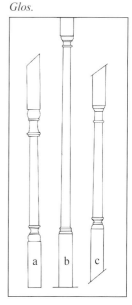

It is not uncommon to find one baluster set upside down, which may be the result of a nailed baluster working loose and being carelessly replaced; it has been claimed, however, that this was done deliberately as a form of good luck charm!

The timber used was generally oak in the 17th century, with pine coming into fashion from the later 17th century and throughout the 18th century. Examples of the latter were often painted, despite the modern fashion for stripping everything wooden.

Victorian turned balusters are generally turned from timber less than two inches square, with long unturned blocks top and bottom. There is a wide variety of designs for the main shaft, with tapered columns, vase shapes, spirals and fluted columns. The use of multiple rings is common and sometimes decorative elements are repeated upside down in a way that would never occur in the 17th or 18th centuries. The stairs are often either painted or varnished, and timber such as teak or mahogany became fashionable.

Fig 4.28 (above): Stairs from the highest social level show the same designs as those in more modest houses, but usually combine more different elements in the one baluster, as in the Queen's Stair of 1691 at Kensington Palace.

Fig 4.29 (right): Victorian turned balusters illustrated in a late 19th century catalogue. One baluster has a pendant on the bottom and was clearly intended for a stair such as that illustrated in Fig 4.17.

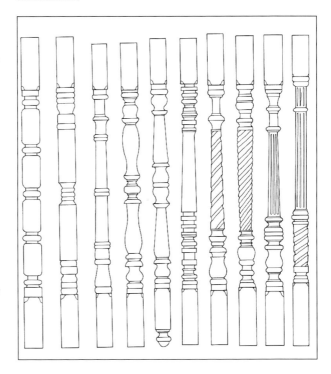

Twisted Balusters

Twisted balusters first appear in Sussex in 1652, but most examples date from the 1670s onwards, with a peak in the 1690s. As with the turned balusters, they gradually become thinner in the 18th century and seem to have fallen out of favour around the middle of the century, with the latest examples dating from the 1760s. They then reappeared in the Victorian period, often with a much tighter spiral (Fig 4.29). In an open-string stair twisted balusters may be combined with other designs, either columnar, or fluted, or both (see Fig 4.14-page 106).

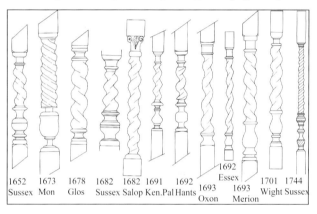

1652 1673 1678 1682 1682 1691 1692 1693 1693 1701 1744
Sussex Mon Glos Sussex Salop Ken.Pal Hants Oxon Merion Wight Sussex
1692 Essex

Fig 4.30 (left): Examples of twisted balusters dating from 1652 to 1744.

Splat Balusters

Splat balusters are carved from a thin plank and their designs follow the same general pattern as turned balusters; those from the early 17th century taper from top to bottom while later ones usually (but not always – see Fig 4.35: 1668 Northants) taper from bottom to top. They differ from turned balusters in that symmetrical mirror balusters appear far more popular in the second half of the 17th century than the first. However, many of the mirror balusters from the mid to late 17th century, both turned and splat, are in Yorkshire and it could be that this is a regional preference. Splat baluster outlines often mimic those of turned balusters, and they were of course much cheaper to produce. Some houses have a main stair with turned balusters and a back stair with splat balusters of the same design. Some are pierced with circles, hearts and other designs, while others are solid; occasionally they have

Fig 4.31 (below): The bar chart shows the numbers of dated examples of twisted balusters from 1660-1750. (dates along the bottom and the quantity of examples up the side). Note how their popularity peaks in the 1680s and 1690s.

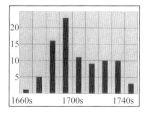

Fig 4.32a (right):
Tapered or vase shape
splat balusters. Their
designs follow the same
general pattern as turned
balusters; those from the
early 17th century taper
from top to bottom while
later ones usually taper
from bottom to top.

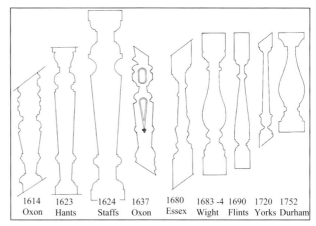

| 1614 | 1623 | 1624 | 1637 | 1680 | 1683-4 | 1690 | 1720 | 1752 |
| Oxon | Hants | Staffs | Oxon | Essex | Wight | Flints | Yorks | Durham |

incised decoration, such as 1637 Oxford (Fig 4.32).

Early 17th century splat balusters tend to be cut from thicker planks than the later ones and are therefore less likely to be pierced. Houses of 1662 in the Cathedral Close in Winchester have pierced balusters for the main stairs and narrower unpierced ones for the back stairs. Pierced balusters are also often seen in church altar rails, as at St Gregory, Castlemorton, Worcs, where they are inscribed

Fig 4.33 (right):
Symmetrical mirror splat
balusters. Unlike turned
balusters, these appear far
more popular in the second
half of the 17th century
than the first.

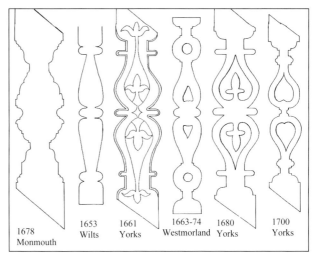

| 1678 | 1653 | 1661 | 1663-74 | 1680 | 1700 |
| Monmouth | Wilts | Yorks | Westmorland | Yorks | Yorks |

with the dates 1683 and 1684 (see Fig 4.35). Splat balusters are also sometimes used in the wall framing of timber-framed houses for decorative effect, especially in Staffordshire and Cheshire (see Fig 4.32: 1624 Staffs).

In the 18th century splat balusters were less common, although in County Durham they continued to be used as dresser legs until at least 1752. Instead the wavy baluster became popular, its outline copying that of twisted balusters. It was sometimes used for staircases, but is perhaps more common in ventilation grilles (see Fig 4.34).

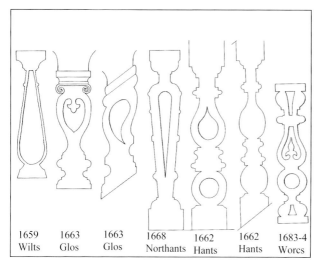

| 1659 Wilts | 1663 Glos | 1663 Glos | 1668 Northants | 1662 Hants | 1662 Hants | 1683-4 Worcs |

Fig 4.35 *(above): Examples of pierced splat balusters.*

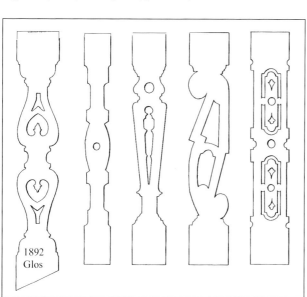

1892
Glos

Fig 4.34 *(above): Wavy splat balusters.*

1713
Cambs

1723
Cornwall
1757
Surrey

Fig 4.36 *(left): Victorian splat balusters. The 1892 design from Gloucestershire is similar to some of the earlier splat balusters, but is fussier in the detail. The others are from a late 19th century catalogue.*

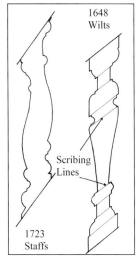

1648
Wilts

Scribing
Lines

1723
Staffs

Fig 4.37 *(above):*
Sometimes rather strange
shapes are produced on
the sloping flights, when
one side of the baluster has
in effect been moved
upwards in relation to the
other side, giving a
distorted vase shape as in
1723 Staffs. Often very
faint scribing lines can be
seen where the carpenter
marked out his design with
a sharp tool in the days
before lead pencils, as in
1648 Wilts.

Splat balusters disappear altogether in the later 18th century, but reappear in the Victorian era with a great variety of designs, many of which bear little resemblance to those of the 17th century (see Fig 4.36).

Carved or Moulded Balusters

Carved or moulded balusters are similar to splat balusters, but are carved from a thicker block of wood and usually have mouldings on all four sides (see Fig 4.38). Unlike the other baluster types, most seem to taper from top to bottom regardless of date, and they seem to be confined to the 17th century. One of the earliest examples may be the grand stair of 1611 at Hatfield House, Hertfordshire. Many incorporate an Ionic capital as part of the design, as in the splendid Leicestershire dog-gate of 1649 whose balusters match those of the stair (see Fig 4.71).

Carved and pierced balustrades occur in a number of stately homes and wealthy houses from the 1630s to the later 17th century, and many are extremely elaborate. Castle Ashby, Northants has two, the west staircase of circa 1630, which has strapwork designs, and the east stair of the 1670s which has openwork panels of acanthus foliage with flowers. The grand stair at Ham House in Surrey, constructed in 1637/8, has very unusual panels decorated with trophies of arms, including highly detailed carvings of cannon with their ramrods, barrels of gunpowder and piles of cannon balls. Documentary

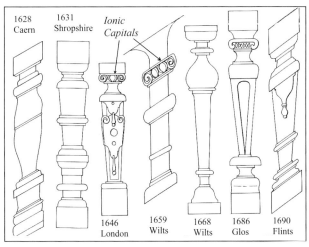

1628
Caern

1631
Shropshire

Ionic
Capitals

1646
London

1659
Wilts

1668
Wilts

1686
Glos

1690
Flints

Fig 4.38 *(right): Carved*
or moulded balusters.

Fig 4.39 (above): An unusual stair of 1655 from Berden Hall, Essex, has carved and pierced balusters with pierced panels between them; the design is very striking and gives an impression of great richness.

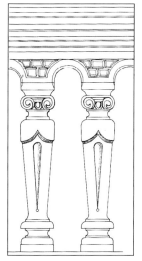

Fig 4.40 (above): The carved balusters with Ionic capitals at Wick Court near Bristol, circa 1665, are linked by round arches with chip carving in the spandrels.

evidence shows that the wood was painted and veined to imitate walnut, with the details picked out in gilding.

At Dunster Castle in Somerset the grand stair of c1680 is framed in oak but the carved foliage panels are of elm. It has elaborate vase finials, and similar ones can be seen at Guildford House in Guildford of the 1660s (see Fig 4.41).

A much plainer type of pierced balustrade occurs at Detton Hall, Neen Savage, Shropshire, which has been tree-ring dated to 1625-59. Here the solid panels are pierced with simple geometric shapes (see Fig 4.10 - page 104).

Pierced balustrades recur in the Victorian period, with a particularly fine one in the Headmaster's House in Malvern of circa 1870 (see Fig 4.42). A totally different type of pierced balustrade, a geometric style commonly called Chinese Chippendale, was popular in the 1750s; its popularity was short-lived but there are examples in Welsh houses as late as 1768 and 1778 (see Fig 4.43 - page 119).

Fig 4.41 (below):Guildford House, Guildford, Surrey: 1660. Open-well stair with high quality pierced balustrades and vase finials.

Metal Balusters

The wrought-iron balustrade, first used in 1625 at the Queen's House, Greenwich, was not copied until 1695 in the King's Stair at Kensington Palace. Both form a

Fig 4.42 *(above): This beautifully carved balustrade is in a house of circa 1870 in Malvern, Worcs. The museum at Ireshopeburn in County Durham, a former manse of 1804, has the usual open-string stair with stick balusters common at this period, but the balustrade along the landing has splendid cast-iron panels. It is not clear if these are contemporary or later insertions.*

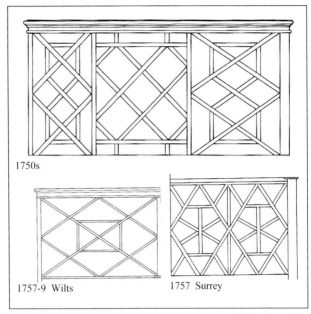

1750s

1757-9 Wilts

1757 Surrey

Fig 4.43 *(above): Examples of Chinese Chippendale balustrades.*

Fig 4.44 *(right): Iron balusters. The Queen's House, Greenwich, uses flat ironwork, unlike later examples. The finest example of free-flowing scrolls is at the Royal Fort House, Bristol, of 1758-61, where the ironwork is gilded. 1759 Bristol has two different cast-iron designs. The wide panel used in c1765 Beverley is found in a pattern book of that date, W. And J.Weldon's 'The Smiths' Right Hand'. Simple geometric designs remained popular until the 1830s.*

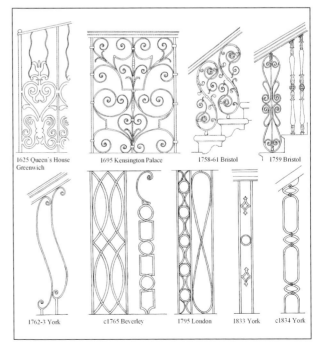

1625 Queen's House Greenwich

1695 Kensington Palace

1758-61 Bristol

1759 Bristol

1762-3 York

c1765 Beverley

1795 London

1833 York

c1834 York

continuous balustrade and include a heart motif. Other grand houses followed suit, but iron balusters only become popular in the second half of the 18th century. They were never used at the bottom end of the social scale and are far more common in urban houses than rural. A variety of geometric or floral patterns were used, and other metals such as lead and brass may form the more decorative elements. In the later 18th century cast- iron became popular and the use of pattern books meant that the same design could be found in houses all over the country; any element of individuality was now lost as Victorian mass-production took over.

Around 1800, stairs became much simpler, with plain stick balusters of pine an inch square under a mahogany handrail. The balusters were painted, which disguised the

Fig 4.45 (above): A typical early 19th century stair from Long Crendon, Bucks. It has stick balusters, a mahogany handrail and carved brackets under the tread ends.

Fig 4.46 (left):Pendants and finials – late 16th to mid 17th century.

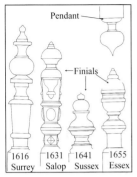

Fig 4.47 (above):
Pendants and finials –
early 17th century.

Fig 4.48 (below): Simple
newel posts of circa 1590
at Chawton House, Hants.
One with a curved top has
two rows of deeply incised
zigzags, the other has a
rudimentary finial and a
band of punched
decoration.

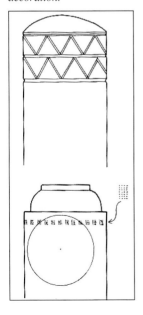

fact that there were iron balusters at intervals to give
strength to the balustrade. This became the standard
Regency stair which remained in vogue until the Victorians
revived the turned baluster (see page 107).

NEWEL POSTS, PENDANTS AND FINIALS

Newel posts at the end of balustrades and at the corners of
open-well and dog-leg stairs became features of great
display, with elaborate finials and pendants of varying
designs.

Stately homes such as Hatfield House may have heraldic
beasts and putti, but geometric shapes were the norm in

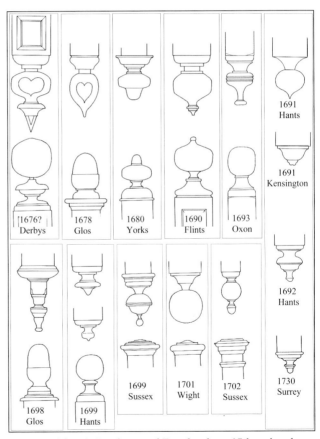

Fig 4.49 (above): Pendants and Finials – later 17th and early
18th century.

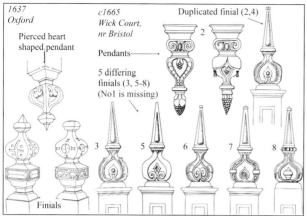

Fig 4.50 (above): Although most stairs have a matching set of finials, this is not always the case. Wick Court, near Bristol, built circa 1665, has only two matching finials out of a set of eight (although the bottom one is missing), and the elaborate pendants are also all different in detail. A smaller house of 1637 in Oxford has two different finials, both highly decorative, and a pendant with a pierced heart shape, a motif seen in several other examples (see Figs 4.46 and 4.49).

Fig 4.51 (above): Some finials are incomplete. The flat top of this one, from St Margaret's, Titchfield, Hampshire, dated 1623, has nail marks showing that a further element has been removed. This is likely to have been some form of vase or urn with carved flowers and fruit; similar features, also nailed onto the top of the finials, exist at a house in Salisbury Cathedral Close, dating from around 1630.

most houses. Pendants and finials may be of matching or very similar designs, but can be completely different. It would appear that they are more likely to match in the first half of the 17th century and to differ in the second half, but it is not a hard and fast rule. Many early finials are also extremely large, dominating the staircase with a profusion of pinnacles. By contrast one of the earliest stairs, in a wing tree-ring dated to circa 1590 at Chawton House,

Fig 4.53 (below): Carved newel post at Batemans, Sussex, of 1634.

Fig 4.52 (below): Victorian newel posts

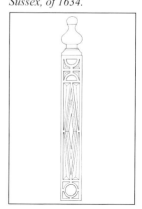

Hampshire, has very simple newel posts (see Fig 4.48). The newel posts themselves are usually square, but may be chamfered and stopped. Occasionally the entire post is covered with carving, as at Hatfield House (1611); even relatively modest stairs such as the one at Batemans, Burwash, Sussex may have this feature (see Fig 4.53).

Fig 4.54 (right): Types of finials: facetted, pyramid variants and polyhedron.

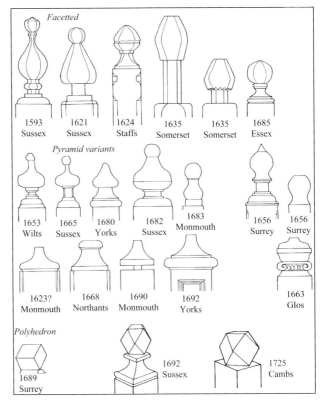

Facetted

| 1593 Sussex | 1621 Sussex | 1624 Staffs | 1635 Somerset | 1635 Somerset | 1685 Essex |

Pyramid variants

| 1653 Wilts | 1665 Sussex | 1680 Yorks | 1682 Sussex | 1683 Monmouth | 1656 Surrey | 1656 Surrey |

| 1623? Monmouth | 1668 Northants | 1690 Monmouth | 1692 Yorks | | 1663 Glos |

Polyhedron

| 1689 Surrey | | 1692 Sussex | 1725 Cambs |

Fig 4.55 (below): Many finials are carved in one piece with the newel post, but some are removable, as in this undated Essex example from the 17th century, and circular holes in the top of newel posts show where they formerly existed.

Alternatively the newel post may have a turned section to match the balusters, as at Odiham Church, Hampshire (see Fig 4.56) and Hall i' th' Wood, Bolton, Lancs (see Fig 4.46). In the second half of the 17th century and into the early 18th century the newel posts may have recessed moulded panels, a feature revived by the Victorians.

Victorian newel posts vary from the relatively slender to the positively massive, with similar or identical designs to the balusters. They have a large unturned block at the base and a smaller one between the turned shaft and the finial. Not all newel posts were turned, and some were

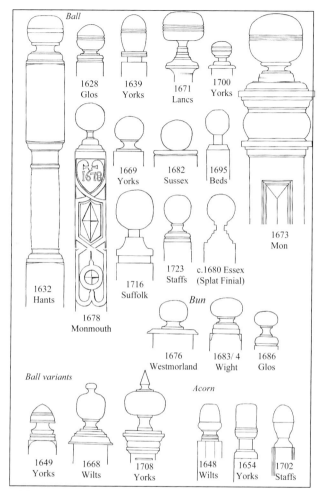

Fig 4.56 (left): Types of finials: ball and acorn.

Ball

1628 Glos
1639 Yorks
1671 Lancs
1700 Yorks

1669 Yorks
1682 Sussex
1695 Beds

1673 Mon

1632 Hants
1678 Monmouth
1716 Suffolk
1723 Staffs
c.1680 Essex (Splat Finial)

Bun

1676 Westmorland
1683/4 Wight
1686 Glos

Ball variants

Acorn

1649 Yorks
1668 Wilts
1708 Yorks
1648 Wilts
1654 Yorks
1702 Staffs

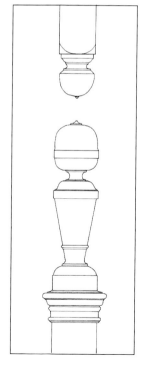

Fig 4.57 (below): A variant on a ball finial and pendant from 1892 Glos.

either square or rectangular in section with carved panels or moulded columns. Some are simply square versions of turned designs. Many of the designs appear fussy in comparison with earlier styles; artistic restraint is not a phrase one associates with Victorian architecture (see Fig 4.52).

Many stairs have more modest balustrades with decorative finials but with no scope for pendants. The finials can be divided into a number of basic types of which the earliest is the facetted finial (see Fig 4.54). These are common up to the 1630s, with occasional later examples. Up to the 1670s, ball finials usually have incised lines like the turned balusters, and are rarely a true sphere, but are slightly flattened or elongated. After 1670 the incised lines disappear and the balls are usually a perfect sphere. A flattened bun shape also occurs in the 1670s and 80s. An Essex house of circa 1680 has a ball finial that is the equivalent of a splat baluster, albeit a very thick one (Fig 4.56).

Acorn finials belong to the second half of the 17th century, with an unusual inverted example from Staffordshire in 1702 (Fig 4.56), and seem to be particularly common in the west and the north. Pyramids

Fig 4.58 (right): Examples of grip handrails and their associated strings.

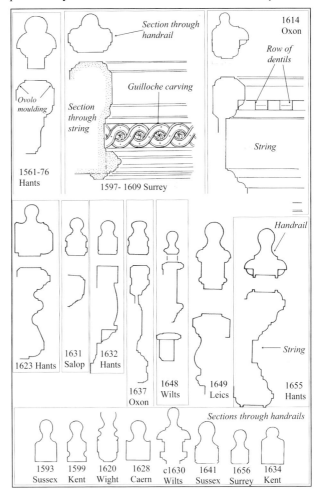

Fig 4.59 (below): Staircase strings – carved bands.

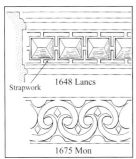

and their variants are mostly from the same period, with an earlier example at Batemans, Burwash, Sussex (1634). A few polyhedrons are known from the end of the 17th and the beginning of the 18th century (Fig 4.54). From the 1690s most stairs no longer have finials; instead the moulded handrail is extended over the newel post to form a flat cap. Some continue to have pendants, however, giving a slightly odd contrast. In the Victorian era, large finials and pendants reappear, and although some are simple balls, many have new designs not seen in earlier periods.

HANDRAILS AND STRINGS

Handrails and strings form the other element of the staircase, and handrails in particular fall into well-defined categories (Figs 4.58, 4.61 and 4.62). The string is the sloping timber which forms the side of the stair, carrying both treads and balusters. Strings vary far more than handrails in design, although the earlier ones tend to have either ovolo (convex) mouldings or chamfers at the top, while later ones have a projecting moulding. Some have a band of decorative carving, such as the strapwork on 1648

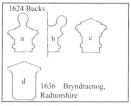

Fig 4.60 (above): A Buckinghamshire manor house displays great sophistication as its stair of 1624 has three variations of handrail. The sloping flights all have the standard grip handrail (a), with an asymmetrical version for the balustrades against the walls (b). Along the landings, however, where there is no need to hold onto the rail, the grip is replaced by a shallow pointed top (c). A handrail similar to the latter was used in 1636 for the gallery around the open hall at Bryndraenog in Radnorshire (d).

Fig 4.61 (Below): Round-topped and miscellaneous handrails.

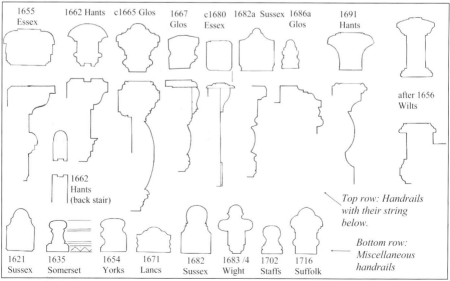

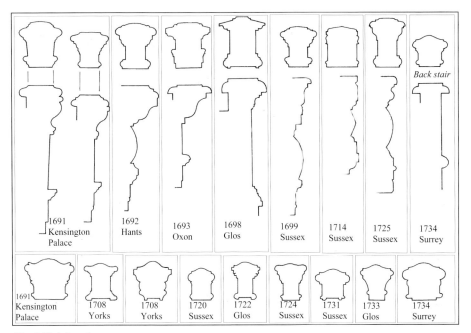

Fig 4.62 *(above): Handrails from the 1690s and the 18th century.*

1691 Kensington Palace | **1692 Hants** | **1693 Oxon** | **1698 Glos** | **1699 Sussex** | **1714 Sussex** | **1725 Sussex** | **1734 Surrey** | **Back stair**

1691 Kensington Palace | **1708 Yorks** | **1708 Yorks** | **1720 Sussex** | **1722 Glos** | **1724 Sussex** | **1731 Sussex** | **1733 Glos** | **1734 Surrey**

Fig 4.63 *(below): The handrail from 1678 Glos has mouldings applied to a rectangular block. 1699 Hants has simply an unadorned rectangle; perhaps it was intended to add mouldings but for some reason it was never finished.*

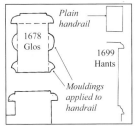

Plain handrail

1678 Glos

1699 Hants

Mouldings applied to handrail

Lancs (Fig 4.59) or a row of dentils, such as 1614 Oxon. Guilloche decoration, comprising two interlacing bands, occur at 1597-1609 Surrey (Fig 4.58) and at Batemans, Burwash, Sussex, (1634).

The earliest type of handrail is the round-topped grip handrail, so called because it is easy to hold onto when going up or down the stairs. The two earliest examples are in fact not true grip handrails, as they lack the characteristic indentations on each side. Grip handrails occur up to the 1650s and, although most are symmetrical, there are a few asymmetrical ones. This date range echoes that of the earliest types of turned and splat balusters, and it appears that a dramatic change of design occurred in the 1650s. Other features show a change in 1660, with the Restoration of Charles II to the monarchy after the Civil War and the Commonwealth, but the revolution in staircase design seems to have occurred slightly earlier.

A miscellaneous variety of other round-topped handrails occurs from about 1620 until the early 18th century; among them 1654 Yorkshire (Fig 4.61) is a flattened version of the grip, while 1702 Staffordshire (Fig 4.61) is a late variant of the same type. Another group of handrails from the second half of the 17th century defies categorisa-

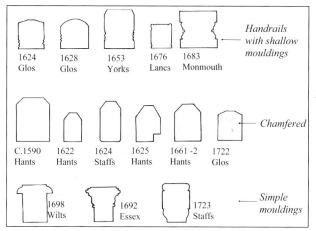

Handrails with shallow mouldings

1624 Glos   1628 Glos   1653 Yorks   1676 Lancs   1683 Monmouth

— Chamfered

C.1590 Hants   1622 Hants   1624 Staffs   1625 Hants   1661-2 Hants   1722 Glos

1698 Wilts   1692 Essex   1723 Staffs   ← Simple mouldings

Fig 4.64 (above): Flat-topped handrails

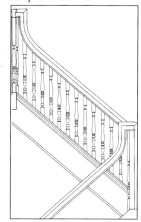

Fig 4.65: Co.Durham balustrade of 1752 with ramped handrail.

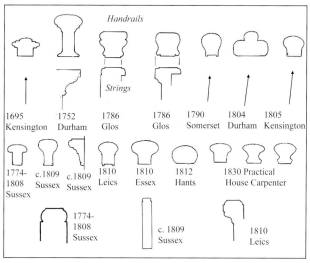

Handrails

Strings

1695 Kensington   1752 Durham   1786 Glos   1786 Glos   1790 Somerset   1804 Durham   1805 Kensington

1774-1808 Sussex   c.1809 Sussex   c.1809 Sussex   1810 Leics   1810 Essex   1812 Hants   1830 Practical House Carpenter

1774-1808 Sussex   c. 1809 Sussex   1810 Leics

Fig 4.66 (above): Later handrails.

Fig 4.67 (below): Victorian handrails

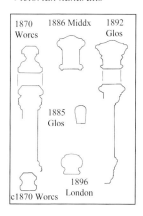

1870 Worcs   1886 Middx   1892 Glos

1885 Glos

1896 London

c1870 Worcs

tion, suggesting a period of experiment before designs settled down in the 1690s into two basic types.

In the 1690s, with a few later examples, handrails were basically rectangular with moulded sides and a flat or slightly rounded top. They may be carved from a solid timber or consist of separate mouldings applied to a central block (Fig 4.63).

This type of handrail was superseded by the toad's-back handrail (Fig 4.62, bottom row); the 1691 Queen's Stair at

Fig 4.68 (right):
Decorative brackets from
open-string stairs.

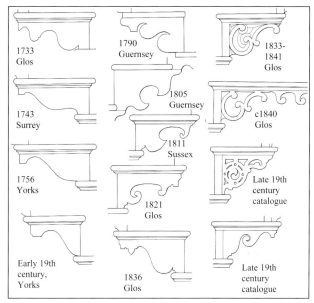

1733
Glos

1790
Guernsey

1833-
1841
Glos

1743
Surrey

1805
Guernsey

c1840
Glos

1756
Yorks

1811
Sussex

Late 19th
century
catalogue

1821
Glos

Early 19th
century,
Yorks

1836
Glos

Late 19th
century
catalogue

Kensington Palace may mark the introduction of this design, and as befits a royal palace, it is one of the largest examples. The type became extremely popular throughout the 18th century, and is usually associated with open-string stairs. Often, too, it is ramped, that is, the handrail is not tenoned into each newel post but instead curves up and over the top, giving a characteristic outline (Fig 4.65).

Fig 4.69 (right):
More decorative brackets
from open-string stairs.
An identical design
occurs in 1722 in Staffs
and in 1886 Middx
(bottom right).

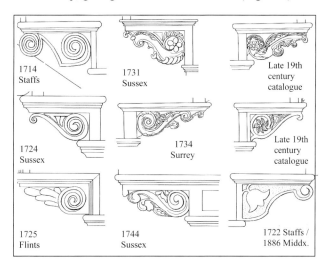

1714
Staffs

1731
Sussex

Late 19th
century
catalogue

1724
Sussex

1734
Surrey

Late 19th
century
catalogue

1725
Flints

1744
Sussex

1722 Staffs /
1886 Middx.

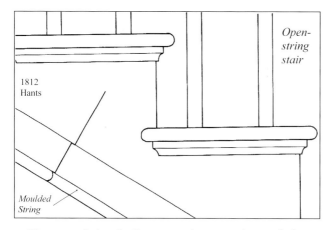

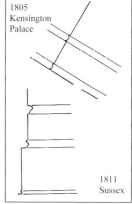

Open-
string
stair

1812
Hants

1805
Kensington
Palace

1811
Sussex

Moulded
String

*Fig 4.70 (left and above):
Early 19th century
moulded strings.*

Flat-topped handrails occur in a variety of forms throughout the 17th and into the 18th centuries. Some have a simple scratch or shadow moulding, others have no embellishment other than chamfered top corners. Three late 17th or early 18th century examples have simple mouldings (Fig 4.64 - see p128).

In the second half of the 18th century, smaller and simpler handrails became popular, in conjunction with much smaller turned balusters or wrought-iron balustrades.

*Fig 4.71 (below): A
highly decorative dog gate
from Cold Overton Manor,
Leics, 1649.*

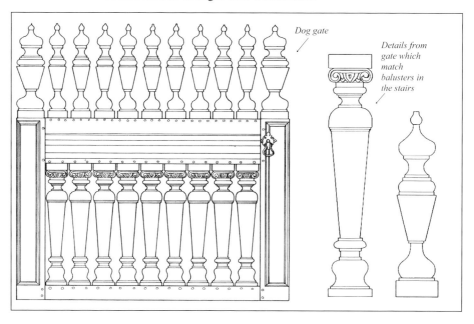

Dog gate

*Details from
gate which
match
balusters in
the stairs*

Fig 4.72a (right): Dog gates with splat balusters. Documentary evidence suggests 1631-42 for Oakwell Hall, Yorks (on the left).

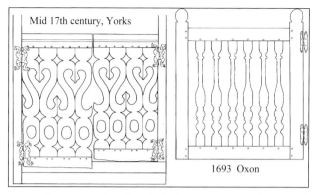

Mid 17th century, Yorks

1693 Oxon

Fig 4.72b (below): A dog gate from Surrey, 1687.

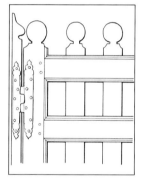

From circa 1800 the stick balusters were associated with very simple handrails of curved section, usually of mahogany (Fig 4.66 - see p129).

In the Victorian period, handrails became larger again and often of very idiosyncratic design, but at the same time the toad's back reappeared in exactly the same form as a century earlier (Fig 4.67).

DECORATIVE BRACKETS

Decorative brackets which featured on open-string stairs (see page 106) may have simple curves or much more elaborate carved spirals or scrolls with assorted foliage. In York and Beverley many open-string stairs had simple rectangular blocks instead of decorative brackets. In the early 19th century, the decorative bracket was sometimes replaced by a simple moulding near the lower edge of the open string (Fig 4.69).

Fig 4.73 (right): Examples of dog gates with straight splats.

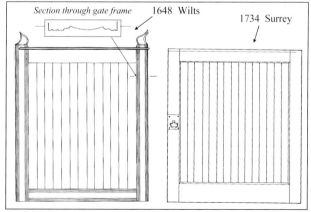

Section through gate frame   1648 Wilts

1734 Surrey

DOG GATES

In medieval open halls and some other later houses, dogs could wander free so gates were fitted to the bottom of stairs to prevent them going up. Although most are in houses some way up the social scale, there are examples in more modest establishments. The earliest surviving may be the grand pair of gates at Hatfield House (1611) although they could be later additions, but most seem to date from the second half of the 17th and the early 18th century. Sometimes they have balusters which match those of the staircase, as at Cold Overton Manor, Leics, (1649), where the gate is a very grand affair surmounted by an impressive row of finials. It also has a very elaborate wrought-iron latch and drop handle (Fig 4.71). Others have splat balusters when the stair itself has turned or twisted balusters, such as 1693 Oxon (Fig 4.72). Other gates consist of a lattice of vertical and horizontal timbers, or have simple straight splats. Examples of the latter are the gate at 1648 Wilts (Fig 4.73), which is not strictly a dog-gate but rather protects the steps down to the cellar, and gates on the back stair at Kew Palace. The function of these is not clear, as the stair is shut off by a door at the bottom, and the gates are at the top of each flight, accessed only from corridors in the servants' quarters.

Frampton Court, Frampton-on-Severn, Glos (1731) has an ingenious gate like a section of garden trellis which folds up into a moulded housing on the wall. Dog-gates are, of course, equally useful as toddler gates, and may always have had a dual function!

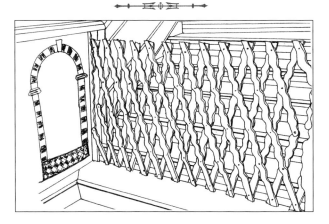

Fig 4.74 (left): An ingenious dog gate from Frampton Court, Frampton-on-Severn, Glos (1731). There is another in a house of 1727-30 in Bath.

5 PANELLING
SCREENS AND DECORATION

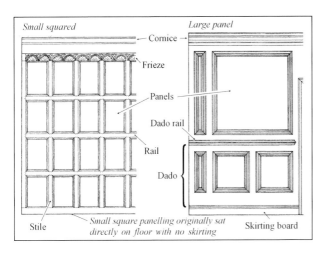

Small squared | Large panel
Cornice
Frieze
Panels
Dado rail
Rail
Dado
Stile | Small square panelling originally sat directly on floor with no skirting | Skirting board

Fig 5.1 (left): Examples of panelling (small square and large panel types) with labels.

SCREENS

In the great hall of a large medieval house, the entrance was usually via opposing doors at the opposite end from the dais, where the owner sat. In order to reduce draughts, a partition or screen was built in front of the doorways creating a passage (the screens passage) behind. The screen could be movable in part or fixed, in the latter case usually with a pair of doorways leading through it and a gallery above which could have been used by musicians.

The most elaborate form occurs in the 15th century at Rufford Old Hall, Lancashire, where short sections of partition called speres form part of the structure at either side of the hall; between them is a massively constructed and (theoretically) movable screen seven feet wide. The panels of the screen are covered with carving and it is surmounted by three enormous pinnacles. The top half of a similar screen dated 1532 can be seen at Samlesbury Hall, also in Lancashire (the lower half was removed to Conishead Priory in the Lake District in 1834).

Fig. 5.2 (below): A sketch showing the position of the screen in a medieval hall. The entrance into the hall was via the open door at the far end of the screens passage and faced one at this end. The two doorways through the screen were opposite two or three openings in the wall on the left side of the passage which led to the service rooms.

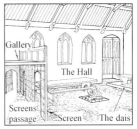

Gallery
The Hall
Screens passage | Screen | The dais

Chawton House, Hampshire, has the Elizabethan successor to this type of screen, a massive panelled construction with two square-headed doorways and a heavy moulded cornice (Fig 5.6). The Tudor House, Southampton, probably built between 1491 and 1518, has a very similar screen, but with four-centred doorheads with traceried spandrels, and a gallery above the passage.

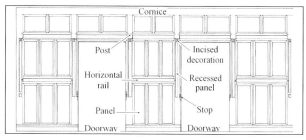

Fig 5.3 (above): A simple screen at St Cross Hospital, Winchester (c.1340?). It has a pair of two-centred arched doorways and coving supporting a gallery above the screens passage (a feature also found at Rufford and Samlesbury), but the doorways and coving appear to have been largely reconstructed. The body of the screen consists of vertical planks within a simple framework.

Fig 5.4 (above): The screen in the great hall at Chawton House, Hampshire was probably part of the primary building phase of the 1580s (see similar screen 1571 Flints, Fig 5.6). The door-frames have ogee mouldings on both sides (Fig 5.5), so did not have doors fitted. The scroll stops are embellished on the side facing the hall with incised saltire crosses, one on the west doorway and two on the east, implying that the latter was the more important doorway. The main posts have thin chamfered recessed panels and above each one there is incised decoration in the form of a zigzag or an M within a rectangle and a background of tiny punched triangles (Fig 5.5). The 'Ms' and crosses may not be simply decoration, but formalised versions of the protective ritual marks found on so many doors, doorways and fireplaces (page 150).

Fig 5.5 (below): Close-up of the decoration on the main posts of the screen at Chawton House (Fig 5.4).

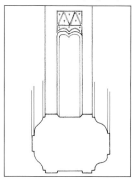

'Post- and- panel' or 'plank- and- muntin' screens are partition walls composed of vertical planks set between wide posts. The posts are usually chamfered and stopped on one or both sides, depending on the relative importance of the room or passage on each side of the screen. More elaborate examples are moulded. Often the chamfers on the side facing the hall are stopped at a height suggesting the former presence of a fixed bench against the screen, and mortises or large peg-holes for brackets may confirm this. Very rarely the actual bench end may survive in situ. Although apparently rare in some counties such as Gloucestershire and Hampshire, plank and muntin screens have a wide distribution; they occur from the medieval

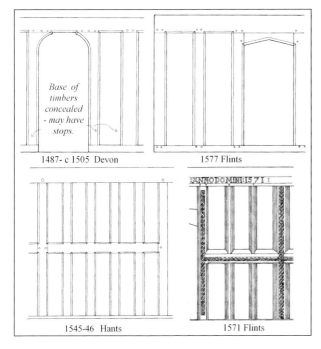

1487- c 1505 Devon

1577 Flints

Base of
timbers
concealed
- may have
stops.

1545-46 Hants

1571 Flints

Fig 5.6 (left): Post-and-panel (plank-and-muntin) screens. 1487-c1505 Devon has a shouldered arched doorway while 1577 Flints has a peaked head. Some screens have a horizontal rail dividing the panels into two equal halves, and they may be embellished with mouldings. Some North Welsh examples, dated between 1571 and 1591, are further decorated with guilloche carving , a pattern of interlacing bands (see page 145).

period to the eighteenth century, with dated examples of 1487- c1505 (Devon), 1564 (Shropshire), 1567 (Sussex) and 1743 (Westmorland). Bramley Manor, Hants (1545-6) has an unusual version with a central rail, while moulded and decorated examples occur in some North Welsh houses of the late 16th century.

In the late 17th century a simplified version of the post and panel screen took the form of 'in-and-out' panelling, composed entirely of planks of equal thickness which overlap at the ends (Fig 5.7).

Some plank and muntin screens retain painted decoration, such as Porch House, Bishop's Castle, Shropshire (1564) which has a chequerboard pattern on the planks and the remains of a different design on the muntins. Other examples are known in Devon, such as the one at St Mary's Cottage, Newton Poppleford. Here the design on the muntins consists of horizontal stripes of black and ochre, with zigzags along the chamfers; the panels have a series of motifs which include flowers, fleur-de-lys and the crowned 'M' of the Virgin Mary, which suggests a   Pre-Reformation date.

Fig 5.7 (below): Profiles through screens showing typical mouldings (1577 Flints is shown in Fig 5.6)

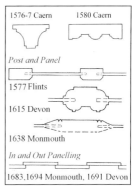

1576-7 Caern   1580 Caern

Post and Panel

1577 Flints

1615 Devon

1638 Monmouth

In and Out Panelling

1683,1694 Monmouth, 1691 Devon

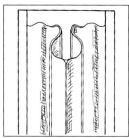

Fig 5.8a (above): Linenfold panelling.

Fig 5.8b (below): A detail from linenfold panelling in situ at the Guildhall, Lavenham, Suffolk.

Fig 5.8c (below): Linenfold panelling from the benches in North Cadbury Church.

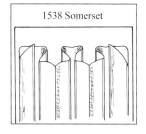

PANELLING
Medieval panelling

The earliest type of panelling, in the sense of a wall covering made of wood, was vertical boards which were used to line a room to make it warmer. There were no decorative mouldings or panels, but the entire surface was painted and may have resembled wall hangings. Such panelling no longer survives, but the Liberate Rolls of Henry III (1216-72) are full of references to 'wainscot' ordered for assorted castles and royal manor houses. His favourite decoration seems to have been green with gold stars, sometimes with the addition of historical or Biblical scenes or, in one instance, a map of the world. Most of this panelling was of oak (wainscot is believed to be a word meaning a particular quality of oak suitable for panelling) but in 1253 the bailiffs of Southampton were ordered to buy 200 Norway boards of fir 'to wainscote the chamber of Prince Edward' at Winchester Castle. This early reference to the import of Scandinavian pine is interesting, as it did not begin to supersede oak in ordinary houses until the late 17th century.

Small-Square Panelling

Panelling consists of a frame of horizontal rails and vertical stiles, tenoned and pegged together, with thin panels set into narrow grooves in the frame; no nails or glue are used. The panels are left rough at the back and the edges are tapered or feathered to fit tightly into the grooves. The frame has mouldings around three sides and a chamfered dust-ledge at the bottom; if the chamfer is at the top or the side it is a sure sign that the panelling has been reset.

The earliest panelling, occurring from the mid 15th century, had linenfold carving in the panels, and this is mentioned in documents of 1532, when 'Dores lyned on both sides with draperye panelle and sealing [panelling] of drapery pannell' were supplied for the great gallery at Westminster Palace. The Oak Gallery at The Vyne, Sherborne St. John, Hampshire (1526) has one of the best displays of linenfold panelling in the country. Badges carved at the top and bottom of each panel include the Tudor Rose of Henry VIII, the pomegranate of Catherine

1538 Somerset

of Aragon and the device and cardinal's hat of Thomas Wolsey. Wolsey's apartments at Hampton Court are also lined with linenfold panelling, but some of it has been reset upside down.

Small-square panelling with plain panels became popular in the later sixteenth century, and usually consists of three, four or five rows of panels; these are generally rectangular rather than square, despite the name. Often there is a decorative frieze at the top, with carvings which may take the form of arcading, strapwork, scrolls and even dragons (Figs 5.21 - 5.31). Godinton House in Kent has panelling of the 1630s which includes a carved frieze of soldiers engaged in musket drill!

Simpler panelling has either an undecorated frieze or no frieze at all. At the bottom the panelling sits directly on the floor and there is no skirting board; if there is a skirting board it has been added later. At this period it is common for smaller houses to have only one panelled room, usually the parlour; often it also has a wooden floor rather than stone flags, both features designed to make the room warmer and more comfortable. Sometimes the room over the parlour, the parlour chamber which would have been

Fig 5.9 (above): Reset linenfold panelling at Kew Palace, Surrey.

Fig 5.10 (bottom left): Examples of small-square panelling from the late 16th to the late 17th century. 1561-76 Hants has been reset to form a corridor and given a deep skirting board. 1662 Hants is original panelling with a plain undecorated frieze. This was one of the houses recorded in 'The Wainscot Book' of Winchester Cathedral which from 1660 to the end of the 18th century recorded the furnishings of the canons' houses. One notable change it recorded was from the use of local joiners producing traditional wainscot in 1660 to the appearance of joiners from London and the new style of large panelling made of deal (pine) instead of oak in the 1670s. This implies that at this period local joiners had not yet learnt about the latest fashions.

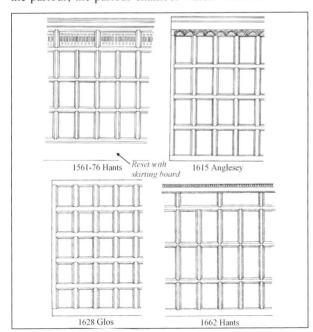

1561-76 Hants — *Reset with skirting board*

1615 Anglesey

1628 Glos

1662 Hants

Fig 5.11 (bottom right): An undisturbed block of small-square panelling in the King's Library at Kew Palace dating from 1631, although the skirting board is a later addition. It is seven panels tall, due to the great height of the ceilings, and the panels reduce in height from the taller ones in the bottom two rows to small ones in the top row. They are arranged in blocks four panels wide, separated by vertical stiles which run the full height of the wall, but the panels are of varying widths. The left-hand block has relatively narrow panels, while the other two have wider ones apart from the very end column next to the window. It appears that the wider panels conform to what was regarded as the ideal, but also that it was easier to have blocks four panels wide than to maintain the same panel width throughout. The block of panelling fits exactly between the window and a doorway; much of the other panelling in the room has been altered or replaced at a later date. This grand house has several other rooms where the panelling has clearly been moved around; one room on the second floor has no less than six different types, all similar in overall style but with different mouldings!

the best bedroom, is also panelled.

Small-square panelling was popular until the second half of the 17th century with examples in dated contexts common from 1580 to 1665 after which it began to be superseded by the type with much larger panels, although there were still occasional examples thereafter. Small-square panelling continued to be used in less important rooms until at least the end of the 17th century and even occurs in a 1732 house in Worcester. There is a possibility that it may be reused, however, as the terms of the 1732 lease allowed the builder to pull down the existing house and to 'make use of all the old matterialls thereof in building the said new house'.

At the end of the 17th century small-square panelling was sometimes made of pine, as in the courtroom of the Guildhall in Guildford; installed in the early 1690s, the pine was the first cargo to use the newly opened Wey Navigation. The choice of an old-fashioned style of panelling is consistent with the idea that buildings such as courtrooms, where traditional values and customs were upheld, needed to look to the past in their architectural style in order to reinforce that tradition.

Larger houses may have many varieties of small-square panelling, with assorted mouldings, and it can be hard to decide which are in situ and which may have been moved or inserted at a later date.

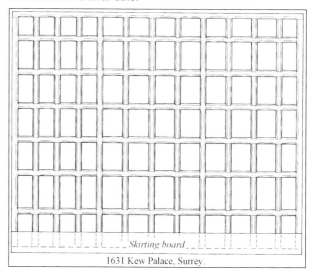

Skirting board

1631 Kew Palace, Surrey.

Panelling is easy to move and has frequently been rearranged within the same house or brought in from elsewhere, thus confusing the historical picture. In addition late 19th and early 20th century antiquarians commonly not only brought in genuine old panelling from another house, but also installed some excellent copies of their own. After 100 years or so this no longer looks new and can be very hard to distinguish from the genuine article. Usually the edges and the mouldings will be sharper and more regular, and the joints of the frame may be fixed with a single peg instead of the two that were almost always used in the 17th century.

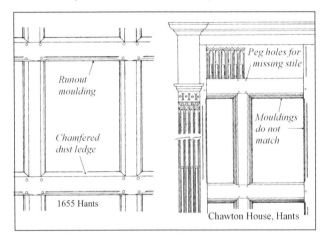

Fig 5.12 (left): Small-square panelling in detail from Chawton House, Hants. On the left unaltered panels with runout mouldings of 1655, and on the right reset panelling evident from the differing mouldings highlighted and the peg holes which once held a stile where there is now a later decorative frieze.

It is important to look carefully at the panelling to see if it has been altered in any way. Sometimes the mouldings do not match, and the example at Chawton House, Hampshire (Fig 5.12) has a more elaborate moulding around two sides of the panels and a simpler runout moulding on the third side. It also has two pegs in the top rail for a missing stile where there is now a frieze of arcading. The runout mouldings appear to be the later type, and are used at Kew in 1631 and on the 1655 staircase at Chawton House.

There are two main types of moulding used with small-square panelling, the ovolo and the ogee. Both types seem to be in use at the same time, although generally the more complex mouldings seem to be the earliest. An alternative form of moulding is the shadow moulding, with dated examples from the 1650s although its true date range is not known.

Fig 5.13 (left): Profiles of the mouldings on the stiles of the panelling. Although generally the more complex mouldings seem to be the earliest, the exception is the panelling used in the rear entrance hall at 1699 Hants, whose moulding would seem to be late 16th century in style. This may be an example of panelling reused from an older house, although it appears to fit its current location.

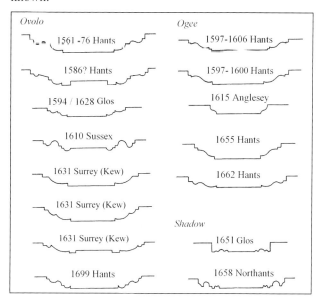

Large-Panel Panelling

Panelling with large panels began to make an appearance in grand houses in the mid 17th century, and became common from about 1670 until panelling went out of fashion in the later 18th century. The earliest examples have prominent bolection mouldings around the panels and the panels are often raised and fielded. Entire rooms, or sometimes just the fireplace wall, were given a unified treatment, with two-panelled doors and bolection-moulded fireplaces (Chapter 7), and the design is usually completed by a moulded cornice and sometimes a skirting board. Many examples have a prominent dado or chair rail between the lower and upper panels; parlours and dining rooms often had large sets of chairs which were set back against the wall when not in use, and the chair rail and skirting boards protected the panelling from damage.

This type of panelling was almost always painted; from the late 17th century the cheaper deal was increasingly used instead of oak, and its knotted surface was less attractive when left bare. 'The Wainscot Book' refers to panelling being painted in the 1670s. Common colours were olive green, brown, cream or a yellow or grey stone colour, and they tended to be darker in the early 18th century and to get lighter as the century progressed. In the late 17th and early 18th century, panelling was sometimes grained to resemble oak, which was still the more desirable material.

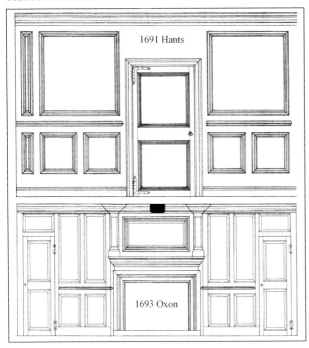

1691 Hants

1693 Oxon

Fig 5.14 (left): Large bolection-moulded panelling of 1691 Hants and 1693 Oxon, showing the complete schemes of décor with doors and fireplaces (both are in the parlour). While most panelling of this type has one upper panel above each lower panel, 1691 Hants has one upper panel to two lower panels and extra narrow panels at the ends of the walls, and the panels are plain rather than fielded. The L-hinge on the door has one arm fixed inside the doorframe instead of on the outer face. 1693 Oxon retains its original paint scheme in three shades of green.

Bolection mouldings were used in the more important houses from about 1660 to 1715, and seem to have been especially common from the 1670s to the 1690s. The earliest examples often have a level field around the panels, while in later ones the field is angled. 1694 Yorks shows some very elaborate panel mouldings, only the first of which is a true bolection moulding; all three have a tiny bead around the edge of the central panels. This amount of elaboration is only found in the grandest houses, with simpler versions further down the social scale.

Later panelling has a much simpler moulding matching that used on doors of the period, with an ogee or more often an ovolo moulding around the frame and a fielded

Fig 5.15 (right): Large panelling: variations in the panel arrangements, with and without a chair rail. As with doors, the panels were made up of several planks glued together; sometimes the lower panels had horizontal planks, but the variations did not matter as the joints were intended to be invisible under the paint.

Fig 5.16 (below): Bolection-moulded panelling, typical of the later 17th century.

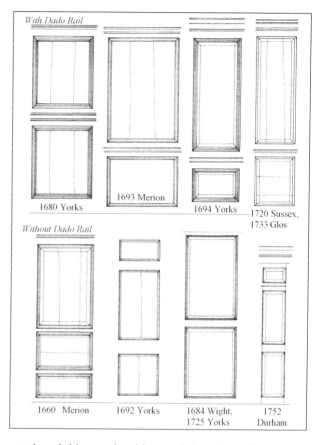

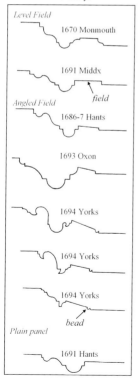

panel, and this type is widespread throughout the country in the later 17th and the 18th century. Enriched versions were used in superior buildings, with decoration such as egg and dart covering the ovolo panel mouldings.

Simplest of all is unmoulded panelling, often found in less important rooms and used as partition walling in the attics at Kew Palace. Full-height panelling began to go out of fashion as early as c1720 in London, but examples can be found as late as the 1760s. Painted plaster, fabric or wallpaper gradually replaced panelling in fashionable houses, although it was often retained up to dado height to protect the lower part of the walls from feet and furniture. This continued throughout the 19th century, when vertical board panelling protected the lower part of the wall from damage. The narrow pine boards often have recessed

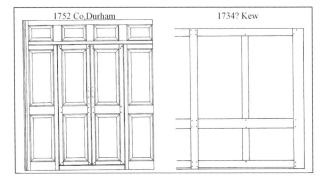

1752 Co,Durham   1734? Kew

Fig 5.17 (left): Later panelling. Fielded panelling used for a recess for a built-in bed at 1752 Co. Durham and plain unmoulded panelling used as partition walls in the attic at Kew Palace, probably dating from the 1734 alterations.

joints and this type of panelling is common in areas most in need of protection, such as passages, service rooms and public buildings such as schools and halls. In family rooms it was common to have prominent skirting boards and chair rails to prevent damage to plaster walls or wallpaper.

Cornices

More important rooms may also have a moulded cornice.

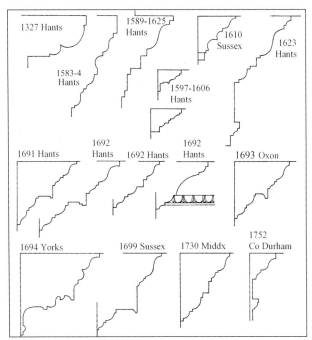

1327 Hants
1589-1625 Hants
1610 Sussex
1623 Hants
1583-4 Hants
1597-1606 Hants
1691 Hants
1692 Hants
1692 Hants
1692 Hants
1693 Oxon
1694 Yorks
1699 Sussex
1730 Middx
1752 Co Durham

Fig 5.18a (left): Profiles of cornices.

Fig 5.18b (below): Profiles of Victorian Cornices.

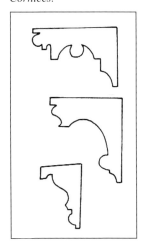

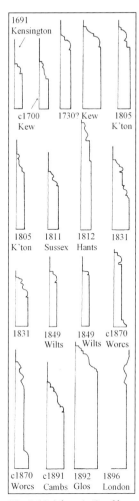

1691
Kensington

c1700
Kew   1730? Kew   1805
                                 K'ton

1805   1811   1812   1831
K'ton   Sussex   Hants

1831   1849   1849   c1870
            Wilts   Wilts   Worcs

c1870   c1891   1892   1896
Worcs   Cambs   Glos   London

Fig 5.19 (above): Profiles of skirting boards.

Fig 5.20 (right): Profiles of dado rails.

The earliest cornices are heavily moulded timbers at the top of the walls of medieval houses and churches, such as 1327 Hants, while 1583-4? Hants has a cornice on top of the hall screen. Most are made of wood, and combine ovolo and ogee mouldings with steps of varying sizes, and designs changed little from the later 17th century until the Victorian period.

Many late 17th and 18th century cornices incorporate a central square projection with a small drip projecting from the bottom; this is a relic of the days when cornices were purely external features, and were provided to enable rainwater to drip clear of the walls. For some reason it remained popular for internal cornices, although one hopes that its practical properties were not required indoors!

Sometimes the cheaper plaster was used instead of moulded wood, or a combination of the two, with plaster detailing added to a basic wooden cornice. More elaborate cornices were enriched with details such as dentils (a row of small blocks called dentils because of their supposed resemblance to teeth), acanthus leaves or other foliage or floral patterns, and the common egg and dart motif (Fig 5.18a: 1692 Hants). In buildings like Hampton Court such details may be picked out in gilding.

Dados and Skirting Boards

Dados or chair rails and skirting boards were nailed onto the panelling as separate elements. The earliest chair rails have a profile similar to the bolection mouldings of the panelling, but various different designs were introduced in

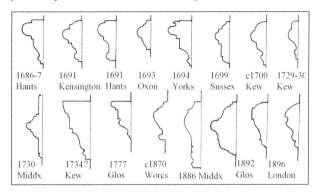

| 1686-7 | 1691 | 1691 | 1693 | 1694 | 1699 | c1700 | 1729-30 |
| Hants | Kensington | Hants | Oxon | Yorks | Sussex | Kew | Kew |

| 1730 | 1734? | 1777 | c1870 | | 1892 | 1896 |
| Middx | Kew | Glos | Worcs | 1886 Middx | Glos | London |

the 18th century, with a further change in the Victorian period. The earliest skirting boards, from the late 17th century, are relatively small but get taller in the 18th and 19th centuries.

DECORATION

Various decorative motifs were in common use from the medieval period until the first half of the 18th century, and can be found adorning external jetty beams, fascias and bargeboards. Internally they are used to embellish panelling, cornices, beams, staircases, overmantels and occasionally doors and doorframes. They also feature prominently on furniture of the period.

In the medieval period designs based on foliage were common, in particular the vine trail, and religious themes were also popular. From the later 16th century designs changed and many were based on geometric shapes, semicircles and S-shaped curves or scrolls. Floral and foliage patterns were still used in and between these shapes, and variations on the many-petalled marigold and the Tudor rose are common. This type of decoration is especially common throughout the 17th century, but continues well into the 18th century in areas such as the Lake District where the tradition of highly-carved built-in furniture remained popular.

Arcading

The type of decoration known as arcading is most often

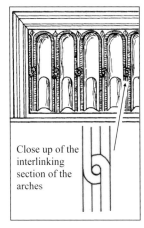

Close up of the interlinking section of the arches

Fig 5.21 (above):At Gawthorpe Hall, Lancs the hall screen of 1605 has unusually elaborate arcading in which the frame of each arch interlinks with its neighbour in a form of guilloche decoration in miniature.

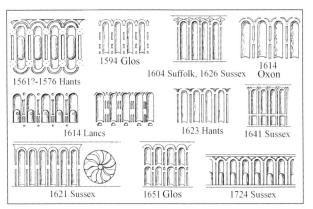

Fig 5.22 (left): Examples of arcading decoration. The unusually late Sussex example of 1724 is from a staircase string.

Fig 5.23 (above): Painted strapwork on the cornice of the Great Chamber at St Margaret's, Titchfield, Hants of 1623.

Fig 5.24 (right): Examples of strapwork and guilloche decoration. 1635 Glos is a band of strapwork on the gates of the large detached porch of the parish church, which formerly served as the town hall; the initials are those of the churchwardens of the time. 1642 Yorks is not strapwork in the strict sense, as the circles and lozenges merely touch at the corners and are not interlinked. 1674 Glos has a most unusual doorframe with guilloche carving and very elaborate stops incorporating a tulip design.

used in the friezes of panelling and of hall screens, as at 1605 Lancashire, or on wooden overmantels. The many variations include punched decoration and /or incised lines between the arches.

Strapwork and Guilloche

Strapwork and guilloche decoration are also commonly used for panelling friezes and are sometimes found on staircase strings, wooden overmantels, and spice cupboards. Strapwork takes the form of geometrical shapes which are usually linked in some way (Fig 5.24: 1561-76 Hants), and the links may intertwine like guilloche decoration (Fig 5.24: 1635 Glos). Painted strapwork is not uncommon and usually occurs on a frieze as part of painted panelling or on a cornice (Fig 5.23: 1623 Hants).

Guilloche derives from Roman times, when it was one of the most common borders for mosaic floors, and consists of two narrow ribbons intertwined to form a series of circles. The circles may be all the same size or may alternate large and small. The centre of each circle is usually filled with some form of flower motif. Dated examples are known between 1570 and 1678, with most occurring before 1640, and there is a lone 18th century

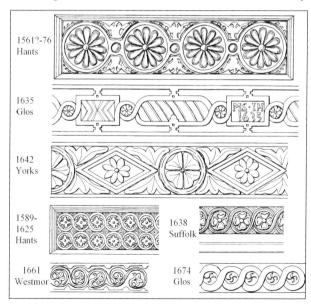

example of 1715 in Westmorland. Both guilloche and strapwork may be used externally; the rich timber framing of the houses in the Butterwalk, Dartmouth (1635-40) have guilloche carving on the vertical members and strapwork on the horizontal ones.

Simpler forms of banded decoration are sometimes found on wooden fireplace lintels, and there are two late 17th century dated examples from Gloucestershire; one had been entirely covered with plaster and paint and there may be others similarly concealed awaiting discovery.

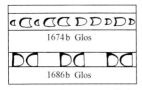

Fig 5.25 (above): Banded decoration.

Fig 5.26 (left): Lunettes and other semi-circular designs. They feature mostly on overmantels and cupboards, although 1615 Anglesey is a panelling frieze (Fig 5.10).

Fig 5.27 (below): The band of decoration from 1638 Suffolk is on the lintel of a single-storey porch added to an older house. Here the curves are not actually semicircles, and they are separated by upside-down tulips, a popular motif in the middle of the 17th century.

Lunettes

Lunettes are a series of semicircles containing foliage designs, some relatively naturalistic and others more stylised. The more elaborate ones have interlinked semicircles, such as 1615 Anglesey, or occasionally a pattern such as 1570 Kent where one set of curves is the opposite way up.

Scroll

Scroll decoration is very common and the more elaborate examples are double scrolls paired in such a way as to

Fig 5.28a (right): Examples of scroll decoration. 1597-1606 Hants is an unusually delicate inlaid frieze above the parlour panelling, while 1626 Sussex has very detailed carving of five-petalled flowers and their leaves, with a central design of five raised bosses. c1656 Shropshire is high relief carving on the external jetty beam of a house in Ludlow, now heavily weathered so that some of the original detail has been lost.

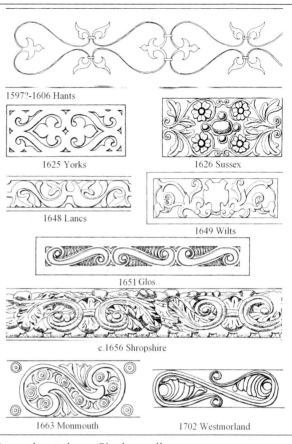

1597?-1606 Hants

1625 Yorks

1626 Sussex

1648 Lancs

1649 Wilts

1651 Glos

c.1656 Shropshire

1663 Monmouth

1702 Westmorland

Fig 5.28b (below): The King's Arms, Sandwich, Kent. A dragon post (the corner post on a building with a jetty on two sides) carved into a mythical figure and bearing the date 1592.

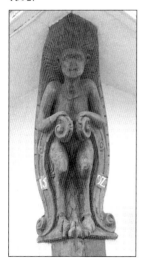

form a heart shape. Single scrolls are even more common and the quality of the carving can vary enormously. Good quality work has beautifully accurate curves and the scrolls will run in alternate directions. In inferior work the scrolls all face the same way and the curves may be very rough and inaccurate. Both single and double scrolls are known in dated contexts in the period 1570 to 1715, and single scrolls are often used to decorate the borders of spice cupboards.

Dragons, Men and Mystical Beasts

Sometimes the scrolls take the form of paired dragons, and it is not always immediately obvious that they are dragons; 1564 Devon (Fig 5.29) is a former doorhead, carved in such a way that it can be read simply as an elaborate foliage design. However, it seems clear that it was also intended to be seen as a pair of dragons in a type of visual double entendre much loved by the Elizabethans. Most are more easily identifiable, however, and paired dragons are especially popular in Shropshire, Worcestershire and the Welsh borders and Wales itself. Dragons sometimes occur further east, but seem to be sufficiently unusual to give their name to the building in which they occur. The Dragon House in Smarden, Kent has a frieze of dragons along the jetty beam of the cross-wing, while Dragon Hall in Norwich (the former Barge Inn) has a dragon in the spandrel of one of the 15th century roof trusses (Fig 5.31).

Fig 5.29 (above): An open hall in Radnorshire, dendro-dated to 1522, has a splendid dragon on the lintel of the inserted hall fireplace, probably dating from the late 16th or early 17th century.

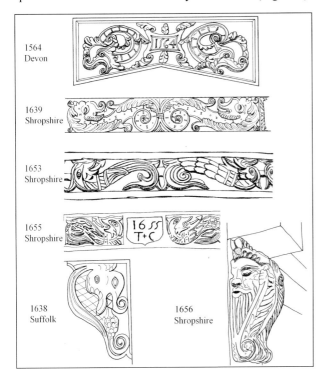

1564 Devon

1639 Shropshire

1653 Shropshire

1655 Shropshire

1638 Suffolk

1656 Shropshire

Fig 5.30 (left): Dragons. 1564 Devon is a former doorhead, 1639 Shropshire is part of an overmantel, and the others are external jetty beams and brackets. The wonderful sleeping giant of c1656 is from Ludlow.

Fig 5.31 (below):Dragon spandrel in the Dragon Hall, Norwich.

Other figures are commonly used for jetty brackets and they may be human, animal or mythical creatures. The Elizabethans favoured squatting figures, often half human, half animal, such as the figure carrying the date 1592 on the King's Head, Sandwich, Kent. Houses in the

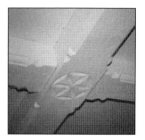

Butterwalk in Dartmouth, built between 1635 and 1640, have heraldic beasts and mythical figures, while number 4, the Quay in the same town, dated 1664, has a bearded man wrestling with a lion. It is not clear if this represents the Biblical story of Samson and the lion, or a Greek myth, one of the labours of Hercules.

Apotropaic marks

Fig 5.32 (above):A carved daisy wheel on the soffit (underside) of the intersecting ceiling beams at Bacon's Castle, Surry County, Virginia, U.S.A,

Apotropaic (literally evil-averting) or ritual marks, often called witch marks, were used to protect a building from evil spirits, witches or their animal familiars. Fear of witches was at its height in the 17th century, and King James I wrote a treatise on the subject, '*Daemonologie*',

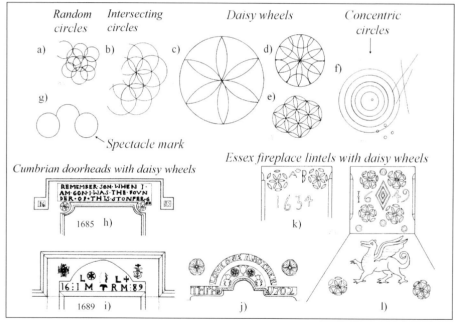

Fig 5.33 (above): Circles and daisy wheels. A fireplace at Samlesbury Hall, Lancs, has two daisy wheels on either side of a tulip, the date 1702 and the text 'Love one another', and the lintel may be a reset doorhead (j). The very neat and elaborate example carved below a window at King John's House, Romsey, Hants is unusually complete (e). Two Essex houses have large deeply carved versions carved into short vertical posts which stand on the lintel of the main fireplace (k and l). In each case the circle surrounding the petals is made up of another six carved petals, and both are dated. The earlier one simply has two circles, the date 1634 and the initials AB, but the 1649 version is more elaborate, with a central lozenge, six daisy wheels and four small sets of concentric circles, as well as a handsome dragon.

published in 1604. He explains the fear of witches as follows: '*for some of them sayeth that being transformed in the likeness of a little beast or fowl, they will come and pierce through whatsoever house or church, though all ordinary passages be closed, by whatsoever open[ing] the air may enter in at*'. Doorways, windows and especially fireplaces were therefore seen as the danger points that needed protection and it is here that these marks, incised on the wood or the stonework, are usually found. Many are very faint and it has been suggested that the carpenters made them as part of their ritual when constructing the building. More obvious ones may have been made by the occupants when they moved in, although this is merely supposition to account for the different character of the marks. Most are in contexts which suggest dates from the mid 16th to the early 18th century, and they are proving to be much more common than had been realised. The faint

Fig 5.34 (below): A reused length of window sill at The Chantry House, Henley is covered with very faint multi-marks and has the initials MW and the date 1747 and IG 1743. The first set is very well carved and the W is positioned exactly within a circle, leading to the suspicion that it refers to Mary rather than being personal initials. The second set, on the other hand, is carved in a much cruder fashion and is clearly someone's initials. What is not clear is whether the supposed ritual marks were carved when the timber was still in place as a window sill, or when it was reused under the floorboards as part of 18th century alterations. Either way, it shows the continuance of the old superstitions until at least the middle of the 18th century.

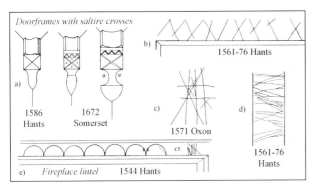

Fig 5.35 (above): Apotropaic marks. Rows of zigzags have been carved onto the stone fireplace at Grove Place, Nursling, Hants (b) although it is not clear if they are meant to be Vs, Ws or saltire crosses; the ambiguity may be deliberate. A single multi-mark (c) can be seen on the transom of a large first-floor oriel window at Priory Cottages, Steventon, Oxon and is above the sole opening casement. It incorporates a large and a small saltire cross. Others are on the stone jamb of a fireplace at Grove Place, Nursling (d). The difficulty of deciding which marks are ritual and which have some other purpose can be seen at Lodge Farm, North Warnborough, Hants where the wooden lintel has a group of intersecting lines, the initials ES twice, and a row of semicircles along one half of the lintel (e). Were these ritual, or did someone intend to cut a pattern of lunettes but give up before they had even marked it all out?

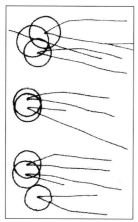

Fig 5.36 (above): Another set of 18th century ritual marks can be seen on the inner face of the west door of St. Mary's church at Abbot's Ann, Hampshire, built in 1716. The marks consist of three sets of very small circles, one above the other, with faint 'tails' streaming out from the centre of each circle rather like comets.

nature of many of the marks means that they are easily overlooked and can often only be seen by the light of a torch held at an oblique angle.

The symbols come in various types. Interlocking circles may appear random but often have been carefully drawn to produce the six-petalled flower or 'daisy wheel' which may represent the sun. Incised daisy wheels can be found everywhere from houses and barns to church pillars and box pews. They are are also a regular feature of the late 17th century carved stone doorheads that are common in Lancashire, Yorkshire and Cumbria. Concentric circles occur in several buildings while the so-called spectacle mark, two circles joined by a semicircle, is also common on fireplace lintels.

Improving texts were often used from the late 16th to the early 18th century, both externally on doorheads and internally on stone fireplace lintels, plaster overmantels or as part of a scheme of wall painting. The fact that they are often associated with doorways and fireplaces suggests that a Biblical text may have been regarded as another type of protective symbol as well as an aid to faith.

The butterfly mark, a saltire cross between two upright lines, is most commonly seen on door latches and bolts, and a Suffolk blacksmith, speaking in the 20th century, said that it represented the cross of St. Andrew between the jambs of the door or window, barring the way to any evil spirits. Saltire crosses also occur as decorative elements in stops on doorframes although in these cases it

Fig 5.37 (right): A drawing of a timber framed fireplace with the heck post highlighted, and close ups of the saltire crosses and decoration which can be found on them.

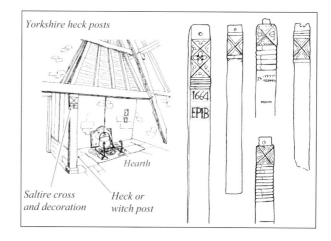

Yorkshire heck posts

Hearth

Saltire cross and decoration

Heck or witch post

is not clear if the motif is purely decorative or has an added symbolic meaning. A Somerset example of 1672 has a prominent bar and two small punched circles which make it resemble the face of an owl. Was this visual pun accidental or an intentional reference to a symbol of wisdom? (Fig 5.35a)

Ms for Mary and Vs or double Vs for Virgin of Virgins (one of the ways of referring to Mary) are common marks especially on fireplace lintels, but often there are so many lines criss-crossing each other (multi-marks) that it is hard to make out anything specific. A Breconshire door knocker dated 1634 also has the initials WM, which could be the initials of the owner, but could equally well be a protective mark invoking the Virgin Mary (see Fig 2.77). Such ambiguity is not uncommon.

Saltire crosses also feature on the so-called witch posts of the North York Moors; the term 'witch post' was only invented in the 20th century and the more traditional name is heck post. In this area timber-framed fireplaces are common, and the side of the fireplace next to the doorway is called the heck. The heck post, which supports the hearth beam, is usually decorated with a large saltire cross as well as a series of roughly moulded bars and one from Postgate Farm, Glaisdale, is dated 1664. Here the crosses clearly form a decorative as well as a protective function (Fig 5.37).

Fig 5.38: The Talbot Hotel in Oundle, Northants, dating from 1626, has an impressive staircase with three different marks, two on finials (left and centre) and one on a newel post (right).

6 CEILINGS
BEAMS, STOPS AND BOARDS

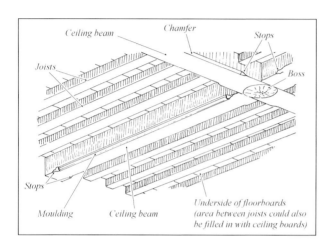

Fig 6.1 *(left): Drawing showing the different parts of a ceiling.*

Ceiling beam · Chamfer · Stops · Joists · Boss · Stops · Moulding · Ceiling beam · Underside of floorboards (area between joists could also be filled in with ceiling boards)

CEILING BEAMS

In medieval and later houses, the 'ceiling' was composed of the beams, joists and floorboards of the upper storey. Both the joists and the main beams into which they were tenoned were usually chamfered, or moulded in the wealthier houses, until the plaster ceiling came into common use in the late 17th century and the joists were concealed. When the joists projected beyond the ground-floor wall of a timber-framed house to form a jetty there may be carvings or mouldings on the jetty beams. Highly complex mouldings are features of the better quality medieval and 16th century houses, and medieval open halls may have mouldings on beams at either end of the hall, on cornices and on the central roof truss.

Moulded dais beams

Medieval houses may have moulded beams to denote the

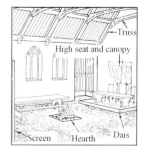

Fig 6.2 *(below): A picture of a medieval hall showing the position of the dais.*

Truss · High seat and canopy · Screen · Hearth · Dais

Fig 6.3 (right): Profiles of moulded dais beams. Most date from the 15th or early 16th century; precise dating by style is not yet possible.

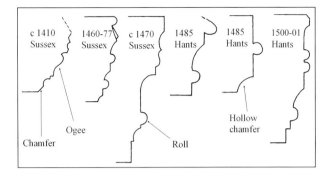

high status of the open hall, either at both ends of the hall or at the more important dais end only. Some are further embellished with small crenellations or brattishing along the top, and in parts of northern England and North Wales they may have supported a dais canopy, although few survive intact. The dais canopy served the dual purpose of emphasising the status of the people sitting at the high table, and offering some protection from particles of soot that may have descended from the smoke from the central open hearth.

A simpler alternative to the coved canopy was the internal jetty, a feature often found in western England; in Wales internal jetties are common in Montgomeryshire, with a few in Breconshire, but otherwise seem rare.

Moulded dais beams seem to be more common in some areas than others; relatively few have been found in Hampshire for example. Dated examples of dais beams in Kent range from 1401 to 1520 and the designs show remarkable consistency over this period; all are very similar to the Hampshire and Sussex examples in Fig 6.3, with prominent roll mouldings in nearly every one.

Fig 6.4 (below): The crenellated dais beam in a Kent house tree-ring dated to circa 1445.

Moulded external jetty beams

Towards the end of the medieval period in the late 15th and early 16th century similar mouldings may be used externally for jetty bressumers or fascia boards, or for internal cornices formed either by moulding the inner face of the wallplate or by adding a separate moulding. Such mouldings are especially common in towns, where rich merchants used the quality of their houses to proclaim their wealth for all to see (Fig 6.5: 1533-4 Hants).

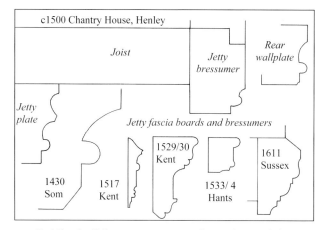

Fig 6.5 (left): Profiles of jetty bressumers and fascia boards. 1533-4 Hants has a continuous jetty and faces the Market Square in Petersfield, a prestigious position demanding the use of a moulding; the moulding is a simple one, but the fascia board was so heavily weathered that it was hard to distinguish the original moulding profile.

Public buildings too were often given elaborate mouldings, and the Chantry House in Henley-on-Thames, a multi-purpose building of circa 1500 which included a school, has mouldings on both the jetty plate (below the jetty) and the jetty bressumer (the beam into which the ends of the joists are tenoned.) Moulded jetty beams are also common in the 17th century, but now the roll has been replaced by the ovolo, which may be double or used with hollows and ogees, such as 1611 Sussex.

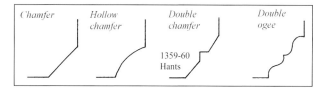

Fig 6.6 (left): Profiles of common mouldings.

Moulded roof trusses

High status medieval buildings may also have mouldings on the posts and tie beam or collar of the central roof truss of the open hall. Some early roof trusses have a double chamfer, a double hollow chamfer, or a mixture of the two (Figs 6.6 and 6.7), but in Hampshire at least the double chamfer also appears on doorframes and stone doorways in much later buildings. One example is on a doorway rebuilt in the 19th century. Some of the more elaborate roof trusses have mouldings with rolls, and 1467 Shropshire shows an unusually early use of the ovolo moulding, a feature normally associated with the Elizabethan period and the 17th century (Fig 6.7).

Fig 6.7 (right): Profiles of medieval roof trusses.

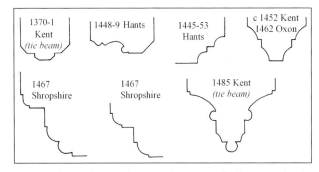

Sometimes the roof truss of an open hall or a solar is further embellished with a carved boss at the centre, and these may survive in what now appear to be quite modest houses. They can provide an object lesson in never judging a house solely on its external appearance. Hampshire has three early bosses. Monk's Cottage, Odiham looks like a small 19th century cottage but is in fact the solar cross-wing of a house of 1300, and the roof has a floral boss at the apex of the steeply cambered tiebeam. The boss at Trees Cottage, Froxfield (1359-60) is a beautifully carved wreath of leaves, while an undated house in Kingsclere, with an 18th century façade, has a delightful head. The serene face has unfortunately lost part of its nose, but its beauty is unaffected. The headdress is a style common around 1400 and has three tiny buttons under the chin; these are scarcely visible even now and must have been even harder to see from ground level before the upper floor was put into the open hall. They are however very easy to feel, and sometimes fingertips can reveal features unnoticed by the eye. Roof bosses occur fairly frequently in North Wales, but are rare in central and South Wales.

Moulded ceiling beams

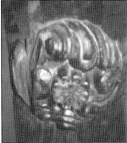

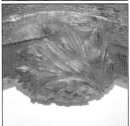

Fig 6.8 (above): Carved roof bosses in three Hampshire houses: a floral boss in Odiham (1300), a foliage wreath in Froxfield (1359-60) and a beautiful head in Kingsclere (circa 1400).

The most frequently used moulding for medieval ceiling beams is the ogee, an S-shaped curve. Usually it is combined with rolls and hollows and tapers to a prominent roll at the base, and in some cases such as 1476 and 1486-7 Hants (Fig 6.9) the moulding is continued down the posts at either end of the beam. Similar mouldings occur as late as 1578 in Devon (Fig 6.9).

The double ogee (Fig 6.6) is a very common moulding

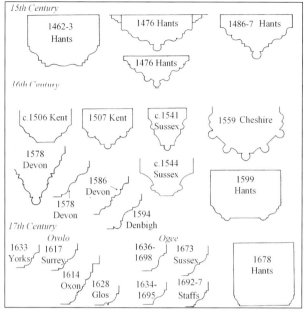

Fig 6.9 (left): Examples of ceiling beams from the 15th -17th century. 1462-3 Hants has an unusual version of a single ogee combined with steps and with a wave moulding on the soffit of the beam. 1599 Hants has parlour beams with an ogee with a tiny hollow and with half-round mouldings on the soffit (underside); similar beams in the parlour chamber have larger roll mouldings on the soffit and scroll (ogee) stops. 1678 Hants has an unusually shallow moulding with no stops. In Gloucestershire the ovolo moulding was enthusiastically adopted in both gentry and yeoman houses from the late 16th century until c1675, after which the ogee moulding was favoured.

with a wide period of use, and may be found on beams, roof trusses, doorways and stone fireplaces. Some dated examples are 1445-53 to 1491-6 in Hampshire, c1520 Suffolk, 1586 Yorkshire and 1654 Glos. Single ogee mouldings are rarely used on beams before the 17th century, with most belonging to the period 1630 to 1700.

Beams in the first half of the 16th century may have prominent rolls and/or hollow chamfers but, in the second half of the century, the ovolo moulding becomes popular, usually combined with hollow chamfers.

The single ovolo moulding first appears on doorframes c1560, but there are no dated examples on ceiling beams until the 17th century. Its popularity varies slightly from area to area; it is relatively rare in Hampshire in comparison with Gloucestershire for example, although this variation may be due to differences in the periods when wealth for building was available as much as to local fashion. The simple chamfer was the cheaper option and is the most commonly used finish for beams and joists.

STOPS

Although the moulding or chamfer along the edge of the beam could continue right to the wall, it was usually

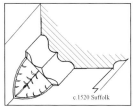

Fig 6.10 (above): Double ogee and complex mouldings are often unstopped, but there are exceptions ranging from simple 90° cuts to this elaborately carved step stop decorated with little incised curves to give a leaf effect from c1520 Suffolk.

c.1520 Suffolk

terminated before the end with a plain or decorative carving called a stop.

Straight cut stops (Fig 6.11)

Many of the earliest chamfer stops were cut in a flat plane. The tiebeams at King John's House, Romsey (1256) have the simplest straight-cut stops, cut at 90° to the chamfer, but straight-cut stops are more often cut at approximately 45° to the chamfer. Diagonal-cut stops are a common variation. All of these types are most commonly found in medieval and 16th century contexts, but occasionally turn up in much later buildings (Fig 6.11: 1730 Surrey).

Step stops (step and runout; step and hollow; fillet and tongue) (Fig 6.11)

The earliest dated examples of step stops are used on the roof timbers of 1368-9 Hants and have a very shallow step. Later the step is more pronounced (1510-38 Hants) and the step stop remained in common use until the early 17th century. It continued in use throughout the 17th century for beams and doorframes in less important rooms, occasionally with additional decoration such as a notch (1685 Oxon) and there are a few dated examples in

Fig 6.11 (right): Examples of beam stops (just the stop is shown rather than the whole beam as in Fig 6.10). One beam at the George Inn, Odiham, Hants (1486-7) has 90° straight-cut stops; this is the simplest type of stop, cut at right angles to the moulding or chamfer. 1656 Wilts has an unusual triangular step, also seen with a roll at 1690 Warwickshire.

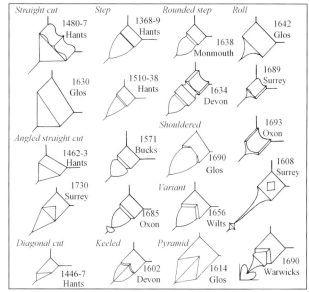

the first half of the 18th century. Variations are the rounded step, which is halfway between a step stop and a scroll stop, the keeled stop, and the shouldered stop.

Pyramid stops (Fig 6.11)

Pyramid stops, common on medieval doorframes and fireplaces, also turn up on ceiling beams in two 17th century houses in Gloucestershire (Fig 6.11: 1614 Glos), and on an undated 16th century house in Radnorshire.

Roll stops (Fig 6.11)

Roll stops seem to be confined to the 17th century; most consist of a simple short curve to a point, but Surrey has an elongated version in the early 17th century (Fig 6.11: 1608 Surrey) and at 1690 Warwickshire a roll is combined with a large notch and a triangular step to give a very decorative stop.

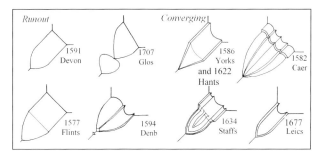

Fig 6.12 (left): Examples of runout and converging stops.

Runout and Converging stops (Fig 6.12)

The runout stop is the simplest of all types, in which the

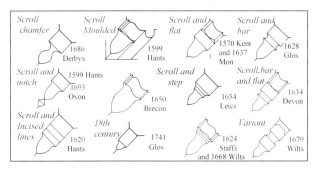

Fig 6.13 (left): Examples of scroll stops, also called ogee, cyma or lamb's tongue.

Fig 6.15 (below): At Hants (1606-8) step stops have a complex variety of deep and shallow incised lines to denote the relative status of each room. At this period the hall is clearly still the room of highest status, with one thick and three thin lines, while the parlour has one thick and two thin and the kitchen a single thick line. The beams at 1647 Staffs show a similar variety to denote status, but this time it is the mouldings rather than the stops that differentiate between the rooms. The parlour is now the most important room, with an ogee moulding to the beam and scroll stops with a wide step. The hall and the hall chamber were of equal status, having ovolo-moulded beams; the stops in the chamber have a slightly different profile, being more leaf-shaped. Lowest in status is the kitchen chamber, with chamfered beams.

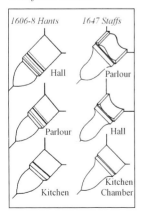

chamfer is curved up to a point where it meets the arris. Usually the curve is smooth and continuous, but sometimes there is an abrupt change of plane (1577 Flints). Moulded beams may also have this type of runout stop, but more often the mouldings converge to a point. Here again the curve may be smooth, but many are sharply angled. Occasionally converging or runout stops are combined with a notch, which can vary in size from the tiny (1594 Denb) to the huge (1707 Glos).

Scroll stops (ogee, cyma or lamb's tongue) (Fig 6.13)

The scroll or ogee stop begins in the late 16th century (1564 Essex) and continues until stops go out of fashion altogether; in more important houses this is at the end of the 17th century, but they can still be found in smaller houses well into the 18th century (1763 Sussex). They are used on beams, doorframes and fireplace lintels with both chamfers and mouldings, and occur in vast numbers throughout the country. They vary slightly in their proportions, and the earliest examples seem to be shorter than the standard 17th century ones. Variants to the basic scroll stop include scroll and notch stops, scroll and flat (used with mouldings), scroll and step, scroll and bar, and assorted combinations of these various elements. Occasionally the ogee profile is more pronounced than usual, giving more of a leaf shape, as 1686 Derbyshire (Fig 6.13).

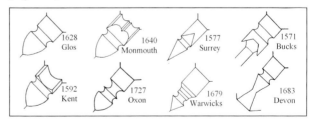

Fig 6.14 (above): Examples of bar stops and their variants.

Bar stops (bar and runout) (Fig 6.14)

Bar stops come into fashion in the Elizabethan period, with dated examples of 1583 Sussex and 1592 Kent (Fig 6.14). One of the earliest, 1577 Surrey, has an angular runout rather than the more usual curve, a feature repeated a century later at 1679 Warwicks. It is quite common for an unusual variant to occur at widely differing dates, and this emphasises the fact that stops can only be used for dating in a very broad way. Nevertheless, bar stops seem to go out of fashion before the end of the 17th century and are rare after about 1680.

Mouldings and stops are often used to denote the different status of the various rooms, with the most elaborate or up-to-date being used in the most important rooms. The early 17th century is a period when room use and status were undergoing subtle changes, as the functions of the hall were gradually taken over by the kitchen and the parlour. Larger houses retained all three rooms but by the second half of the 17th century many smaller ones only had two, perhaps with a service room such as a dairy or buttery, and the hall gradually lost its former status.

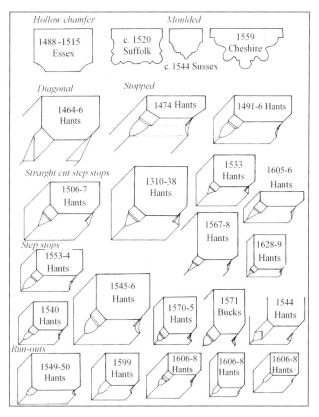

Fig 6.16a (left):
Examples of joists with stops. An unusual lozenge-shaped stop occurs at 1544 Hants, while other joists of this date have simple run-outs. The latest example of chamfered and stopped joists in Hampshire occur in 1628-9, but unstopped chamfers can occur as late as 1686. An Essex house of 1488-1515 has large joists with hollow chamfers, and in the 16th century moulded joists may be used in the wealthiest houses, particularly in the towns. C1520 Suffolk and c1544 Sussex are wealthy town-houses, while Little Moreton Hall (1559 Cheshire) has massive moulded beams and joists in the parlour. The largest joists (top left) are 7 inches (177mm) wide, the smallest (bottom right) are 3½ inches (89mm).

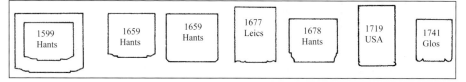

Fig 6.16b (above): Profiles of unstopped joists. A few joists have a shallow ogee moulding, with almost identical Hampshire examples in 1599 and 1659 and a slightly different version at 1677 Leics. A later Hampshire variant of 1678 has a more upright ogee moulding. Bead mouldings occur at the side in 1719 USA and on the soffit at 1741 Glos. The joists vary in width from 5 inches (127mm) on the left to 2½ inches (64mm) on the right.

1622 Hants, for example, has ovolo-moulded beams with sharply converging stops in both the hall and the parlour, which at this period seem to have had more-or-less equal status; the parlour has a fine brick fireplace to mark its slightly superior status, while the kitchen has plain chamfered beams.

Chamfer size is not greatly significant in relation to date, although most chamfers before 1650 are 2 to 2½ inches (50-63mm), while most after 1650 are less than 2 inches. Beams in the parlour at 1540 Hants have exceptionally large hollow chamfers (over 4½ inches or 115mm).

JOISTS
Chamfered and moulded joists

Many early joists (the lesser timbers between the main ceiling beams) are either unchamfered or have stopped chamfers, but where stops are used they tend to vary from those used on the main beams. The diagonal-cut stop appears at 1464-6 Hants (Fig 6.16a), but most are step stops, either curved as seen on the beams or flat or triangular-shaped, a style popular in the 16th century.

Fig 6.18a (above): An example of ceiling boards set into grooved joists at 10 The Close, Lichfield, where they probably date from the 17th century.

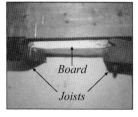

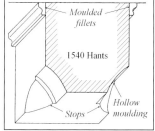

Fig 6.17 (left): Moulded fillets have been nailed onto the beam and the joists to carry ceiling boards at 1540 Hants, where the parlour beams have a large hollow chamfer and step stop; this arrangement seems to be unknown outside Hampshire.

In the 16th century moulded joists may be used in the wealthiest houses, particularly in the towns (Fig 6.16: c1520 Suffolk and c1544 Sussex). All these moulded and chamfered joists were, of course, intended to be seen and any plaster was confined to the spaces between them. Sometimes the upstairs floorboards were left exposed below. At 1567-8 Hants (Fig 6.16) the joints between the floorboards are covered by nailed-on battens; although many are clearly more recent replacements, some are fixed with old hand-made nails and look original. This may have been a common technique, concealed when later plaster ceilings were added. Many houses now have the joists as well as the floorboards concealed by later plaster ceilings, although it is impossible to know how many are original and how many have been added later.

Ceiling boards

An alternative to exposed floorboards was the use of ceiling boards, thin boards which run between the joists. At 1476 Hants (Fig 6.9) and 1540 Hants (Fig 6.17) moulded fillets have been nailed to the beams and joists to carry ceiling boards. Elsewhere the usual technique was to have grooves in the joists to take the boards (Fig 6.18).

Ceiling boards were only used in houses at the upper end of the social scale, such as Great Dixter, Northiam, Sussex (circa 1470), where the boards were placed below the joists which were thus concealed. The same feature occurs in the Bishop's Palace in Chichester, where the parlour has a magnificent early 16th century painted ceiling. The main beams and smaller intermediate beams are all moulded, with applied tracery at the intersections, and the heraldic painting is applied directly onto the boards in each panel.

Joist dimensions

Early joists are always laid flat, having a width noticeably greater than the depth, but from the end of the 16th century joists began to be set on edge in some houses. By the second half of the 17th century this had become standard practice, although sometimes joists were square rather than rectangular in section.

Analysis of the widths of exposed ceiling joists in fifty houses in Hampshire has shown a marked progression from wide joists in the 14th century to much narrower ones in the 17th century. Joists over 8 inches (200mm) wide are confined to the 14th century, while before 1500 most are between 6½ and 7 inches (165-180mm); 5 inches (130mm) is the absolute minimum width before 1540, but after that date joists of between 4 and 4¼ inches

Fig 6.18b (above): An early 16th century painted ceiling in the parlour of the Bishop's Palace, Chichester, Sussex.

Fig 6.19a (above): Ceiling boss from Radnor (see Fig 6. 22).

(100-110mm) are almost universal. However, there are a few wider ones in the mid-16th century, a period of transition. Joists under 3½ inches (90mm) wide are confined to the 17th century. Within that spectrum there is a certain amount of overlap, but the general trend is clear. Chamfers above 1½ inches (40mm) are likely to be early 16th century or earlier, while tiny chamfers of less than half an inch (10mm) date from the 17th century. The spaces between the joists show a similar progression, with all joists after 1550 being a foot or more apart (305mm). However, spacing in the medieval period is more varied; all joists less than 11 inches (280mm) apart are before 1550 but some early joists are as far apart as the later ones.

A smaller sample of 32 houses from East Sussex for the period 1400 to 1760 shows a similar pattern of change in joist sizes, with the widest in the 15th century and most 17th century joists being 3½ inches (90mm) or less. As with most features, there are always a few houses that buck the general trend, and joists 6 inches (150mm) wide are recorded in 1611 and 5 inches (130mm) in a relatively modest house of 1656.

Floorboards

Floorboards also get narrower over time. Early floorboards may be over a foot (300mm) wide, and, like joists, are often of elm rather than oak. The width gradually reduces and eventually narrow machine-sawn pine boards become the norm. Many are simply butted together and nailed to the joists, but some are rebated to prevent the joints opening up to create a gap as the timbers shrink. Usually the floorboards run at right angles to the joists, but occasionally in good quality work they run parallel; in this case they are set in rebates cut in the upper face of the joists. Others are joined or 'splined' by a narrow thin timber set into thin grooves in each floorboard.

PANELLED CEILINGS

Ceiling beams in the more important rooms of the wealthier houses were often arranged with secondary beams tenoned into the main beams to produce a ceiling of four or more panels. Dated examples in Sussex occur between 1470 and 1669, but most date from the 16th

Fig 6.19b (below) : Ovolo mouldings and scroll stops at the intersection of ceiling beams at St Margaret's, Titchfield, Hants (1623).

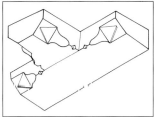

Fig 6.20 (left): Intersecting ceiling beams with very elaborate scroll, notch and triangle stops at 1668 Shropshire.

century, and the beams may be either chamfered or moulded.

Some of the more elaborate panelled ceilings with moulded beams also have carved bosses at the intersections, giving a very rich appearance. It would seem that once the open hall had gone out of fashion some of the decorative elements were transferred to the ceilings of the most important rooms. The Tudor rose design was popular throughout the 16th century, but religious subjects sometimes figure in earlier ceilings, as well as various types of foliage (Fig 6.19a).

The successor to this in the 17th century was the panelled ceiling in which all the beams are stopped at each intersection. This gives a fairly impressive appearance even with simple scroll stops, as at 1623 Hants (Fig 6.19) and even more so with more elaborate stops such as 1668 Shropshire (Fig 6.20).

Nearly 20 houses in Shropshire have panelled ceilings in which the joists are set in a chequerboard pattern, running in alternate directions in each panel of the ceiling. This means that the floorboards also run in different directions, creating a patterned floor in the room above. Most of these seem to date from the second half of the 16th century, although one is in a house dated 1653. Others are known in Breconshire, Radnorshire and Montgomeryshire in the same period; most have chequerboard ceilings in either the hall or the parlour, but one Radnorshire house has them in all three rooms, with very decorative carved bosses of Tudor rose design at the intersections of the ceiling beams. There are also examples in Devon including Larkbeare House, Exeter which dates from the first half of the 16th century.

Fig 6.21 (above): Two chequerboard ceilings in 16th century Radnorshire houses. One has very unusual joists of triangular section, with bosses of Tudor rose design (see Fig 6.19a).

Painted Decoration

Some ceiling beams and joists have the remains of painted

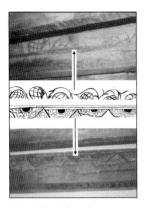

Fig 6.22 *(above): Photos with close up drawings of painted decoration on beams at 1571 Bucks.*

patterns which give a suggestion as to how richly decorated many houses once were. Geometric patterns such as chevrons were popular, and one example has given its name to the Chevron Room at the Guildhall in Newport, Shropshire (dendro-dated to 1546). The colours used are black, beige and orange. At 1571 Bucks (Fig 6.22a) two different decorative schemes have survived in fragmentary form on the ceiling beams in two rooms. Both are painted in black and may have had a white background, and they have only survived above the level of inserted ceilings since removed. One has a geometric pattern, the other a very rough vine trail; both were clearly painted freehand and probably painted fairly rapidly.

PLASTERED CEILINGS

Joists that were intended to be concealed by plaster ceilings have different profiles from those that were meant to be seen, and are neither moulded nor chamfered. They are much deeper than they are wide, and are set level with the soffits of the main beams to give a suitable surface for lath and plaster ceilings. They can occur relatively early, and a townhouse built in Rye between 1556 and 1560 was clearly designed to have plaster ceilings from the start. The technique was much more common from the end of the 17th century, when moulded and chamfered beams and joists began to go out of fashion; one example is 1699 Hampshire, where the joists, never intended to be seen, have now been exposed.

This construction became normal in many 18th century houses, although the old-fashioned beams and exposed joists continued to be used in the smallest houses and cottages. In Sussex chamfered beams and scroll stops were still in occasional use as late as 1731, 1744 and 1763, and ceiling beams with small bead mouldings to match the doorframes occur in 1725 and 1736.

Fig 6.23 *(right): Examples of plasterwork ceilings typical of Elizabethan and Jacobean houses where the geometric patterns were deep and pronounced below the surface of the ceiling.*

The older styles lingered longest in service rooms, partly because they would not be seen by visitors and partly for practical reasons. At 1810 Leics most of the rooms have concealed beams, but the dairy has exposed beams and joists, presumably to provide somewhere to fix hooks for hanging sides of bacon and other produce or implements. In order to modernise older houses, ceiling beams were often concealed totally behind inserted plaster ceilings if the ceilings were high enough to allow for this. If not, the beams were either plastered over or boxed in and painted white to match the plaster ceiling and make them less conspicuous. If this covering is later removed, it may reveal the original chamfers, mouldings and stops, but may also produce beams that have been badly scarred to provide a key for the plaster. Alternatively, they may have a striped appearance from the laths which were nailed on to provide a base for the plaster.

Although most plaster ceilings were plain the more important rooms in grand houses had raised patterns. In the 16th and early 17th centuries these tended to be prominent geometric patterns, with the slender moulded ribs popular in Elizabethan times being replaced by wider ribs in the Jacobean era. By the late 17th century skilled plasterers were creating Classical styled ceilings with large oval or rectangular centrepieces featuring paintings surrounded by swags and flowers.

In the later 18th century Neo-Classical and Adam interiors had less prominent mouldings so colours were used to lift the patterns. Combinations of pinks and greens, blues and reds, and green, yellow and black, were popular.

In the 19th century, ceilings again reflected the historic style chosen for the larger houses, with ceiling beams and geometric patterned ceilings reappearing. For most, the ceiling remained plain but a central moulded medallion or rose became popular as a feature above the light or chandelier hanging below.

Fig 6.24a (above): A plastered ceiling from the parlour chamber at Hill Farm, Christow, Devon.

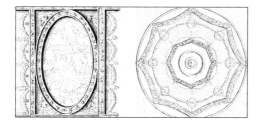

Fig 6.24b (above): The example on the left is typical of that found in late 17th and early 18th century houses with a painting framed by oval or rectangular mouldings which are still deep and decorated with Baroque motifs. The example on the right is a late 18th century Robert Adam design which uses more delicate Neo-Classical features and has a notably shallower relief.

7 FIREPLACES
HEARTHS AND OVERMANTELS

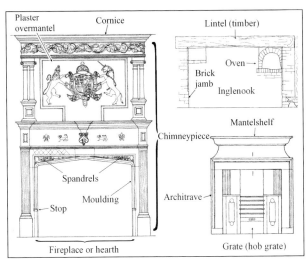

Fig 7.1 (left): Fireplaces with labels of parts.

Fig 7.2 (below): Open hearths reconstructed in a house from North Cray, Kent (top) and 'Bayleaf' (bottom) at the Weald and Downland Open Air Museum near Chichester. The Bayleaf hearth has been furnished with iron firedogs for holding the burning logs, iron trivets for cooking pots and a pottery curfew (couvre-feu) for covering the smouldering remains at night (the origin of the modern term 'curfew').

MEDIEVAL HEARTHS

In the medieval period most houses had an open hearth in the middle of the floor of the open hall, and occasionally the physical evidence is found beneath the floor when renovations are done or if an archaeological investigation is undertaken. Sometimes there is simply an area of fire-hardened clay, or there may be a stone or tile hearth beneath the later floor. Such hearths have been recon-structed at buildings in the various open-air museums (Fig 7.2) and in the great hall of St Cross Hospital, Winchester; the original octagonal tiled hearth survives at Penshurst Place, Kent. At Barley Hall in York the reconstructed 15th century hall includes a central hearth set into a floor of glazed tiles, reproducing those found in the excavations. The hearth itself has a border of bricks and the centre is laid with thin tiles set on edge, with the square divided into four triangles in which the tiles are laid in opposite directions (Fig 7.3).

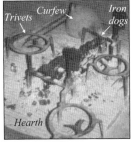

FIREPLACES
Medieval Stone Fireplaces

The larger houses had stone-built fireplaces in first-floor chambers and sometimes also in the parlour, and the earliest to survive date from the late 12th and the 13th centuries. Most have a large stone hood carried on corbels supported by columns, although the remains of such a fireplace at Stokesay Castle (Shropshire) appear to have held a timber hood. At Abingdon Abbey the late 13th century fireplace has lost its stone lintel and hood, but the surviving columns and carved capitals show work of the highest quality (Fig 7.4). The fireplace is connected to the famous original chimney which has a tiny gabled roof with smoke outlets in the sides.

Fig 7.3 (above): Barley Hall, York; the open hearth. The surrounding glazed tile floor was reconstructed from excavated evidence.

A much smaller version of a corbelled fireplace has survived in the solar of Daubeney's Farm, Colerne, Wilts; it has simple rounded corbels and the hood consists of a single massive stone and a row of three smaller stones, with a moulded mantelshelf. The date 1390 is inscribed on it, and although it is very rare to find inscribed dates this early it could be authentic. This, too, has its original pinnacle chimney, with a narrow smoke vent in each of the eight sides and a conical roof on top. Although medieval chimneys are rare, Wiltshire has several, and there is another at St Briavel's Castle in the Forest of Dean.

From the mid 14th century the fireplace with a stone surround gradually replaced the corbelled fireplace, although the latter survived in the Channel Islands until a much later period. Most 15th century stone fireplaces have some variation of the four-centred arch, often elaborately moulded; the spandrels may be plain, sunk or hollow, recessed or embellished with carving such as the mouchettes at 1500-1 Hants (Fig 7.5). Some open halls were provided with a fireplace from the start, usually on the long wall (a lateral fireplace); a lack of smoke-blackening on the roof timbers will usually indicate that the fireplace is original. The advent of the storeyed hall from the later 15th century meant that the hall inevitably had a fireplace. Fireplaces were also inserted into open halls and sometimes predate the insertion of an upper floor.

Some 15th century stone fireplaces have square heads and it is possible that this was an earlier type than the

Fig 7.4 (below): The remains of the late 13th century corbelled fireplace at Abingdon Abbey (Berks), and detail of a carved capital.

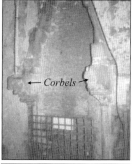

← Corbels →

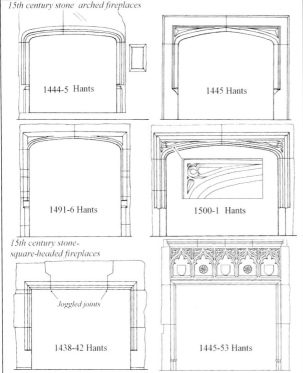

15th century stone arched fireplaces

1444-5 Hants

1445 Hants

1491-6 Hants

1500-1 Hants

15th century stone-square-headed fireplaces

Joggled joints

1438-42 Hants

1445-53 Hants

Fig 7.5 (left):15th century arched and square-headed stone fireplaces from Hampshire. The arched examples show the variations in the treatment of the spandrels. 1444-5 has none, 1445 has hollow or sunk spandrels, 1491-6 has plain recessed spandrels and 1500-1 has carvings of mouchettes. The square headed fireplace 1445-53 disappeared from the Angel Inn, Andover sometime after 1970. The lintel is covered with the most elaborate carving with five cusped recesses containing alternately shields and roses; these were probably painted. Such elaborate carving is not uncommon in high-status buildings on both arched and square-headed fireplaces.

four-centred arch (Fig 7.5). Structurally a square head was harder to achieve than an arch, which is inherently more stable. The fireplace of 1438-42 in the lodgings range of the bishop's palace at Bishop's Waltham solves the problem by the use of joggled joints between the central stone and the two side stones of the lintel. One alternative to joggled joints was to have a central keystone between two side blocks or to have a lintel made from a

Fig 7.7 (below): A decorative lamp bracket carved with a green man, set close to the fireplace in the parlour chamber at Manstone Old House, Sidmouth, Devon and probably dating from the 15th century.

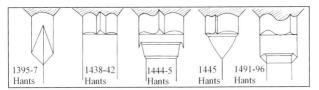

1395-7 Hants	1438-42 Hants	1444-5 Hants	1445 Hants	1491-96 Hants

Fig 7.6 (above): Mouldings and stops of stone fireplaces. The mouldings show a progression from the simple hollow chamfer of the late 14th century example at East Meon Courthouse, Hampshire to more complex mouldings in the 15th century with double hollows or hollows with ogees.

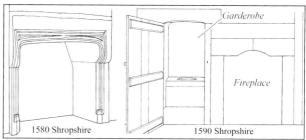

1580 Shropshire   1590 Shropshire

Fig 7.9 *(above): Variations in the later 16th century include a corbelled fireplace with an elaborate moulding at 1580 Shropshire and one of 1590 from the same county which has a very simple straight stone lintel with a segmental arch in the centre. Like many fireplaces of the period, this one has a garderobe (toilet) next to it (this kept the garderobe warm and it was structurally easier to include it in the projection for the chimney stack).*

Fig 7.8 *(above): the parlour fireplace at Samlesbury Hall, Lancs is unusual in bearing the date 1545 in Roman numerals. The lintel is decorated with three shields in the centre, flanked on each side by three circles containing varied motifs, all contained within a twisted cable frame. Below this the spandrels have delicate floral decoration with, rather oddly, a dagger at one end. The whole has been repainted and the original fireplace opening filled in with elaborately carved and painted mock-medieval decoration, but it gives a good impression of what many of these fireplaces may have looked like when new.*

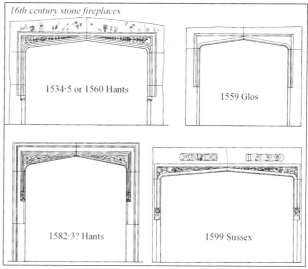

16th century stone fireplaces

1534-5 or 1560 Hants   1559 Glos

1582-3? Hants   1599 Sussex

Fig 7.10 *(above): 16th century stone fireplaces. The date of the example from Kimpton Manor, Hants is not certain as the house has two dated phases in the middle of the 16th century and stylistically the fireplaces could belong to either. The straight-stemmed foliage carving in the spandrels is similar to that at Samlesbury Hall of 1545 and to a fireplace in the Archbishop's Palace at Maidstone, Kent of circa 1500, so the earlier date is the more likely (later foliage is more sinuous in design). The 1599 fireplace, originally from East Grinstead, Sussex, is now in a Leicestershire manor house. It has vine trail decoration in the spandrels and vase and rose stops (Fig 7.13).*

single piece of stone (Fig 7.5: 1445-53 Hants).

Some medieval fireplaces incorporate a projection on one or both sides, commonly referred to as lamp brackets; Manstone Old House, Sidmouth (Devon) has a separate bracket in the parlour chamber, set above and to one side of the plain square-headed fireplace. The bracket is carved with a green man (Fig 7.7).

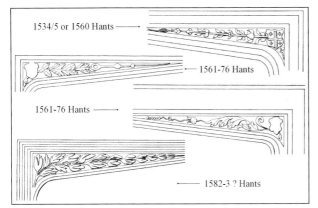

Fig 7.12 (above): Foliage carving in the spandrels of 16th century Hampshire houses.

16th Century Stone Fireplaces

Fireplace design changed little in the 16th century except that the four-centred arch, which remained extremely common, was now usually a depressed arch with a more angular appearance (Fig 7.10). The grandest houses continued to have the grandest fireplaces. Floral or foliage

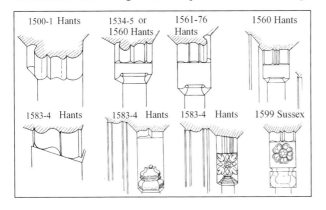

Sunk chamfer

1559 Glos	1594 Glos

Ovolo and hollow

1576 Sussex	1594 Glos

Ogee and hollow

1582 Brecon	1594 Glos

Fig 7.11 *(above): Profiles of stone fireplace mouldings of the 16th century.*

Fig 7.13 *(left): 16th century fireplace mouldings and stops. From about 1500 to 1560 mouldings combine ogees or hollows with pronounced rolls, while stops, as in the earlier period, are simple. From 1560 the ovolo moulding makes an appearance and quickly becomes a standard feature, while stops become much more elaborate from about 1580. Another feature that arrives in Hampshire in 1560 is the sunk chamfer, which also occurs on Gloucestershire fireplaces of 1559 and 1594 (Fig 7.11).*

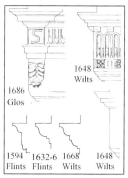

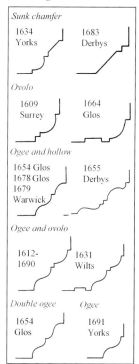

Fig 7.14 *(above): Stone mantelshelf mouldings of the 17th century.*

Fig 7.16 *(below): Profiles of 17th century fireplace mouldings.*

decoration was popular for the spandrels of 16th century fireplaces in the larger houses (Figs 7.10 and 7.12) and in the Elizabethan period elaborately carved stops came into fashion (Fig 7.13). These stops are often set much higher than later examples and can look slightly odd. Plainer fireplaces sometimes occur, even in manor houses, such as 1559 Gloucestershire, which has completely plain spandrels and stops (Fig 7.10).

17th century stone fireplaces

The four-centred arch continued in use for much of the 17th century, with the depressed arch becoming universal. Many fireplaces were relatively plain, with a simple moulding and stops, a large blank area above the arch, and a moulded mantelshelf (Fig 7.14). Some, however, include carved decoration on the lintel, with features such as

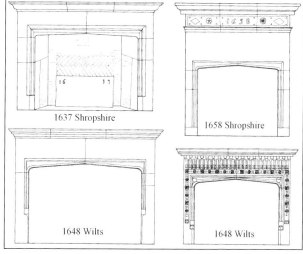

Fig 7.15 *(above): 17th century stone fireplaces. 1648 Wilts has an abundance of carved decoration on the lintel, but there is a mystery, as an early 20th century detailed drawing of the room shows the fireplace as plain and unadorned, a smaller version of the hall fireplace also shown to the left. A story of the fireplace having been rebuilt suggests that the stones may have been taken away, given carved decoration and then rebuilt in the original location. Although the style of the carved decoration is correct for the period the overall effect is rather overwhelming in a way that most genuine examples are not.*

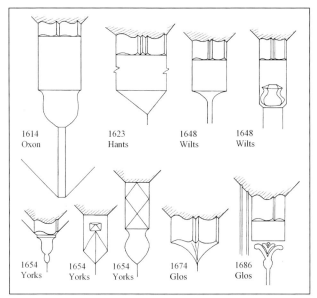

1614
Oxon

1623
Hants

1648
Wilts

1648
Wilts

1654
Yorks

1654
Yorks

1654
Yorks

1674
Glos

1686
Glos

Fig 7.17 *(above): Stone fireplace mouldings and stops of the 17th century. Sunk chamfers continue into the 17th century, with an example as late as 1683 in Derbyshire (Fig 7.16).The ovolo moulding continues into the 17th century and is found until the 1660s on its own and up to 1690 in combination with an ogee. The ogee, after its use in the 15th century, has a similar date range, from the 1580s to the 1690s. The 17th century stops on stone fireplaces tend to be less elaborate than the late 16th century examples, and they show considerable variety which, with such a small sample, is not susceptible to any sort of analysis. Stone mantelshelves likewise show little variation throughout the 17th century (Fig 7.14). N.B: 1623 Hants is in fact a brick fireplace plastered to resemble stone.*

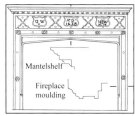

Mantelshelf

Fireplace moulding

Fig 7.18 *(above): A dated fireplace of 1638 in the parlour of a farm in Hinton, South Gloucestershire with profiles of the mantelshelf and fireplace moulding within.*

Fig 7.19 *(below): Fireplaces with stone 'Yorkshire arches' at Shibden Hall, Halifax (top), at a house in Warley, Yorks, 1691 (middle) and Wilts, 1648 (bottom).*

arcading or a recessed panel around the opening containing roses and other motifs (the parlour fireplace at 1648 Wilts: Fig 7.15 has these features in abundance).

The decorative effect at Healey Court Farm Fig 7.18) is much more restrained, despite the 20th century blue and white colour scheme. The initials are believed to refer to George Weare and his son Henry, and the story is that George was taken ill and, believing he was dying, made a will. When he made an unexpected recovery he was so grateful that he decided to renovate the house and installed new stone fireplaces in the parlour and the chamber above.

17th century segmental arch fireplaces

A particularly distinctive style of 17th century stone fire-place is the wide segmental arch that is a feature of many Yorkshire houses, with some across the border in the Lancashire Pennines and another group in North Wales (Fig 7.19). Dated examples occur throughout the 17th century, with a late and unusually small one of 1691 at Peel House, Warley. By contrast the great kitchen fire-place at East Riddlesden Hall (1648) is nearly nine feet wide and five feet six inches high at the centre of the arch.

There is also a group of kitchen fireplaces of this type in the north-west Wiltshire/Gloucestershire area, like the large arched kitchen fireplace at Wilts 1648 (Fig 7.19). In Gloucestershire, Doughton Manor near Tetbury has yet another; the date 1641 on a gatepost may mark the completion of the house. The history of Doughton may explain the presence of a Yorkshire feature in the south, as it was built by the Tallboys family who originated in Yorkshire.

Fig 7.20 (above): A fireplace carved with a mirror baluster outline at Lower Old Hall, Norland, Yorks (1634).

Fig 7.21 (below): A plain brick fireplace in the parlour of a 1622 Hampshire house (top), and two elaborate examples from undated houses in Essex, probably early 16th century below.

Other regional variations may be found in fireplace design. In parts of Devon and Cornwall granite is used, giving rise to distinctive heavy and rather crude mouldings while some West Yorkshire fireplaces of the 1630s have jambs carved with shapes which are reminiscent of mirror balusters (Fig 7.20). Unusual low-relief carving can also be seen on the fireplace in the main first-floor room of the Merchant's House in Marlborough, built in 1656 (Fig 7.55), which has a strapwork design across the lintel.

16th and 17th century brick fireplaces

In areas where good building stone was not readily available houses slightly lower down the social scale may use brick in the later 16th and the 17th century. Sometimes this was plastered over to resemble stone, and usually the bricks were chamfered. Hampshire brick fireplaces tend to be plain, with a simple four-centred arch, but were occasionally moulded (Fig 7.17: 1623 Hants). In Essex and Suffolk much more decorative brickwork is found and fireplaces may have elaborate mouldings and incorporate corner columns and moulded mantelshelves (Fig 7.21).

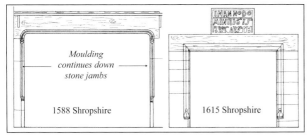

Fig 7.22 (above): Fireplaces with moulded wooden lintels. 1588 Shropshire has the date inscribed on the right-hand jamb and a wooden mantelshelf carried on simple brackets.

Timber hoods

Many houses once had a timber chimney or firehood, with a heavy wooden lintel carrying a hood made of timber studs and infilled with wattle and daub. Although such a structure sounds inherently unsafe, in fact the daub and plaster rendered it reasonably fire-proof and a number have survived to the present day (Fig 7.23).

Most have had brick chimneys built inside them, but occasionally the sloping face of the hood in an upstairs chamber will indicate the original structure. More often only the lintel survives, although there may be a small part of the original structure within the roof. A house in Montgomeryshire has a very rare survival, a timber chimney which contains two back-to-back fireplaces (Fig 7.25). This was inserted into the medieval house in 1630-1 and the carpenter's marks on the frame show that it must have projected some five feet above the roof ridge.

Fig 7.23 (above):A timber firehood at Stang End Farmhouse, reconstructed at the Ryedale Folk Museum, North Yorkshire.

Fig 7.25 (below): A very rare timber chimney of 1630-1 with back-to-back fireplaces in a Montgomeryshire house (top). Some of the original smoke-blackened plaster and wattle survives inside (bottom).

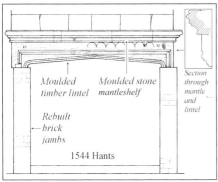

Fig 7.24 (left): A fireplace with a moulded wooden lintel. The brick jambs of 1544 Hants have been rebuilt, as they do not match or line up with the moulding of the lintel.

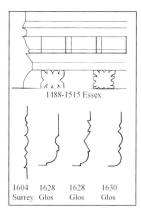

1488-1515 Essex

1604	1628	1628	1630
Surrey	Glos	Glos	Glos

Fig 7.26 (above): A detail from a wooden fireplace lintel moulding from Essex and profiles of later examples.

Fig 7.27 (below): The 16th century carved wooden lintel at the Sun Inn, Feering, Essex.

Fireplaces with timber lintels

Although moulded stone fireplaces are surprisingly common the vast majority of fireplaces had a timber lintel on stone or brick jambs. Some occasionally survive from the medieval period; 1488-1515 Essex has a very elaborate moulding to the deep lintel (Fig 7.26), while the early 16th century fireplace at the Sun Inn, Feering, Essex has foliage carving covering the entire face of the lintel (Fig 7.27).

Some are similar to stone fireplaces, with four-centred or depressed arches and foliage carving in the spandrels or sunk spandrels. One Welsh house has a splendid dragon carved at one end of the fireplace lintel (see Fig 5.29). 1544 Hampshire has an unusual combination of materials, with rebuilt brick jambs, a moulded wooden lintel and a moulded stone mantelshelf, while Shropshire has some fireplaces with wooden lintels whose moulding matches that of the stone jambs (Fig 7.24).

1604 Surrey (Fig 7.26) has an unusual moulding carved along the flat of the lintel, while many 17th century Gloucestershire fireplaces have an ovolo moulding. Most are a simple ovolo, but some have more complex arrangements (Fig 7.26). In the second half of the 17th

Fig 7.28 (below): Hampshire fireplaces with chamfered wooden lintels. Note the plain mantelshelf at 1510-38 and the marks for such a shelf at 1675. 1622 Hants has the relatively rare use of a mason's mitre to link the lintel and jamb chamfers. The 1678 example has mortises for a solid mantelshelf; despite the optical illusion created by the shape of the lintel these are actually in a straight line. The lintel has a series of notches and scribed marks which may be protective witch marks (see Chapter 5).

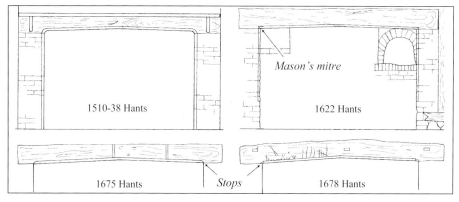

1510-38 Hants

Mason's mitre

1622 Hants

1675 Hants

Stops

1678 Hants

century the ogee moulding is equally common and seems to take over from the ovolo, which may now be relegated to the less important upstairs rooms. Chamfered wooden lintels are the most common type and in the smallest houses and cottages continued well into the 18th century or even later.

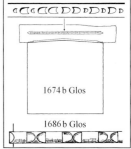

1674 b Glos

1686 b Glos

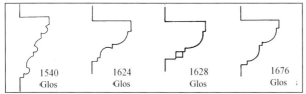

| 1540 | 1624 | 1628 | 1676 |
| Glos | Glos | Glos | Glos |

Fig 7.30 (above): Profiles of moulded mantleshelves. Some wooden lintels bear marks showing the former existence of mantelshelves, either a plank shelf held by vertical brackets (Fig 7.28: 1675 Hants) or a solid moulded mantelshelf tenoned into the lintel (Fig 7.28: 1678 Hants). Several such mantelshelves survive in Gloucestershire houses, all with ovolo mouldings.

In Gloucestershire some of the earliest wooden lintels, dating from the 16th century, are extremely deep, well over a foot, and may include an integral or separate mantelshelf which can be moulded or chamfered. In most of the 16th century fireplaces in Hampshire the lintel is less deep and is rounded at the corners, with the chamfer running through to form a continuous chamfer with the jambs (Fig 7.28: 1510-38).

By contrast most 17th century fireplaces in Hampshire and elsewhere have the chamfer stopped so that even if the jambs are chamfered there is no connection between the two. 1622 Hampshire has a relatively rare variation in which the two chamfers are linked by the use of the mason's mitre (Fig 7.28). Although some wooden lintels are straight, particularly in the later period, many have a slight camber; this can be so small as to be barely noticeable, with the centre only an inch higher than the sides.

Stone jambs may be made up of several stones of varying sizes, but often the side of the fireplace away from the main house wall is composed of a single massive slab of stone. The reason for this is not clear, and it must have involved considerable effort to both find and transport such a large piece of stone. It has the effect of making the

Fig 7.29 (above): Two late 17th century houses in the same county have a band of carved decoration running along the lintel. Chamber fireplace (1674 Glos) had been covered over with a layer of plaster and was only revealed by careful use of a screwdriver to prise out the plaster.

Fig 7.31 (below): Painted fireplace at the museum in Totnes, Devon.

Fig 7.32 *(above):Painted scroll decoration discovered on the inner edge of the hall fireplace during restoration work at Moorend Farm, Hambrook, Glos (1676).*

Fig 7.33 *(below): Profiles of late 17th and early 18th century fireplace bolection mouldings.*

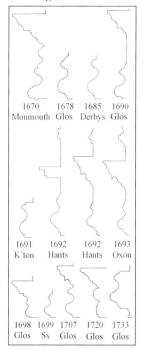

side wall of the fireplace relatively thin when compared with walls built up more conventionally of smaller stones. At one house in west Somerset the stone has a number of grooves worn in it from the constant sharpening of knives over the centuries!

It is very common for fireplace lintels to have been wholly or partially plastered over at a later date. Unfortunately when they are uncovered again the surface of the wood is often found to have been scored to provide a key for the plaster; alternatively laths have been nailed on to take the plaster, and their removal leaves the lintel with a stripey effect. It was also fairly common for the inner surface of the fireplace to be plastered as an original feature, although now it is all too often removed on the assumption that it was added later. The purpose of this 'pargetting mortar' was to stop smoke from penetrating between the joints of the brickwork or stonework.

Strange as it may seem, some even had painted decoration inside the fireplace, a feature that is particularly common in Devon and Somerset. This usually took the form of geometric patterns, with squares divided diagonally into black and white triangles being the most common (Fig 7.31). Occasionally foliage decoration was used, and at Moorend Farm, Hambrook, Glos, a fragment of scroll decoration was discovered during renovation work (Fig 7.32). It was a totally unexpected discovery and as such was nearly overlooked in the process of unblocking the fireplace; one wonders how many other examples have been inadvertently destroyed. It shows the care needed when any sort of restoration work is undertaken and the necessity for obtaining expert advice both before and during such work.

18th century fireplaces

In the late 17th century fireplace design changed and became much plainer. Instead of arched fireplaces with mouldings and stops the square-headed opening with a large bolection moulding became popular in the more fashionable houses, and decorative stops disappeared altogether (Fig 7.33). The bolection moulded fireplace surrounds may be either wood or stone; the wood was usually pine and was always painted.

The earliest bolection mouldings date from 1670 and the

1692 Hants

1692 Hants

Fig 7.34 (left):Two wooden bolection - moulded fireplaces at Otterbourne Manor, Hampshire of 1692.

feature was especially popular in the 1690s; its use continues until the early 1730s. This style of fireplace was often used in a panelled room, with a large framed panel above the fireplace (Fig 7.34). Although most are now blank, a number of original overmantel paintings have survived in these panels; one can be seen at Tintinhull House in Somerset, and there are several others in the county.

Plain bolection-moulded fireplaces can be found in many less important rooms or in smaller houses; in 1691 Kensington Palace took delivery of a bulk order from the Portland quarries in Dorset for fireplaces for the large number of rooms for the staff and servants (Fig 7.35).

Sometimes wooden fireplace surrounds have a very simplified version of the bolection moulding, as at circa c.1680 Essex (Fig 7.35). Others in both stone and wood have a section of bolection moulding below the moulded

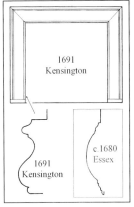

1691
Kensington

1691
Kensington

c.1680
Essex

Fig 7.35 (above): A simple stone bolection-moulded fireplace of 1691 at Kensington Palace. Circa 1680 Essex is a wooden fireplace surround with a very simplified bolection moulding.

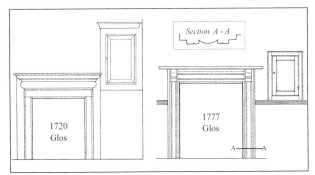

Section A - A

1720
Glos

1777
Glos

A———A

Fig 7.36 (left): Two Gloucestershire fireplaces with adjacent cupboards. 1777 Glos is a parlour fireplace with a profile of the moulding between A and A.

mantelshelf, while the rest of the architrave has a simpler moulding, as at 1720 Glos (Fig 7.36). The arrangement of fireplace and cupboard here is one that is repeated time and again in the late 17th and the 18th century. At 1777 Glos, the layout and the cupboard, with its bead-moulded door and frame, are definitely of 1777; the fireplace surround, however, may be later as the moulding seems more like those of the early 19th century (Fig 7.36).

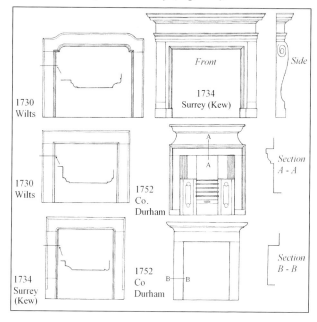

The smaller farmhouses and cottages in the 18th century continued to have simple fireplaces with wooden lintels, but in the more important houses and in towns the structure of the fireplace was usually hidden behind an architrave, however plain. Stone fireplace surrounds were now planted onto the front of the wall, unlike the earlier fireplaces where the moulded or chamfered stones formed the jambs and lintel of the opening, and a great variety of designs were in common use. Sometimes the original large open fireplace was partly filled in and a new architrave added inside the old opening (see Fig 7.37).

Eared or lugged fireplace surrounds were popular from the 1720s, but can occur as late as about 1770, with several examples in Beverley (Fig 7.39). Designs for eared fire-

Fig 7.38 (above): Late 18th century Adam-style fireplace. Although this fireplace is in a wing which was modernised in 1771, an early photograph of the room does not show the fireplace, implying that it was introduced some time in the early 20th century. Nevertheless the style is correct for the date.

places are found in Batty Langley's *The City and Country Builder's and Workman's Treasury of Design* of 1745 and York has an example in Colliergate of 1748 which matches one of these designs almost exactly. In the later 18th century fireplace surrounds often have more delicate designs, with Classical vases, swags of fruit and flowers, wheatear drops and bows all based on designs by Robert Adam (Fig 7.38).

Fig 7.39 (above): Some 18th century eared fireplace surrounds.

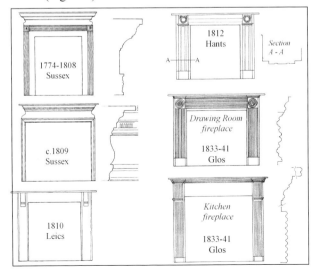

Fig 7.40 (left):Early 19th century (left side) and Regency fireplaces (right side) with profiles of their mouldings.

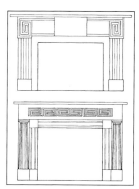

Fig 7.41 *(above): Fireplaces designs showing Greek influence, published in 1830.*

Fig 7.42 *(right): Some 19th century fireplaces of unusual materials, Coade stone (1849 Wilts), plaster-of-Paris and cast-iron (1892 Glos).*

Fig 7.43 *(below): Variations on the bolection moulding from 1892 Glos (Fig 7.42).*

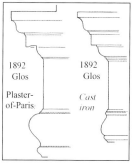

19th century fireplaces

Similar delicate designs continue into the early 19th century, with two examples from Slinfold in Sussex being typical (Fig 7.40). One has the square corner blocks which became such a feature of design in the Regency period.

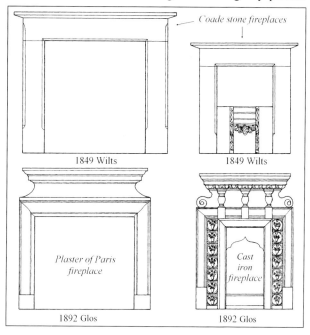

Coade stone fireplaces

1849 Wilts

1849 Wilts

Plaster of Paris fireplace

Cast iron fireplace

1892 Glos

1892 Glos

1812 Hampshire has an interesting variation on these, with a marble fireplace surround with garlands of leaves and ribbons in the corner blocks. More typical of the slightly later Regency period are the concentric circles which are equally common on doorframes of the period as are the multiple ribbed mouldings. Other fireplaces of the period show Greek influence, with variations on the Greek key pattern and tapered reeded columns (Fig 7.41).

The Victorian period shows a huge variety of fireplace design, with ideas drawn from all previous periods and other features that were completely new. Amongst the latter was the use of new materials; the plain chamfered fireplace surrounds at 1849 Wilts are made of Coade stone, a type of terracotta invented in 1767 by George and Eleanor Coade and much used for doorways and other decorative details in London (Fig 7.42). At the end of the century fireplaces at the former Literary Institute (now Tower House) in Almondsbury, Glos are made of plaster-of-Paris and cast iron (Fig 7.42). The latter incorporates pretty blue and white tiles in imitation of the Delft tiles which were used in some 17th and early 18th century fireplaces, and forms of bolection moulding (Fig 7.43).

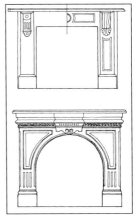

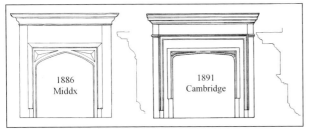

Fig 7.44 (above): Sample designs from a late Victorian catalogue.

Fig 7.45 (above):The Arts and Crafts movement produced a four-centred arch at 1886 Middx and a depressed arch at 1891 Cambs; both lack the decorative stops of the 16th and 17th centuries and the mouldings are fussier

Late Victorian catalogues are full of designs for fireplaces of wood, marble or cast-iron, which could be ordered in a variety of sizes and colours. Round arches were extremely popular, both for the main fireplace surround and for the smaller grate that was inserted within a square-headed surround. Most designs incorporate some sort of mantelshelf, often a plain shelf carried on two heavy brackets of varying designs (Fig 7.40: 1810 Leics).

With the influence of the Arts and Crafts movement in the late 19th century came a return to traditional four-centred and depressed arches and sunk spandrels, but the mouldings are generally fussier in the details and comprise more and smaller elements than earlier ones. The same fussiness can be seen in the square-headed bedroom fireplaces of 1886 Middx, while the kitchen and scullery fireplaces have plain surrounds with tiny chamfers and a

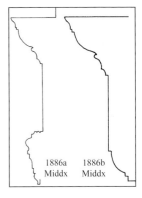

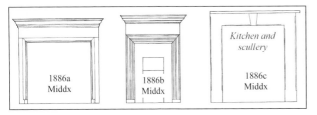

Fig 7.46 (left and above): Square-headed fireplaces of the late 19th century with the profile of the moulding from 1886a and 1886 b illustrated above.

Fig 7.47 (right): The splendid dining room fireplace with built-in L-shaped benches at St Saviour's Vicarage, Sunbury-on Thames, Middx, built in 1886 by J. R. Sedding.

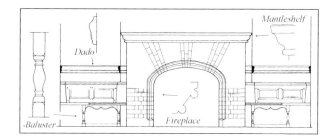

central keystone, a design found in thousands of 18th and 19th century kitchens (Fig 7.46).

The large dining room in the same house has a splendid moulded brick and stone fireplace with built-in benches on either side, all set within a huge recess at one end of the room (Fig 7.47). The radiating bands of brick above the arch are a forerunner of the sunburst pattern which became so popular in the 1930s and the whole design seems to signal the end of the Victorian period and to usher in the 20th century.

INGLENOOKS, OVERMANTELS AND FIREBACKS
Inglenook seats and ovens

Fig 7.48 (above): Inglenook seat in an undated Gloucestershire farmhouse.

Larger fireplaces often have an inglenook seat built into one or both sides, where the farmer could sit and warm himself after a cold day in the fields. Often there are small ledges, some acting as elbow rests and others for parking one's tankard of ale or cider (Fig 7.48).

Bread ovens are also commonly built into the side or back of the fireplace, either as original features or as later additions. One of the earliest types is the clay or cloam oven, commonly called Barnstaple ovens after the centre of manufacture. This is a pottery oven complete with a clay door which could be bought as a complete unit and built into the fireplace (Fig 7.49); they were common in the west country in the 17th century and were even exported to America by the early settlers. Elsewhere ovens were built of brick.

Fig 7.49 (below):A cloam oven built into the fireplace of a farmhouse in South Gloucestershire; it has lost its door.

The earliest had heavy doors made of elm, which is relatively fire-proof, with a large vertical handle in the centre; they were simply lifted into place when needed (Fig 7.50). In the 19th century these were replaced by cast-iron frames with hinged doors, often bearing the name of the manufacturer. These have unfortunately become prized collectibles and it is not uncommon for the door to have been lifted off its hinges and removed, leaving only the frame in situ.

Bacon-smoking chambers may also be found next to the kitchen fireplace, especially in Somerset and other parts of the west country. They take a variety of forms, some being a cupboard in the side of the stack reached from the first floor room, and these occur in many parts of the country and in America (Fig 7.51). Others are a large circular chamber three or four feet in diameter, opening into the side of the fireplace. Some survive intact, while others have been turned into cupboards or cut through to create new access from one room to another.

Some fireplaces have an original ash pit to collect the ashes which were used both in the creation of a form of soap and to sprinkle on the contents of the privy. Gloucestershire probate inventories include frequent references to the ash pit grate, suggesting that ash pits were once more common than they are now.

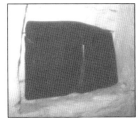

Fig 7.50 (above): A bread oven with a heavy elm door.

Fig 7.51 (below): A bacon-smoking chamber in a house in New England.

Wooden overmantels

In the more important houses in the later 16th and the 17th century the fireplace in the most important room, whether the hall or the parlour, may have a decorative overmantel. This can either be of wood, especially if the room is panelled, or of plasterwork.

Wooden overmantels often incorporate either round arches or geometric patterns of the same designs used for

Fig 7.52 (below): Overmantels with round arches

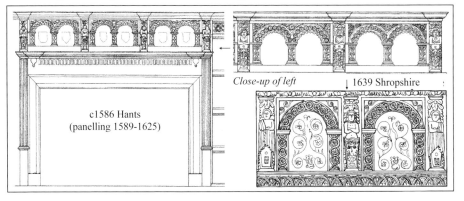

c1586 Hants
(panelling 1589-1625)

Close-up of left

1639 Shropshire

1604 Suffolk ↑

1570? Kent   1623 Hants

Fig 7.53 *(above): A Dartmouth overmantel dated 1595 has flattened arches of a type more usually seen in Yorkshire.*

Fig 7.55 *(below): An overmantel of 1656 at the Merchant's House in Marlborough, Wilts (bottom) and a close up detail (top). It incorporates small recesses which have cross-hatching at the back; this was possibly to display small items of china or other precious objects.*

Fig 7.54 *(right): Overmantels with geometric shapes. 1604 Suffolk combines geometric patterns with round arches in a very rich design, while 1623 Hants has a contemporary painting in the central panel. The brick arched fireplace was probably originally plastered over to resemble stonework. The side columns may have been added, perhaps from a 17th century bed.*

the myriad 'Jacobean' pulpits found throughout the country. Indeed, sometimes the overmantel is actually made up of bits of a dismantled pulpit, as in the example at Bitterley Court in Shropshire; one of the three arches contains the inscription 'ES GS Churchewardenes: Ano Dni 1630'. Others have been made up of sections of 17th century chairs, chests and tester beds and it always pays to look at the details carefully to see if all the wood matches. Often the genuine old panels have been set in a newer framework whose wood will be slightly different in colour and in general appearance.

There are, however, many genuine overmantels, either in

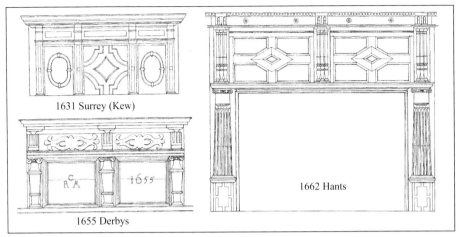

1631 Surrey (Kew)

1655 Derbys

1662 Hants

Fig 7.56 (above): A simpler geometric designs.

their original locations or moved bodily from one house to another; Blakesley Hall, Yardley, Birmingham has an overmantel from Little Aston Hall, Staffordshire. The round arches often have guilloche decoration around the arch, and some have figures called terms on the columns (Fig 7.52). These consist of the upper half of a usually naked figure emerging from a column and having a basket of fruit (or a degenerate version thereof) on their heads, and they are equally common on plaster overmantels. The

1561-76 Hants
but with later
Royal Arms

Fig 7.57 (above and left): At Grove Place, Nursling, Hampshire, built between 1561 and 1576 the grand fireplace in the west wing has a fine royal arms as an overmantel. However, the supporters are the lion and the unicorn, which places the arms after the accession of James I in 1603; before that date, the lion was paired with a dragon. Although now painted white, the royal arms may originally have been painted in more colourful fashion; a good example is the overmantel, also of James I, at a house in Sandwich, Kent (above).

Fig 7.58 (above):The Sloping Deck restaurant in the Butterwalk, Dartmouth, (1635-40) has a scene of the Holy Spirit descending as tongues of flame on the disciples at Pentecost, flanked by large figures of Moses, holding the tablets with the Ten Commandments, and David with his lyre.

Fig 7.60 (below):A Derbyshire overmantel with an improving text.

Fig 7.61 (below): An overmantel in the main chamber of the Lamb Inn, Iron Acton, Glos, 1690, still with its original colour. Next to the fireplace are the remains of a painted royal arms.

example at Chawton House, Hampshire has alternate male and female figures, with strapwork decoration on the columns.

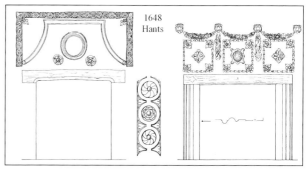

Fig 7.59 (above): Queen's Lodge, Wickham, Hants, dated 1648, has two very unusual plaster overmantels, one relatively plain with a guilloche border and the other much more elaborate with swags of fruit and flowers hanging from lion's mask heads and square panels with fleur-de-lis at the corners. The finer detail of both overmantels has been lost under layers of paint, disguising the high quality of the work.

The panels within the arches may be plain or carved, while some have delicate inlaid decoration in the form of floral scrolls (Fig 7.52). An example of this is at East Riddlesden Hall, Yorkshire, of 1648; here the round arches have a flattened form that is common in Yorkshire but rare elsewhere. An example in Dartmouth, Devon has geometric patterns within the arches, while on the capitals of the two main columns a hound chases a hare (Fig 7.53).

The round arch was especially popular between 1610 and 1630 but had gone out of fashion by 1650; geometric patterns however continue until the 1660s. The earlier ones tend to have much richer carving and more elaborate designs (Fig 7.54), while the later ones are simpler (Fig 7.56).

Plaster overmantels

Plaster overmantels feature in some of the grandest houses from the Elizabethan period until the mid 17th century and they can be extremely elaborate. Many of the best are in Somerset and Devon, where there was a strong tradition of plasterwork at this period and there are other good

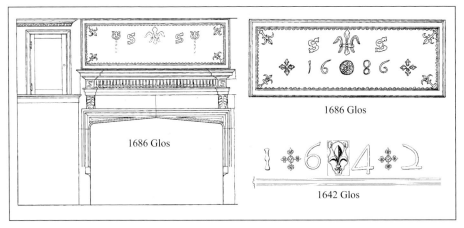

1686 Glos

1686 Glos

1642 Glos

Fig 7.62 *(above): South Gloucestershire overmantels. The 1686 fireplace, at Commonwealth House, Latteridge, has the initials of the owner, Simon Sloper 'Gentleman' on the stonework of the hall fireplace and on both overmantels; he clearly did not wish to be overlooked. The hall overmantel had been covered with many layers of paint, obscuring the detail, but careful restoration has recently revealed the remains of the design, which included two tulips. It is not clear if this panel also included the date, but clearly something is missing from the lower half of the panel. The centre of the fireplace arch has been hacked away, but has been restored in the drawing. There is an almost identical overmantel also of 1686 in a small house in Westerleigh with no other embellishments apart from a band of carving on the main fireplace lintel, and one wonders whether it could be the home of the plasterer himself.*

examples in West Yorkshire. Coats of arms, Biblical scenes (Fig 7.58) and allegorical figures such as Peace and Plenty all feature prominently; the coats of arms may be those of the family or the royal arms of the day (Fig 7.57). Other plaster overmantels have texts rather than Biblical scenes (Fig 7.60).

Smaller houses may have rather more modest plaster overmantels and sometimes it is possible to detect the work of a single craftsman by the style of his work. South Gloucestershire has two distinct groups of overmantels, and nearly all of them are found in first-floor chambers. One has the date in large figures with a central shield containing a fleur-de-lis and two lozenge-shaped designs formed from a central rose with a small fleur-de-lis at each corner (Fig 7.62: 1462 Glos). This motif is clearly created from a wooden mould and it recurs in a group of later overmantels in the second half of the 17th century. The second distinct group has a moulded rectangular panel with a small fleur-de-lis at each corner and a large one in

Fig 7.63 *(above): Hampshire firebacks. The 1588 example at Chawton House (top) is original to the house, which was begun in 1583 or 1584, but the 1664 (middle) and 1687 (bottom) examples seem unrelated to the history of the houses in which they are located.*

the centre, with the date and the owner's initials. Examples date from 1686 (Fig 7.62) and 1690 (Fig 7.61). These overmantels could all be the work of one man who changed his designs at intervals, or perhaps they represent a father and son. The 1690 example is unusual in retaining what appears to be its original colour scheme, with the main elements picked out in red ochre and additional flowers sketched in black.

17th century firebacks

Cast-iron firebacks of the 17th century are common, but they are rarely built into the structure and it is often impossible to be certain whether their dates bear any relation to the date of the fireplace or to the house as a whole (however, 1637 Shropshire, Fig 7.15 is dated by the fireback built into the rear wall). There are also many very good reproductions, which can be very misleading.

Chawton House, Hampshire has a fireback dated 1588 which bears the initials of John Knight, who built the house after he inherited in 1583, so there can be little doubt about its authenticity. Its design of repeating patterns is typical of early firebacks, whereas after the Restoration in 1660 most bear the royal arms. Other Hampshire houses have firebacks whose dates however seem totally irrelevant to the overall history of the house (Fig 7.63).

8 FIXED FURNITURE
CUPBOARDS AND SHELVES

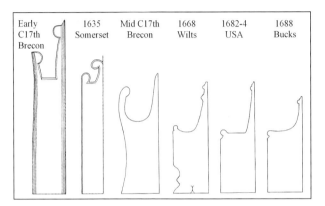

Early C17th Brecon	1635 Somerset	Mid C17th Brecon	1668 Wilts	1682-4 USA	1688 Bucks

Fixed furniture comes in many forms and is particularly vulnerable to being moved or removed, at great detriment to the historic character of the house. It is also illegal to move or remove *anything at all* from a listed building without listed building consent, whether it be a 1950s fireplace or an original 17th century dresser! Fixed furniture includes dressers and wall shelves, benches and settles, lamp brackets, spit racks and dog-wheels, bacon racks, cheese shelves, and assorted cupboards. Much of it is connected with the everyday tasks of preparing and storing food and is a reminder that every farm produced its own cheese and bacon; this needed special fixtures for both preparation and for long-term storage. Documentary evidence such as probate inventories can shed much light on the way houses were used and what furnishings were in which room, and many of the above items are listed in 17th and 18th century inventories.

BENCH ENDS AND SETTLES

Many medieval houses had a fixed bench at the upper end of the open hall, but few survive in situ and fewer still have

Fig 8.1 (left): Examples of bench ends. Two survive in houses in Breconshire, both undated; the bench end from Pen-y-Bryn, Llangatwg dates from the early 17th century and is similar to that of 1635 from Somerset. The one at Cwm-Gu-Fach, Llanfihangel Cwm Du, may date from the mid 17th century. The benches at Jordans Meeting House (1688 Bucks) were recently destroyed by fire.

Fig 8.2 (below): At a small Gloucestershire farmhouse a settle forms part of the partition opposite the fireplace, which divides off a passage from the back door; its date is uncertain, but it may be early 19th century.

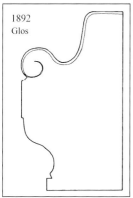

1892
Glos

Fig 8.3 (above): In the late 19th century the fixed bench reappears in Arts and Crafts buildings, such as Tower House, Almondsbury, Glos. This was built in 1892 as a Reading Institute, and fixed benches survive in what is now the entrance hall. Others may be built into large inglenook fireplaces.

Fig 8.5 (below): Cupboard built into the central well of a closed-well stair of 1560 at Abbot's Barton near Winchester.

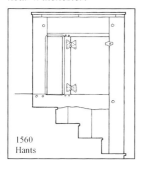

1560
Hants

the original bench ends in place (Fig 8.1). Such features are far more likely to survive in the common halls of almshouses and in meeting houses, both in England and America.

Fixed settles can occasionally be seen, and there is a good example in Kennixton Farmhouse at the Welsh Folk Museum at St Fagan's near Cardiff and another at the George and Dragon at Potterne in Wiltshire. In both cases there is a door next to the chimney stack and the settle is positioned at right angles to reduce the draughts from the door. Sometimes marks in the ceiling beams or joists show where such a settle has been removed (Fig 8.2).

CUPBOARDS AND DRESSERS

Cupboards were built into recesses next to the fireplace, under the stairs, or set into the wall. They may be concealed behind panelling, with a panelled door to match, or built into odd spaces around staircases. Closed-well stairs in particular may have one or more cupboards built in to utilise otherwise wasted space in the central well (Fig 8.5).

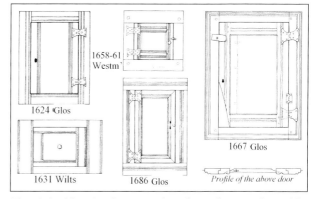

1658-61
Westm'

1624 Glos

1631 Wilts

1686 Glos

1667 Glos

Profile of the above door

Fig 8.4 (above): Spice cupboards with scratch-moulded decoration.

Spice cupboards

The most decorative cupboards are usually the so-called spice cupboards; these are small wall cupboards most often found near the chimney stack and sometimes actually in the back wall of the fireplace itself (Fig 8.6).

The name spice cupboard implies a use in storing the expensive spices which were imported to improve the flavour of many dishes, and the position close to the fireplace prevented the contents from getting damp. Salt may also have been stored in them, although there are many references in probate inventories to salt boxes as separate moveable items from the later 17th century. Other likely uses are for documents, money, and jewellery, especially when the cupboard is located in a bedroom, and there are also examples in Devon and Yorkshire which were used for storage of Bibles.

Fig 8.6 (above): Two cupboards are found close together in the back of the fireplace, at Stang End farm house, reconstructed at the Ryedale Folk Museum in North Yorkshire. These may date from 1709, the date inscribed over the front door recording the rebuilding of the outer walls in stone to replace the medieval timber framing. In this case the lower one has lost its door, and it is not uncommon to find only the frame remaining of a former spice cupboard (Fig 8.8).

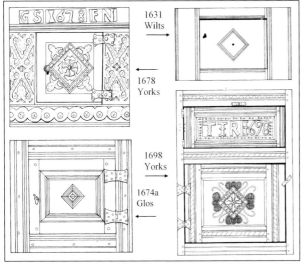

1631 Wilts
1678 Yorks
1698 Yorks
1674a Glos

Fig 8.7 (above): Spice cupboards with lozenge decoration. 1631 Wilts has a rare harr-hung door, which pivots on small pegs top and bottom.

The double cupboard at 1698 Yorks (Fig 8.7) may also have contained a Bible in the smaller upper cupboard. Double cupboards are rare, although there is another at 1664 Glos (Fig 8.9), but sometimes two cupboards are found close together in the back of the fireplace (Fig 8.6.)

Many spice cupboards are relatively plain, with decoration confined to shallow scratch mouldings on the outer frame and the outer sections of the door (Fig 8.4). Alternatively the central panel may be surrounded by mouldings, either applied as separate pieces to the rails and stiles or carved in the solid. Sometimes the central

Fig 8.8 (below):A spice cupboard which has lost its door.

1642 Glos

Fig 8.9 (right): Gloucestershire spice cupboards. The double cupboard at 1664 Glos is unusual and the carving, although elaborate, is relatively crude in its execution. So is the much simpler door at 1659 Glos, which has the same four-petalled motif. In contrast the carving at 1674 Glos, although covered in black gloss paint, is extremely fine. The door has an acanthus in the central panel with reversed scrolls around the edge, while the frame has strapwork top and bottom and tulips and daisies at the sides.

1659 Glos

1664 Glos

1674 Glos

panel is decorated with a lozenge, either carved on the panels or formed from applied mouldings (Fig 8.7: 1674a Glos).

In the west and the north there is a strong tradition of highly decorative spice cupboards covered with incised carving, and many northern examples include the date and the owner's initials (Fig 8.11). Lozenges feature on many of these, along with a variety of motifs such as scrolls, lunettes and strapwork. Flowers such as acanthus, daisies and tulips sometimes feature, as on the extremely fine cupboard at 1674 Glos (Fig 8.9).

The carving varies enormously in quality, from the relatively crude carving of 1659 and 1664 Glos (Fig 8.9) to the extremely skilful work, unfortunately not dated, at another Gloucestershire house (Fig 8.10).

Spice cupboards continued into the 18th century, but by the middle of the century decorative carving had died out, even in the far north. Instead the doors had fielded or sunk panels to match the doors and panelling in use at the time, as at 1752 Co. Durham (Fig 8.12).

Most spice cupboards now have butterfly hinges, although these may have been replaced by modern hinges as at 1698 Yorks (Fig 8.7), where the nail marks of the original hinge can still be seen on the upper door. Some were originally harr hung, a technique in which the door

Fig 8.10 (below):A beautifully carved Gloucestershire spice cupboard (undated).

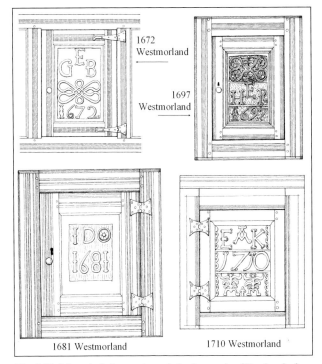

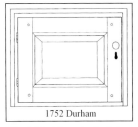

1752 Durham

Fig 8.12 (above): A plain 18th century spice cupboard with a fielded panel door.

Fig 8.13 (below): Display cupboards (from Glos) with shaped shelves with a central projection (top) and elaborate carving like a shell hood in the top of the cupboards (middle and bottom).

1672 Westmorland

1697 Westmorland

1681 Westmorland

1710 Westmorland

Fig 8.11 (above): Spice cupboards in the north of England often include the date and the initials of the owner and his wife.

pivots upon small wooden pegs which protrude from the top and bottom rails and are set into holes in the frame. These pegs frequently broke, and were replaced by conventional hinges, but occasionally they still survive, as at 1631 Wilts (Fig 8.7).

Display cupboards

Display cupboards became popular in the 18th century, when people were beginning to have items of china and glassware to show off to their less wealthy neighbours. Often they are built in on either side of the parlour fireplace, with one closed cupboard with panelled doors and one open one. The latter usually has a curved back and specially shaped shelves, which follow the curve and have a large round projection in the centre for the prize items to be displayed. Some early 18th century examples have

Fig 8.14 (right): Display cupboards. The upper cupboard at c1809 Sussex has shaped shelves behind the double doors which have beautiful brass keyplates. The panels of the upper doors have a decorative shape which is similar to the one at 1849 Wilts, where open display shelves have curved brackets at the top corners. Here the lower shelf and the enclosed cupboard below have all been removed at some time, leaving only the moulded architrave and the upper shelf.

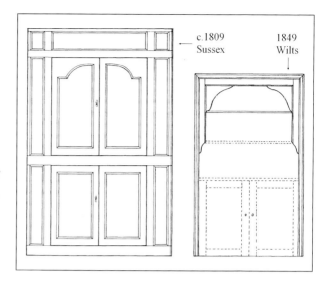

1731 Bucks

1760 Flints ——

Fig 8.15 (above): A small cupboard in a house in Buckinghamshire (left) has the date 1731 formed by tiny holes pierced in the door. On the right is a wall cupboard with a dated door, in a north Welsh house.

elaborate carving in the top of the cupboard, rather like a shell hood above a door (Fig 8.13). Shaped shelves are found surprisingly often in closed cupboards; presumably the doors were left open on special occasions to display the items within, but were usually kept closed for protection.

Single display cupboards were often added to earlier houses, and are frequently built into the recess where a door or a window has been blocked. Plainer storage cupboards are also inserted into blocked openings, and occasionally a date may be inscribed on the door (Fig 8.15).

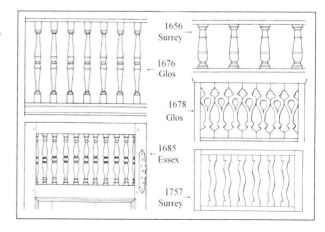

Fig 8.16 (right): Ventilation grilles with turned (1656, 1676 and 1685) and splat balusters (1678 and 1757).

Ventilation grilles

Ventilation grilles consist of a row of balusters set above or occasionally into a door (Fig 8.16). The balusters may be turned or splat and the designs are comparable to staircase balusters (see Chapter 4). Most date from the 17th century, but splat balusters with a wavy profile are common in the 18th century, and simple straight slats are sometimes used in the 19th century. They provided both ventilation and borrowed light, and are most often found above the doors of cupboards built into the recess next to the fireplace.

Fig 8.17 (above):A grille with turned balusters of late 17th century design over the dairy door of a house in Keynsham, Somerset.

On the ground floor such cupboards are usually found in the kitchen, or in the hall if that was used for cooking, and are assumed to be pantry cupboards. They also occur in first-floor chambers, when a more likely use is clothes storage, and occasionally a cupboard under the stairs has a grille (Fig 8.16: 1678 Glos). Ventilation grilles are also used above the doors of dairies (Fig 8.17), or to light a windowless box room in the attic (Fig 8.16: 1676 Glos). Sometimes they have been blocked at a later date and may only be visible from inside the cupboard or pantry .

Fig 8.18 (below): Mid to late 17th century spindles in the door of a bedroom cupboard in South Glos.

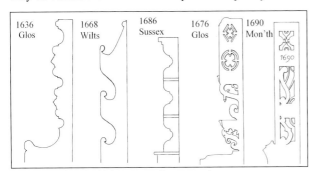

Fig 8.19 (above): 17th century dresser ends.

Fig 8.20 (below): The Merchant's House at Marlborough has a ventilated closet at the top of the main stairs; the date is sometime after the completion of the front range in 1656 and as such it is an early example of wavy balusters.

Dressers and trencher racks

Built-in dressers are fairly common and continued to be popular kitchen fittings well into the 20th century. The earliest date from the 17th century, and consist of decoratively shaped ends (Fig 8.19) which support a wide bottom shelf and two or sometimes three narrow shelves which function as plate racks.

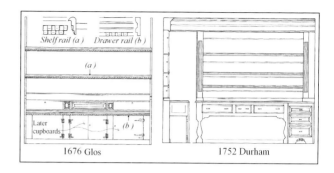

Fig 8.21 (right):The dresser at Moorend Farm, Hambrook, Glos (1676) has the central drawer embellished with applied mouldings and there are dentils along the fronts of the shelves, while the ends have very elaborate pierced decoration. This dresser was later given cupboard doors to enclose the lower part. High Green, Mickleton, Co. Durham (1752) has the typical Co. Durham splat baluster supporting the dresser at one end, with an unusual arrangement of three drawers one above the other at the opposite end.

The piece of furniture we know as a dresser evolved from the dresser board, a wide board on which food was dressed or prepared, and a wall-mounted trencher rack. Even in 1741 a Gloucestershire inventory referred to 'a Dresser Board on a frame with a Plate Rack and a Chopping Block', together worth 5 shillings. The dresser at 1636 Glos (Fig 8.19) takes this simple form of shelves with carved ends, but the next stage was to add drawers below the wide shelf, as at 1676 Glos (Fig 8.21).

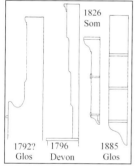

Fig 8.22 (above): Plain dresser ends of the late 18th century and two 19th century wall-mounted shelves. The smaller one is a plate rack, but the larger could have held pots, pans and dishes as well as plates.

Fig 8.23 (right): Late 18th and 19th century dressers.

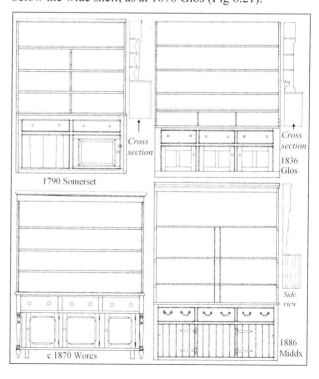

Many 18th and 19th century dressers incorporated cupboards from the start, but some regional variations can be recognised. In County Durham there is often an open area below the drawers, with the end of the wide shelf supported on a carved splat baluster (Fig 8.21). In the later period, dresser ends became much plainer, often with just a simple curve at each shelf, but there may still be decorative carved brackets at the mid point of each shelf, as at 1790 Somerset (Fig 8.23) and 1796 Devon (Fig 8.22), and most have a moulded cornice applied to the top. The dresser in the kitchen of a Malvern house (c1870 Worcs, Fig 8.23) has cupboards which appear to be later insertions into a formerly open area below the drawers. The cupboard doors have chamfers and stops around the panels which match those on the doors throughout the house, implying that the basic dresser is earlier than 1870. Sometimes simple trencher racks survive mounted to a wall, but they are becoming increasingly scarce (Fig 8.24).

Fig 8.24 (above): Trencher rack of uncertain date, formerly in a house in Cromhall, South Glos, but now at Blaise Castle Folk Museum, Bristol.

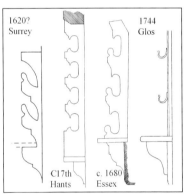

Fig 8.25 (left): Decorative uprights are arranged in twos, threes or fours to form spit racks and also support a mantelshelf at the bottom.

Fig 8.26 (below): Fixed shelves in the pantry of a South Gloucestershire house (top) and a small shelf above the stair of a house in Ticehurst, Sussex, probably to hold a candlestick to light the stair (bottom).

Fixed shelves

Fixed shelves carried on simple curved brackets like those used for mantelshelves were once common, but many have fallen victim to the fitted kitchen syndrome. Usually they can be found in pantries and butteries, and dairies which were often lined with shelves around two or three walls. Dairies also had stone or slate shelves to provide a cool surface for preparing and storing cheese, butter and other food. Others were fitted into odd corners in closets or even over the staircase, where they may have held a candle or lantern to light an otherwise dark stair (Fig 8.26).

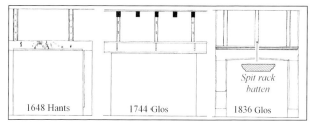

| 1648 Hants | 1744 Glos | Spit rack batten 1836 Glos |

Fig 8.28 (above): Fireplaces with vertical battens mounted on the wall above to carry hooks or pegs for a spit rack..

Fig 8.27(above):Spit racks at Cogges Farm Museum, Witney, Oxon, (top) where rather strangely it is in the parlour, and at Blakesley Hall, Yardley, Birmingham, (bottom). Both are undated but probably belong to the later 17th century. Note the corner of bacon rack in the lower picture.

Fig 8.29 (below): A dog wheel at Wick Court, near Bristol. It is not clear whether the wheel is in its original location.

Dog Wheel

Spit racks

Many houses originally had a rack above the fireplace to store all the spits. Often they had more than one spit, and there are frequent references in probate inventories to spits or 'broaches', an alternative name for a spit for much of the 17th century in western England.

There is documentary evidence for spit racks in the houses of the Canons of Winchester Cathedral. Nos 5, 6 and 8 The Close had 'One dresser & 4 shelves round the wall, wooden racks for Spitts' in the kitchen, dating from 1662. Although these do not survive, spit racks are fairly common elsewhere, and there are some good examples in buildings that are open to the public such as Cogges Farm Museum at Witney, Oxon, Blakesley Hall, Yardley, Birmingham, and the museum in Worcester.

Spit racks are often combined with a mantelshelf, supported on curved brackets, and have from two to four carved wooden uprights which carried the spits (Fig 8.25). They are commonly thought to be gun racks, but if they have been used for guns they have usually been mutilated as the original slots are not large enough for the gunstock.

Although the type of spit rack with carved wooden uprights is the most decorative, and may be the most common, other types exist in which simple vertical battens, usually moulded, carry either large turned pegs like giant coat pegs, or iron hooks. Often it is only the battens that remain (Fig 8.28). Battens presumably for some form of spit rack exist as late as 1836 in the kitchen of a Gloucestershire house.

Spit racks with turned pegs were more adaptable than the carved wooden uprights, and a drawing by Sydney Jones of a farmhouse kitchen at Weston Patrick, Hampshire in about 1905 shows one holding two spits, two guns and a bread peel. The Gloucestershire inventory reference in 1709 to 'One Jack, two Guns and three Spitts' suggests that this may not have been uncommon.

Dog wheels

There was a variety of ways by which the spit could be turned while cooking meat and one type used in some of the larger 17th century houses was a wheel turned by a dog. They were usually mounted on the wall above and to one side of the fireplace (Fig 8.29). A cooler location for the poor animal was around the corner on the side of the chimney stack, and a Shropshire house still has the recess in the wall that once housed such a wheel. A few survive in situ, and they can be seen at St Briavel's Castle in the Forest of Dean and St Fagan's Castle in Glamorgan.

Fig 8.30 (above): A clockwork spit jack at Shibden Hall, West Yorks, operated by a large stone weight.

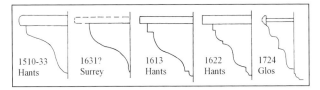

1510-33 Hants	1631? Surrey	1613 Hants	1622 Hants	1724 Glos

St Fagan's Castle also has an 18th century 'smoke-jack' which used the hot air from the fire to drive the spit; the rising air turned a horizontal vane mounted in the chimney, and this was attached to the end of the spit by a chain. More common are the clockwork spit jacks, mounted on the wall above the fireplace or sometimes on the fireplace lintel (Fig 8.30). Large holes and cut-out housings often show where such jacks have been removed from a wooden lintel, and sometimes holes have been cut in an earlier mantelshelf to accommodate the chain.

Fig 8.31 (left): Mantel shelves and brackets. Dating is difficult, as the mantelshelf may have been added later, but 1613 and 1622 Hants have similar brackets and dates suggesting that the shelves are original. 1724 Glos has a separate moulding applied to the front of the shelf.

Fig 8.32 (below): West country cheese racks. These racks at Oxwick Farm, Yate, Glos (1722) still have a few shelves in situ.

Mantelshelves

Many fireplaces have or had a mantelshelf above the lintel (Fig 8.31). Some 16th century wooden lintels have an integral mantelshelf which is either chamfered or has a complex moulding, and many stone fireplaces also incorporate a mantelshelf (see Chapter 7). Separate mantelshelves consisting of a thick plank supported on

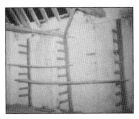

two or more carved brackets are also common, and many more have been removed, leaving only the scars on the lintel as evidence of their former existence.

Dairy and Cheese Room fittings

In the 17th century it was usual for cheese to be stored in the attic of the larger farmhouses, and many have the remains of cheese shelves; many more, sadly, have been removed or have rotted away. Most farms would have made cheese for their own consumption, but in major cheese-producing areas such as south Gloucestershire vast quantities were made and sold to the big cities. One of the largest houses had as much as three tons of cheese in the attics in 1717, worth £78. It is therefore not surprising that the evidence of this once major industry is still there.

Fig 8.33 (above): An early cheese press reproduced at the Ryedale Folk Museum in North Yorkshire.

Fig 8.34 (below): A base stone from a cheese press with a run-off channel, which has been laid as a paving stone at an 18th century house in the Hudson Valley near New York.

Cheese shelves, usually referred to as cheese racks in Gloucestershire, consist of loose boards set on fixed supports (Fig 8.32). The supports may be set against the wall or free-standing and usually either have ladder-shaped ends or a series of brackets projecting from a central post. The shelves are always loose so that they can easily be removed for cleaning, and often they have been used for other purposes leaving only the supports.

Cheese was made in a mould which had to stand on a

Fig 8.35 (below):A lattice dairy window formerly at a South Gloucestershire farmhouse.

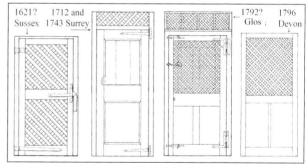

Fig 8.36 (above): Latticework doors and ventilation grilles for dairies and cheese lofts. 1792? Glos from Northwick House Farm, Pilning which was built in 1707 and extended in 1792, has a lattice grille above the pantry door which also has a lattice upper section. Behind the latter is a hinged panel which can be let down to ventilate the room. It is not clear if this belongs to the first or second phase of construction, but most securely dated examples of lattice doors date from the later 18th century.

press for the excess moisture to be squeezed out. Early cheese presses are rarely seen outside museum (Fig 8.33), but their base stones may be found lying around the garden or farmyard or reset in a stone path. They are usually roughly circular, 12 to 15 inches across and with a channel around the edge for the liquid to run off (Fig 8.34).

Dairies and cheese rooms needed to be well ventilated and some have lattice grilles above the doors, lattice doors or even entire lattice partitions in cheese lofts or cellars (Fig 8.36). Dairies may have two doors, one solid and one slatted, and some had lattice windows instead of glazing (Fig 8.35). As such lattice work is generally extremely fragile very few have survived.

Dairies and cheese rooms were both exempt from the window tax that was introduced in the late 17th century and continued until the 1850s, but the rooms had to be labelled as such. Sometimes the words 'Dairy' or 'Cheese Room' were painted directly on the door but some houses have separate wooden boards nailed up over the window to identify the rooms in question (Fig 8.37). A house in the main square in Montacute in Somerset even has the word 'Milkhouse' carved in the stonework of the window; along with 'Whitehouse' this was a common term for a dairy.

Bacon racks

Bacon was generally stored on bacon racks suspended from the kitchen ceiling, and there are numerous inventory references to them throughout the 17th and 18th centuries. Some racks have survived and the simplest form is the ladder shape which seems to continue into the 19th

Fig 8.37 (above):A wooden board with the word 'Diry' (recte Dairy) painted on it, fixed above the dairy window at Oakwell Hall, Birstall, West Yorkshire.

Fig 8.38 (above): Ladder-type bacon rack at High Wycombe Museum, Bucks.

Fig 8.40 (below): Square bacon racks subdivided into four panels; the turned pendants at the corners suggest a 17th century date. Undated Glos house (top) and Blakesley Hall, Yardley, Birmingham (bottom).

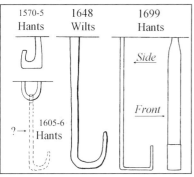

1570-5	1648	1699
Hants	Wilts	Hants
1605-6		
? Hants		

Side

Front

Fig 8.39 (left): Bacon rack hooks in dated houses. While it can never be absolutely certain that the hooks belong with the dated phase of the house, many are found in 17th century contexts. They also occur in later buildings , however.

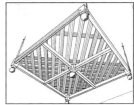

Fig 8.41 *(above): A salting trough set into a recess in the cellar of the Grey House, Pucklechurch, Glos, built in 1678.*

Fig 8.42 *(above): A salting stone set against the wall of the small dairy wing at Moorend Farm, Hambrook, Glos. The house was built in 1676 and the wing extended in 1723, and the stone, on its decorative stone pillars, may date from the first phase.*

Fig 8.43 *(below): Turned coat pegs at a house in Charlton Kings, Glos. Comparison of its features with dated houses suggests a date in the 1720s.*

century (Fig 8.38). Some 17th century racks are more decorative and the square frame may be subdivided by cross-members into four squares spanned by smaller timbers running at right angles or by diagonal slats forming a sort of lattice (Fig 8.40). The outer frame may have carved decoration and there may even be small turned pendants at the corners.

Although some bacon racks survive far more have been lost and often all that is left are four substantial hooks set into the hall or kitchen ceiling in a rectangle or square measuring three or four feet in each direction (Fig 8.39). If the ceiling has later been covered with multiple layers of plaster, all that may be visible are the curved bases of the hooks.

Bacon rack hooks should not be confused with the sundry hooks fixed to beams and joists for hanging all manner of things from sides of meat to bunches of herbs. These are usually arranged randomly and the hooks often have sharp points, whereas bacon rack hooks are always blunt and arranged in a precise rectangle. Sometimes a simpler form of bacon rack is created by nailing a number of slats across some of the ceiling joists, but this type is fixed permanently and cannot be taken down for cleaning.

Salting troughs and slabs

Further evidence for bacon production is found in the salting troughs and slabs which sometimes survive, occasionally in their original locations but more often as plant troughs or paving slabs around the garden. The Grey House, Pucklechurch, Glos (1678) has a salting trough in a recess in the cellar (Fig 8.41), and the 'Two Sides of bacon in Salt' in the cellar in 1711 are typical of many inventory references. In Gloucestershire one salting slab

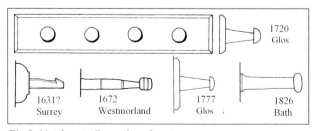

Fig 8.44 *(above): Examples of coat pegs.*

survives in the cellar of a house of 1733, while another, formerly in the dairy of a 1624 house now stands outside the back door. At Moorend Farm, Hambrook, built in 1676, the salting slab is also just outside the back door next to the dairy wing. As it is set on stone pillars which have been given primitive capitals this is almost certainly its original location (Fig 8.42).

Coat pegs

Rows of coat pegs mounted on heavy moulded or chamfered battens are not uncommon, and many are in contexts suggesting an 18th century date (Fig 8.43). Some however appear to be earlier, such as the turned pegs decorated with incised lines found at Townend, Troutbeck, Westmorland dating from 1672 (Fig 8.44). A row of carved pegs on a thick ovolo-moulded batten in the attic of Kew Palace may date from the first phase of the house in 1631, while another set of carved pegs in a Sussex house may date from the 17th century (Fig 8.45). These are fixed inside a first-floor closet, a common location for coat pegs. The most unusual set of coat hooks is a row of four iron hooks set into the stonework of the chimney breast next to the front door of a Wiltshire house of 1648 (Fig 8.47). Anyone coming in through the door could immediately take off their wet coat and hang it where the warmth of the chimney stack would soon dry it.

Fig 8.45 (above): Carved coat pegs in a first-floor closet in a Sussex house.

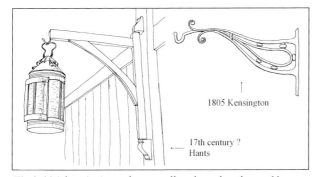

1805 Kensington

17th century ?
Hants

Fig 8.46 (above): A wooden swivelling lamp bracket and lantern to be found in Hampshire (left) and a wrought-iron bracket for a candelabrum above one of the back stairs at Kensington Palace, dating from 1805 (right).

Fig 8.47 (below): Possibly unique iron hooks set into the side of the chimney stack next to the front door at a Wilts house. They are almost certainly original features of 1648.

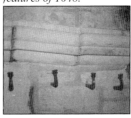

Lamp brackets

Most lighting was by candles and rushlights until the invention of the oil lamp, followed by gas lamps and finally electricity in the 19th century. Some medieval stone fireplaces incorporate projecting brackets or small shelves on one or both sides which are generally referred to as lamp brackets and may have held candlesticks. 17th and 18th century inventories are full of references to candlesticks of various sorts, some clearly large and free-standing.

There are also slightly less numerous references to 'lanthorns' or lanterns, which were the equivalent of the modern torch that could be taken wherever needed. It is not clear if the lanterns had a permanent location inside the house, but one in Hampshire has a remarkable wooden bracket fixed to the back of the hall screen (Fig 8.46). The bracket is mounted so as to be moveable, and it carries an ancient lantern to light the screens passage. The date of both bracket and lantern are uncertain.

One of the back staircases at Kensington Palace has a very graceful wrought-iron bracket projecting from the string at the top of the stair in the attic (Fig 8.46). It has a large hook on the end and was almost certainly intended to carry a candelabrum to light the otherwise rather gloomy stairwell. It is not clear how common such features were or how many survive.

9 APPENDICES
NOTES ON DATING FITTINGS

If we relied purely on inscribed dates somewhere on the house the scope of the book would be limited, as such carvings are extremely rare before the middle of the 16th century. They can also be misleading; the Lecturer's House, Old Street, Ludlow, has an inscribed date of 1611, but this refers to the appointment of one Thomas Kay as Town Preacher. Documentary records suggest that the house was in fact rebuilt in 1622 for the sum of £26 7s 9d.

The dating criteria has therefore been widened to include houses dated by documentary evidence or by dendrochronology, enabling a much wider period to be covered. Documentary evidence includes references to 'my house newly built', details of a change of ownership suggesting a likely building date, and actual building accounts. Accounts often survive for buildings at the top end of the social scale and may give the name of the carpenter and details of the wood used for different items. For example, the 1822 accounts for the Old Rectory, Slimbridge (Gloucestershire) list such items as '35 feet run of oak beams 11 inches by 9½ inches, 300 feet run of oak joists 5 by 2¼ inches, 200 feet run of elm quarter 5 by 3 inches, 890 feet run of deal coffer joists 9 by 2½ inches, 54 feet run of oak, 5 by 4 for doorframes', right down to 'deal laths for the tiling'.

Some documents reveal that, unsurprisingly, English carpenters went to America and used their skills to carry out and supervise building work there. Dedham in Massachusetts had five recorded carpenters in the 1630s, three of whom came from the same small area on the Suffolk/Norfolk border. Fairbanks House, Dedham, tree-ring dated to 1641 and the oldest timber-framed building in North America, has carpentry details in the roof that are only found in the same parts of Suffolk, although the family for whom it was built came from Sowerby in West Yorkshire. Emigration of both settlers and craftsmen did not stop with the first wave of settlement, of course, but continued throughout the 17th and 18th century. Account books survive for one John Drew, detailing his joiner's work in Deptford, East London, between 1706 and 1709. He acted as a general contractor and oversaw carpentry, brick-laying, plastering, tile work, painting and glazing, and both domestic and ships' joinery. In 1715/16 he, along with two other English joiners, turned up in Portsmouth, New Hampshire, where he oversaw the construction of the MacPheadris-Warner House between 1716 and 1718. The house survives virtually unaltered and would not look out of place in many an English town.

It was not only the craftsmen who were imported from England; many of the materials also travelled across the Atlantic, not just the small items such as brass doorhandles and keyplates but also brick and stone. Window glass was imported from England until the end of the 18th century; it was commonly referred to as 'Bristol glass' as Bristol was the main port of export. It was not until 1787 that the first American glass factory was established at Boston. Many old houses in Virginia and New England are both well documented and full of original features and thus provide useful parallels with English buildings. A few items have therefore been included in this book, and some relevant books added to the bibliography.

Dendrochronology (tree-ring dating) works on the basis that a tree produces a growth ring each year. The relative widths will vary according to the climatic conditions each year, with drought years producing extra-thin rings. By working backwards from living trees it has proved possible to build up an unbroken sequence reaching back more than 1,500 years in Britain, and samples taken from standing buildings can be matched against this sequence. The most accurate dates are obtained when the sample includes all the sapwood (the outer rings) to the underside of the bark; if some of the sapwood is absent, an estimate has to be made as to how many years might be missing, based on regional sapwood studies. If all of the sapwood is missing, plus some of the heartwood rings, there will be no way of knowing how many rings were trimmed off the tree when it was converted into a beam or plank, and only a terminus post quem or 'felled after' date can be given. Not all wood is suitable for dating, however. The growth pattern varies in different parts of the country depending on the local climatic conditions, so it is necessary to have a sequence from the same area for the most successful dating. The more work that is done in this field, the easier this becomes. Some English dendrochronologists are also dating buildings in America, providing much useful information to complement the documentary and architectural evidence in that country.

At present sequences are common for oak, although elm is often used for floorboards and sometimes for structural timbers. Other timbers such as deal (pine) came into more general use in the later 17th century for doors, panelling and staircases. Some research has been carried out by Cathy Groves at Sheffield University in the dating of pine, but there can be problems in determining the place of origin of imported timber. Some oak was especially fast grown, in which case the growth rings are too wide to conform to the pattern produced by the majority of trees. The date obtained by dendrochronology is that at which the tree was felled, but documentary evidence shows that it was almost always used within a year or two of felling. Sometimes a building with an inscribed date has been tree-ring dated, and the close correlation again shows little time-lag between felling and use. For example, the recut inscribed date of 1583 at Oakwell Hall, Birstall, Yorkshire, has now been confirmed by dendrochronology which produced exactly the same date.

This, however, is only part of the story. Few houses were built entirely at one time with no subsequent alterations, and they may produce several tree-ring dates or have more than one inscribed date. Alternatively only one part of the house may be dated, but this may be an addition to an earlier house, or refer to minor alterations. The date may apply to the basic structure, but it may have been substantially refitted at a later date;

Oakwell Hall has a splendid staircase with dog-gates, but this was put in later in the 17th century and does not belong with the 1583 inscribed date. It is therefore still necessary to decide which features belong with the given date or dates and which to other periods. Often it is obvious to the trained researcher, with 18th century and Victorian additions usually being easily distinguished from those of earlier periods. One of the aims of this book is to enable the untrained observer to make such distinctions for themselves.

Equally often, however, even the architectural historian can have problems in deciding which features belong with the early 17th century datestone and which were added later in the same century; some features and styles remained popular over a long period. Also it must be remembered that houses may have undergone minor alterations with each subsequent occupant, even if they remained in the ownership of one family for centuries. All of today's house make-over programmes on television are merely reflecting the fact that everyone likes to make their own mark upon their home, whether by simply repainting the walls and doors or by building a porch, moving a door, or adding a whole new wing; our ancestors were no different in this respect.

Modernising can take many forms, one of the most common being to insert new windows in the current fashion. Sometimes the entire front façade has been rebuilt, leaving old-fashioned features out of sight inside and at the back of the house. Timber-framed houses are particularly likely to have been treated in this way, with fashionable brick fronts or rendering added to conceal the timbers, and sash windows inserted to replace the old mullioned windows. A house should therefore never be dated by its façade alone, as this may conceal a much older structure.

Although houses and other buildings are primarily designed to perform a specific function, there is often scope for architectural display which fulfills a quite different purpose – to reveal the status and wealth of the occupant. Elaborately carved doorframes and projecting oriel windows are external displays of wealth; internally the grand staircase or the panelled parlour performs the same function. The wealthy will therefore have the most up-to-date features, while the poor peasant may continue with few if any embellishments to his house, replacing functional items with ones of similar design when they wear out. New ideas in architectural styles and details were introduced at the very top of the social scale and gradually filtered downwards and outwards. What is not certain is how long this process took. Did a new fashion starting in London take longer to reach Yorkshire than Devon for example? Insufficient research has been carried out to be able to answer this question satisfactorily, but the recent research on Hampshire buildings has shown that crown-post roofs went out of fashion nearly 100 years earlier in Hampshire than in East Sussex. Clearly factors other than simple distance were involved. Evidence so far suggests that the styles of internal features such as doors and staircases show far more consistency in date across the country, implying that ideas spread rapidly. Craftsmen such as carpenters and joiners could travel easily, taking ideas as well as tools and skills with them. One of the first open-string stairs was built in 1691 at Kensington Palace (the Queen's Stair), but by 1710 open-string stairs were to be found in many upper class houses across the country. Blacksmiths on the other hand were far more static, being confined to their forge. Looking again at Hampshire, it appears that ironwork, and hinges in particular, were generally simpler in design than those in Gloucestershire, Wales and the borders, but more detailed studies of individual counties are needed to reveal the full extent of such regional variations. Similarly it would appear that doorheads vary in design across the country, with simpler examples in the south-east and Gloucestershire, ogee shapes in Shropshire and the north, and highly elaborate ones in Monmouthshire. There is a further tradition of highly carved and dated stone doorheads in Lancashire, Yorkshire and the far north-west which find no counterparts further south. Some features found in more than one area may be similar in form but dissimilar in date; the ogee doorheads of Shropshire belong to the 14th and 15th centuries, while in Cumbria they persist to the end of the 17th century. This implies that new ideas were initially spread by travelling craftsmen who worked for the upper classes, and were later taken up by more local craftsmen who stayed in their own area.

These variations generally occur in buildings up to the end of the 17th century, with some persistence into the 18th century in the north. Most fixtures and fittings were becoming far more standardised in the 18th century, with few regional differences, even though woodwork and ironwork was generally still produced by local craftsmen. This is partly due to the influence of pattern books such as Batty Langley's *The Builder's Jewel*, published in 1754. This enabled every carpenter or blacksmith to have access to the latest ideas and to copy them more or less accurately, depending on their skill. It is also interesting to compare the fixtures and fittings of the grandest houses with the lowliest. Kew Palace, used by the royal family in the 18th century, was built in 1631 as a very grand merchant's house, but has panelling of the same type as that found in far more modest farmhouses. The only difference is that the ceilings at Kew are so tall that there is far more of it and most of the rooms are or were panelled; the humbler farmhouse often had panelling only in the parlour. Kensington Palace underwent refurbishment in 1805, and in the areas used by the servants the stairs, fireplaces and doorcases are no different from those found in ordinary houses of the same period. In the state rooms, however, the same basic designs are used but with the addition of elaborately carved borders with the decoration highlighted by gilding. By the Victorian period, hand-crafted work was being replaced by machine-made items, losing the charm that irregularity of line so often brings. But even at this period rural cottages may still have hand-made window catches, for example, continuing the tradition of earlier work. Later in the 19th century there was a reaction against factory-made conformity, and the Arts and Crafts movement returned to the old hand-made traditions. In some areas, such as the villages near Stroud in Gloucestershire, the tradition has continued almost to the present day; the nephew of Alfred Bucknell, the Arts and Crafts blacksmith, made his last pair of strap hinges for a front door about twenty years ago. He used the same designs as his uncle, and exemplifies one of the main problems of dating by style – it only takes one old-fashioned craftsman, doing things in exactly the same way as his grandfather, to mislead one completely. It is with that proviso that this book is offered as a guide to dating.

GLOSSARY

Baluster:	A small column supporting a handrail
Balustrade:	A series of balusters, with handrail, etc
Bargeboard:	Decorated boards placed at the gable ends of a roof to hide the ends of the roof.
Bastle House:	A defensive house found in the far north, which has a byre on the ground floor and living rooms above.
Bolection moulding:	A projecting S-shaped moulding around a doorway, fireplace, etc.
Boss:	Carved decoration at the intersection of ceiling beams or the centre of a roof truss.
Brattishing:	Decoration resembling miniature battlements used along the top of a moulded beam.
Bressumer:	A horizontal beam, especially a jetty beam.
Cames:	Strips of lead of H-shaped cross-section which hold the panes of glass in a leaded light window.
Casement window:	A window hinged on one side to open outwards or inwards.
Cornice:	A horizontal moulded projection at the top of a wall, fireplace, etc.
Crenellations:	An alternative name for battlements.
Cross-passage:	A passage with only one external door; the term is often used instead of through-passage
Cruck truss:	A pair of curved or angled timbers which rise from ground level, or not far above it, and curve over to meet at the apex. Each crucks is called a blade.
Dais:	A raised platform at the upper (i.e. Superior) end of an open hall.
Dendrochronology:	The science of dating timber by the pattern of growth rings.
Finial:	A decorative feature at the apex of a gable or on top of a newel post.
Hood-Mould:	A projecting moulding above a stone doorway or window to throw off the rainwater.
Inglenook:	Term commonly used to describe a large open fireplace with seats on one or both sides.
Jamb:	The straight side of an archway, doorway or window.
Label mould:	See Hood-Mould
Lintel:	A horizontal beam or stone which bridges an opening.
Mortise:	A slot in one timber designed to receive the tenon of another timber; hence 'mortise and tenon joint'.

Mullion:	A vertical bar of stone or wood which divides a window into lights.
Newel post:	The central post of a spiral stair; the posts at each corner of a framed stair and at the end of the balustrade.
Ogee:	An S-shaped curve, also called a cyma or scroll.
Oriel:	A projecting window, either on the first floor or a bay rising through two storeys.
Overmantel:	A decorative panel, usually of plasterwork, above a fireplace.
Pendant:	A decorative feature, similar to a finial but hanging down; commonly found on the lower end of the newel posts of a framed stair.
Quarrels or Quarries:	Diamond-shaped panes of glass in a leaded-light window.
Sash window:	A window comprising of sashes (a frame holding glazing) which slide vertically in grooves. A sash window which slides horizontally is also known as a Yorkshire Sash.
Screens passage:	Passage with opposed doorways, separated from the open hall by fixed or movable screens.
Sill:	The beam at the base of a timber framed wall.
Soffit:	The underside of a beam or lintel.
Solar:	The upper living room of a medieval house; the private room of the owner of the house or lord of the manor.
Spandrel:	The triangular space between one side of an arch and the rectangular frame enclosing it.
Stanchion:	A vertical bar in a window light between the mullions, usually of iron but sometimes of wood.
String:	The sloping timber supporting the treads of a staircase at their outer edge; often decorated. A closed string is where the treads are framed into the string, and an open string is where they project over the top of the string.
String course:	A moulding or narrow projecting course of stone or brick running horizontally along the face of a wall.
Stops:	The termination of a chamfer or moulding, usually decorative.
Tenon:	The end of a piece of wood shaped to fit into a mortise in another piece of wood.
Transom:	A horizontal cross-bar in a window.
Truss:	A pair of principals or principal rafters, usually joined by a collar or a tie-beam, set at intervals along a roof to support the purlins, which in turn support the common rafters.
Wall-plate:	A horizontal timber laid along the top of a wall to which the feet of the rafters are joined.

BIBLIOGRAPHY

* = particularly useful for fixtures and fittings

General

Brown, R. J., *English Farmhouses*, (Hale, 1982)
Brunskill, R. W., *Illustrated Handbook of Vernacular Architecture* (Faber, 1970 and reprints)
Cooper, Nicholas, *Houses of the Gentry 1480-1680*, (Yale, 1999)
Forrester, Harry, *The Smaller Queen Anne and Georgian House* (Chelmsford, 1964)
Gray, Edmund, *The British House* (London, 1994)
Hewett, Cecil A., *English Historic Carpentry* (London and Chichester, 1980)
Jekyll, Gertrude and Jones, Sidney R., *Old English Household Life*, (London, 1944-5)
*Lloyd, Nathaniel, *A History of the English House,* (1931, reprint 1975*)*
Osband, Linda, *Victorian House Style* (Newton Abbott 1991, 2001)
Parissien, Steven, *The Georgian House* (London, 1995)
Parker, J. H., *Some Account of Domestic Architecture in England, II, from Edward I to Richard II* (Oxford, 1853)
Parker, J. H., *Some Account of Domestic Architecture in England, III, Parts I and II, from Richard II to Henry VIII* (Oxford, 1859)
Turner, T. Hudson, *Some Account of Domestic Architecture in England from the Conquest to the end of the Thirteenth Century,* (London, 1851)
Wood, Margaret, *The English Medieval House,* (London 1965)

Regional

*Barnwell, P. S. and Adams, A. T., *The House Within: Interpreting Medieval Houses in Kent* (RCHME, 1994)
Beacham, Peter (ed), *Devon Building* (Exeter, 1990)
Black, D.W; Goodall, Dr I.H. and Pattison, I.R., *Houses of the North York Moors* (RCHME, 1987)
Brinton, Marion, *Farmhouses and Cottages of the Isle of Wight* (Isle of Wight County Council, 1987)
Britnell, W. J. (ed), *Ty-mawr, Castle Caereinion* (The Powysland Club, 2001)
Denyer, Susan, *Traditional Buildings and Life in the Lake District* (London, 1991)
*Forrester, Harry, *Timber Framed Houses of Essex*, (London, 1959, 3rd ed 1976)
*Fox, Sir Cyril and Raglan, Lord, *Monmouthshire Houses* (Cardiff, 1951-4)
Giles, Colum, *Rural Houses of West Yorkshire 1400-1830* (RCHME, 1986)
*Hall, Ivan and Hall, Elisabeth, *Historic Beverley* (Beverley, 1973)
Hall, Linda J., *Rural Houses of North Avon and South Gloucestershire 1400-1720* (Bristol, 1983)
Hutton, Barbara and Martin, Joyce, *Doorways in the Dales* (York, 1986)

Jones, S.R. and Smith, J.T., "The Houses of Breconshire", *Brycheiniog* 9 (1963), 1-78

Jones, S.R. and Smith, J.T., "The Houses of Breconshire", *Brycheiniog* 10 (1964), 69-183

Jones, S.R. and Smith, J.T., "The Houses of Breconshire", *Brycheiniog* 11 (1965), 1-149

Jones, S.R. and Smith, J.T., "The Houses of Breconshire", *Brycheiniog* 12 (1966-7), 1-91

Jones, S.R. and Smith, J.T., "The Houses of Breconshire", *Brycheiniog* 13 (1968-9), 1-85

*Martin, David and Martin, Barbara, *A Selection of Dated Houses in Eastern Sussex 1400-1750* (Robertsbridge, 1987)

Martin, David and Martin, Barbara, *New Winchelsea, Sussex* (English Heritage, 2004)

Moran, Madge, *Vernacular Buildings of Whitchurch and Area [Shropshire]* (Logaston Press, 1999)

Moran, Madge, *Vernacular Buildings of Shropshire* (Logaston Press, 2003)

Musson, Ann and Thorp, John, *Topsham Houses, Warehouses and Trades 1700s and earlier* (Topsham, 1998)

Palmer, J. H. (revised and edited by McIntire, W. T.), *Historic Farmhouses in and around Westmorland* (Kendal, 1952)

Pearson, Sarah, *Rural Houses of the Lancashire Pennines 1560-1760* (RCHME, 1985)

Pearson, Sarah, *The Medieval Houses of Kent: An Historical Analysis* (RCHME, 1994)

*Penoyre, Jane, *Traditional Houses of Somerset*, (Somerset Books, 2005)

Pevsner, Sir Nikolaus, *Buildings of England* (individual counties, various dates from 1951 to the present day)

Portman, D., *Exeter Houses 1400-1700* (Exeter, 1966)

*Roberts, Edward, *Hampshire Houses 1250-1700*, (Hampshire County Council, 2003)

*RCHM(E), *The City of York, Vol III: South-West of the Ouse* (1972)

RCHM(E), *York: Historic Buildings in the Central Area* (1981)

*RCHM(E), *Salisbury: Houses of the Close*, (1993)

Slocombe, Pamela: *Wiltshire Farmhouses and Cottages 1500-1850* (Wiltshire Buildings Record, 1988)

Slocombe, Pamela: *Medieval Houses of Wiltshire* (Wiltshire Buildings Record, 1992)

*Slocombe, Pamela: *Wiltshire Town Houses 1500-1900* (Wiltshire Buildings Record, 2001)

Smith, Peter, *Houses of the Welsh Countryside* (London, 2nd ed 1988)

Thorp, John R.L., "4 The Quay, Dartmouth: a Devon Town-House of 1664", *Devon Archaeological Society Proc No 41,* 1983, 107-122

Wilson, R. E., "Tudor and Merton Cottages, Sidmouth", *Trans Devon Ass* 106 (1974), 155-9

Wood-Jones, R. B., *Traditional Domestic Architecture in the Banbury Region* (Manchester, 1963)

*Internal features
Alcock, N. W. and Hall, Linda J., *Fixtures and Fittings in Dated Houses 1567-1763* (CBA, 1994)
Ayres, James, *The Shell Book of the Home in Britain* (London, 1981)
Ayres, James, *Domestic Interiors: The British Tradition 1500-1850* (London, 2003)
Calloway, Stephen (ed), *Elements of Style: an Encyclopedia [sic] of Domestic Architectural Details* (London, 1991)
Chinnery, Victor, *Oak Furniture; The British Tradition* (Woodbridge, Suffolk, 1979)
Easton, Tim, *'Ritual Marks on Historic Timber'*, Weald and Downland Open Air Museum Newsletter (Spring 1999)
English Heritage, *Georgian joinery, 1660-1840* (London, 1993) [guidance leaflet]
Eveleigh, David J., *Firegrates and Kitchen Ranges,* (Shire, 1983)
Jourdain, M., *English Interiors in Smaller Houses, 1660-1830* (London, 1923)
Lander, Hugh, *House and Cottage Interiors* (Redruth, Cornwall, 1982)
Lindsay, Seymour, *An Anatomy of English Wrought Iron* (Tiranti Press, 1964)
Martin, David and Martin, Barbara, *Domestic Building in the Eastern High Weald 1300-1750: Part 2 – Windows and Doorways* (Robertsbridge, 1991)
McCann, John, *'The Introduction of the Lamb's Tongue Stop – some new evidence',* Historic Buildings in Essex, Issue 2, September 1985, 2-5
Pearce, Walter, J., *The Glazed Windows of Moreton Old Hall, Cheshire,* J. Brit. Soc. Master Glass Painters, 1938, 68-75
Penoyre, John and Penoyre, Jane, *Decorative Plasterwork in the Houses of Somerset 1500-1700* (Tiverton, 1994)
Sambrook, John, *Fanlights* (Chatto and Windus, 1989)
Small, Tunstall and Woodbridge, Christopher, *Architectural Turned Woodwork of the 16th, 17th and 18th centuries* (London, undated)
Williams, Commander E. H. D.,*'Curing Chambers and Domestic Corn Drying Kilns',* Trans Somerset Archaeological and Natural History Soc 120 (1976), 57-61
Williams, Commander E. H. D., *'Bacon Curing Chambers - Some Recent Discoveries',* Trans Somerset Archaeological and Natural History Soc 122 (1978), 53-56
Woodward, Christopher, *Windows* (The Building of Bath Museum, 1994)

Documentary
*Crook, John, *The Wainscot Book* (Hampshire County Council, 1984)
Moore, John S. (ed), *Goods and Chattels of our Forefathers: Frampton Cotterell and District Probate Inventories, 1539-1804,* (London and Chichester, 1976)
*Salzman, L.F., *Building in England Down to 1540: A Documentary History,* (Oxford, 1952, 1997)
Steer, Francis W. (ed), *Farm and cottage inventories of Mid-Essex 1635 to 1749,* (Chichester, 1969)
Trinder, Barrie and Cox, Jeff (eds), *Yeomen and Colliers in Telford: Probate Inventories for Dawley, Lilleshall, Wellington and Wrockwardine, 1660-1750,* (London and Chichester, 1980)

America

*Comstock, William T., *Victorian Domestic Architectural Plans and Details,* (New York, 1881, reprinted 1987)

*Garvin, James L., *A Building History of Northern New England* (Hanover NH, 2001)

*Kelly, J. Frederick, *Early Domestic Architecture of Connecticut* (New York, 1924, reissued 1963)

*Wilson, Kenneth M., *'Window Glass in America', Building Early America,* ed Charles E. Peterson, (Radnor, Pennsylvania, 1976) p150-164

INDEX

BUILDINGS FEATURED IN THIS BOOK WHICH ARE OPEN TO THE PUBLIC

Buckinghamshire
Chenies Manor House: 100
High Wycombe Museum: 205
Jordans Meeting House: 193
Cheshire
Little Moreton Hall: 84, 85, 86, 162
Cumbria
Rydal Hall: 61
Derbyshire
George Hotel Tideswell: 78
Haddon Hall: 85, 86
Hardwick Hall: 25, 85 (1590-3 Derbys)
Devon
The Butterwalk, Dartmouth (Museum, Sloping Deck restaurant): 35, 70,147, 150, 190
Totnes Museum: 179
County Durham
Crook Hall, Durham: 100
Museum, Ireshopeburn: 119
Dorset
Sherborne Castle: 66
Essex
Sun Inn, Feering: 178
Glamorgan
Llancaiach Fawr, Gelligaer: 65
The Welsh Folk Museum, St Fagan's Cardiff: 194, 203
Gloucestershire
Blaise Castle Folk Museum, Bristol: 201
Dyrham Park: 76
Lamb Inn, Iron Acton: 190
Hampshire
St Mary's Church, Abbot's Ann: 152
Angel Inn, Andover: 171
Bishop's Palace, Bishop's Waltham: 19, 83, 171
Chawton House, Chawton: 121, 122, 134, 139, 190, 192

All Saints' Church, Odiham: 110, 123
George Inn, Odiham: 20, 159
King John's House, Romsey: 150, 159
The Red Lion, Southampton: 101
Tudor House Museum, Southampton: 134
The Vyne, Sherborne St John: 136
St Cross Hospital, Winchester: 83, 134, 169
Hertfordshire
Hatfield House: 104, 117, 121, 123, 132
Kent
Godinton House, near Ashford: 137
Archbishop's Palace, Maidstone: 172
King's Head, Sandwich: 149
Knole, Sevenoaks: 104
Penshurst Place: 169
The Guildhall, Sandwich: 104
Lancashire
Gawthorpe Hall, Padiham: 23, 74,145
Hall I' th' Wood, Bolton: 110, 120, 123, 125
Hoghton Tower: 54
Rufford Old Hall: 133
Samlesbury Hall: 133, 150, 172
London
Kensington Palace: 27, 75, 105, 107, 113, 118, 119, 127, 128, 129, 181, 207, 208
Queen's House, Greenwich: 118, 119
Middlesex
Hampton Court Palace: 86, 137, 144
Norfolk
Dragon Hall, Norwich: 149
Northamptonshire
Castle Ashby: 117
Talbot Hotel, Oundle: 153
Triangular Lodge, Rushton: 25, 33, 49, 55, 108
Oxfordshire
Abingdon Abbey: 170 (NB Berks in Caption)
Broughton Castle: 104